STICKS AND STONES

STICKS AND STONES

THE PHILOSOPHY OF INSULTS

JEROME NEU

OXFORD
UNIVERSITY PRESS

2008

OXFORD
UNIVERSITY PRESS

Oxford University Press, Inc., publishes works that further
Oxford University's objective of excellence
in research, scholarship, and education.

Oxford   New York
Auckland   Cape Town   Dar es Salaam   Hong Kong   Karachi
Kuala Lumpur   Madrid   Melbourne   Mexico City   Nairobi
New Delhi   Shanghai   Taipei   Toronto

With offices in
Argentina   Austria   Brazil   Chile   Czech Republic   France   Greece
Guatemala   Hungary   Italy   Japan   Poland   Portugal   Singapore
South Korea   Switzerland   Thailand   Turkey   Ukraine   Vietnam

Published by Oxford University Press, Inc.
198 Madison Avenue, New York, New York 10016

www.oup.com

Oxford is a registered trademark of Oxford University Press

Library of Congress Cataloging-in-Publication Data
Neu, Jerome.
Sticks and stones : the philosophy of insults / Jerome Neu.
p. cm.
Includes bibliographical references and index.
ISBN 978-0-19-531431-1
1. Invective. I. Title.
BF463.I58N48 2007
179—dc22   2007006256

9 8 7 6 5 4 3 2 1

Printed in the United States of America
on acid-free paper

Sticks and stones may break my bones, but words will never hurt me.

—Children's chant

Words, like sticks and stones, can assault; they can injure; they can exclude.

—Blurb for *Words That Wound: Critical Race Theory, Assaultive Speech, and the First Amendment*

A gentleman never insults anyone unintentionally.

—Oscar Wilde

I am enclosing two tickets to the first night of my new play, bring a friend ... if you have one.

—George Bernard Shaw to Winston Churchill

Cannot possibly attend first night, will attend second . . . if there is one.

—Winston Churchill, in reply

Let's give a welcome to macaca here.

—Senator George Allen

You scullion! You rampallian! You fustilarian! I'll tickle your catastrophe!

—Shakespeare, *Henry IV, Part 2* II.1.56–57

ACKNOWLEDGMENTS

Ever think, "I've never felt so insulted in my life"? And then, somewhat later, think it anew? Lovers will do that to you. At least some of them will. That is how I got into the subject. Such lovers are masters of your heart, and so masters of humiliation. They forget you and their commitments to you. They neglect you in favor of people they assure you don't really matter. They disappoint expectations you didn't even know you had.

Of course, strangers can insult one too, but perhaps not repeatedly. One is less ready to forgive and more ready to back away.

To insult is to assert or assume dominance, either intentionally claiming superiority or unintentionally revealing lack of regard. To be insulted is to suffer a shock, a disruption of one's sense of self and one's place in the world. To accept an insult is to submit, in certain worlds to be dishonored. How is one to retrieve self-respect?

The schoolyard wisdom about "sticks and stones" does not take one very far: insults do not take the form only of words, in truth even words have effects, and in the end the popular as well as the standard legal distinctions between speech and conduct are at least as problematic as they are helpful. How are we to defend ourselves, if a chant won't do it? While being insulted is painful, invulnerability to insult has its costs. Excessive servility, so that it is not possible for others to show one less respect than one feels for oneself, and excessive arrogance, so that the actions and attitudes of others are dismissed with the same contempt as those others themselves are dismissed, are not attractive models for living. Neither, however, is an excessive sensitivity, so that one is always and readily insulted. It means that others must constantly walk on eggshells to protect one's delicate sensibilities or pander to one's self-importance. On the other hand, an excessive self-sufficiency, so that the concerns of others cease to be of concern to one, makes one equally insufferable. Where is the Aristotelian mean that will tell us just how sensitive and vulnerable to insult it makes sense to be? The conventions of etiquette, morality, and the law, as well as the counsels of religion, provide us with norms and guidelines that are of some help, but they too are subject to critique and raise issues of their own.

For example: What is it exactly to look at someone "the wrong way"? How, given that our legal system both values freedom of speech and is concerned to prevent harm, offense, and emotional distress caused by speech, are we to delimit protected groups and unprotected speech? Who may insult whom and how? And what is it to "respect" another religion? Must one follow its dictates? Must one follow all of those dictates (whether having to do with depictions of Muhammad or the eating of pork)?

To find guidance on how to live in the world with the many others who impinge on our boundaries, to think about how much we should put up with those who would put us down, it is necessary to explore the nature and place of insult in our lives. What kind of injury is an insult? Is its infliction determined by the insulter or the insulted? What does it reveal of the character of each and of the character of society and its conventions? What is its role in social and legal life (from play to jokes to ritual to war and from blasphemy to defamation to hate speech)? In what follows, I emphasize philosophical, anthropological, psychoanalytic, and legal approaches to these questions.

I much appreciate the encouragement and suggestions of Peter Ohlin, my editor at Oxford University Press. A version of the final chapter of this book was previously published in Sharon Lamb and Jeffrie Murphy, eds., *Before Forgiving: Cautionary Views of Forgiveness in Psychotherapy* (New York: Oxford University Press, 2002). Able research assistance was provided by Thomas Del Monte and Gary Maushardt. I have also benefited from the participants in a seminar, "On Insults" (*not* a "how-to" course), that I have taught at the University of California, Santa Cruz over recent years. Carter Wilson, as always, has been particularly generous with helpful comments and feedback. Finally, while their names are too numerous to mention, I am grateful to all those who have shared their thoughts on insults and also to those who have, however unintentionally, given me occasion to think about the place of slights, slurs, slander, and yet deeper wounds in the lives we, sometimes uneasily and uncomfortably, lead together.

CONTENTS

STICKS AND STONES

ONE

∎ ∎ ∎

ON FEELING INSULTED

AT ITS CORE, AN INSULT IS (OR AIMS AT) A KIND OF INJURY. WE SPEAK OF "adding insult to injury," but in certain contexts the two may be equivalent. In one of its senses, one of its earliest senses, an "insult" denotes a physical injury. Even today, doctors will speak of "an insult to the brain."[1] *The Oxford English Dictionary* gives as the first meaning of "an insult" an attack or assault, which in medicine can refer to anything that tends to cause disease or bodily injury (and the resulting reaction, lesion, or injury). It also has a literal meaning in the military, referring to an open and sudden attack or assault. An eighteenth-century military writer reports, "The others were obliged to retire into fenced Cities, for fear of our Insults." In its most familiar meaning, however, it refers to speech or behavior "intended to wound self-respect." The injury is personal—one might say, mental or moral—rather than physical; though I shall be arguing that it may often be unintentional, due to thoughtlessness or negligence rather than self-conscious ill will.

---

1. Just before Dylan Thomas lapsed into his final coma in 1953, he was diagnosed with "a severe insult to the brain" caused by alcohol poisoning (Wetzsteon 2002, 485). I myself once suffered from what the ear, nose, and throat specialist I went to see referred to as "an insult to the tongue." (I think I had—literally—bitten it. Usually, of course, it is the tongue that lashes out to cause injury.) *Time*, the newsmagazine, extends this usage of insult to speak of the polystyrene foam used in cups, boxes, and packing peanuts as an "insult to the environment" ("A Burger to Go—Hold the Plastic," 11/12/1990).

The *OED* gives as an obsolete meaning, "the act of leaping upon; 'covering', " as in the following Dryden quote, "The Mother Cow must wear a low'ring Look. The Bull's Insult at Four she may sustain." The sexual significance is of interest. Etymologists trace the word insult to the Latin *salīre* to leap, and its frequentative form *saltāre, saltus* a leap, *insultāre* to leap upon (also translated as jump or trample on, which is close to the early meaning of insult as exult or act arrogantly). Assault and assail come from the same family of words. (For the etymological situation, see Partridge, 582–83; Onions, 479, 56; Chantrell, 277.) In the Bible, leaping (like knowing) has a sexual sense. The line about those "ten lords a leaping" in the Christmas carol may be obscene. Of course, what is probably the most common verbal insult today, "fuck you," speaks directly to the issue. I believe it may also speak directly to the central psychological significance of insult. "Fuck you" and its more specific variant, "up yours," make explicit sexual anxieties about activity and passivity, masculinity and femininity, domination and submission. Insult is about humiliation and the assertion of superiority, the assertion or assumption of dominance. It is an interesting question, given the etymology, how a physical insult can become an insult to dignity, bringing the two modern usages of "insult" together. The language (which preserves the word's etymological source in the rare, "leaping upon," usage just noted) takes us to a physical act that is sexual.

Understanding disrespect in terms of violation and breaking of boundaries translates into the sexual sphere as rape. (Of course there are other sexual prohibitions and boundaries, such as incest taboos, but they do not necessarily involve a shock, an affront, to the person involved. The violation—however serious—may be merely of social norms. Rape is inevitably personal, necessarily unconsented to.) Understanding disrespect as involving an assertion or assumption of dominance translates into sexual zones as anal erotism. Unconscious *a tergo* rape ("Up yours!") thus becomes the hidden psychological significance of insult. Why assume insult has such a general, hidden, significance? It is sometimes written large in insult rituals (e.g., among Turkish boys and in "the dozens" engaged in especially by African-American male adolescents) and in other relevant social practices and attitudes (in ancient Greece and elsewhere—discussed by Dover, Foucault, and others). Freud's teachings on the pervasiveness of anal erotism in particular and sexuality in general offer some clues. Is there a drive to "put down" and insult others? The sense of "violation" and of "shock" in insult needs exploration. But both the anthropology and psychoanalysis of insult are stories for later.

ANGER AND DEJECTION

Feeling insulted is a species of anger — or so it might seem. Aristotle actually defines anger as "a desire accompanied by pain, for a conspicuous revenge for a conspicuous slight at the hands of men who have no call to slight oneself or one's friends" (*Rhetoric*, trans. W. Rhys Roberts, 1378a). "Slighting," Aristotle further clarifies, involves thinking of someone "as obviously of no importance" and can be subdivided into "contempt, spite, and insolence" (1378b) — that is, various forms of insult. We moderns might regard the sort of publicity suggested by talk of "conspicuous" revenge and "conspicuous" slights as inessential, the external audience that judges status and honor playing perhaps less of a role for us than for Aristotle's rhetorician. We might also recognize more occasions for, and so more species of, anger. (Aristotle himself at one point associates anger broadly with "suffering without justification" — 1380b.)

But, despite the apparently natural — if not essential — ties of anger to insult, the experience of insult may feel more like dejection. While some may respond to insult with outrage, others (at least sometimes) suffer inwardly. (Aristotle's definition actually leaves an explicit place for pain alongside the various pleasures he ascribes to thoughts of vengeance.) Does "the experience of insult" itself have a distinctive character? Might outrage, might dejection, simply be reactions — perhaps separate and subsequent reactions — to that experience? To get clearer on the question, I think we must probe the nature of insult and its place in human life. Just as to understand feeling afraid, we must first understand the concept of danger, so to understand the nature of the experience of insult, and perhaps separable reactions to it, we must first look to the situations to which the experience is itself a reaction.

People take offense more often than it is meant to be given. This may be due to mistake or to hypersensitivity (or even to strategic victimhood), but it may also be due to the fact that insult can be given independent of the intentions of the insulter. Insult can be given through thoughtlessness, by negligence, as the result of the failure to care or to care enough. The insulter need not directly intend offense.

Is insult determined by the insulter or the insulted? It is well to remember that hypersensitivity has its opposites. Even if one does not take offense, one may in fact have been insulted. This may be due to social conventions that operate and establish standards independent of one's subjective response. It may be due to the attitudes and intentions of the insulter. Further, subjective responses may be distorted by failures to understand as well as by insufficient self-regard.

BEING INSULTED VERSUS FEELING INSULTED: EXPECTATIONS OF RESPECT

What does it take to feel insulted? Before too quickly answering "not much," we should first enter a caution. Actually two cautions. There is a difference between feeling insulted and properly feeling insulted and also between feeling insulted and being insulted.

Is the victim the final authority on whether or not insult has been given? As noted, there is a difference between feeling insulted and properly feeling insulted. The first may be wholly subjective, leaving the sufferer as the ultimate authority, but the second raises issues of justification that may bring social and other external standards to bear. A person may be excessively sensitive or even irrational. Imagine a person feeling offended because someone calls them by the name they themselves have asked to be called by. (With some people, one just can't win.) The notion of being too sensitive, having too thin a skin, presupposes a more-or-less objective standard that provides a norm for sensitivity. By such norms, some people are indeed oversensitive. On occasion at least, individuals may be excessively sensitive even when they deny it. Of course, one needs to recognize that these matters are arguable and that the individual who refuses to acknowledge they are being oversensitive may ultimately be right—given a clear-headed reading of the facts of the case, given an accurate reading of the prevailing norms, or finally, given a persuasive critique of those norms.

In Freud's case of Dora (1905e), his understanding of her emotional reactions imposed norms that she rejected and that later times would agree with her in rejecting. When Dora was fourteen years old, her father's married friend, Herr K, cornered her and kissed her. While

Freud might have been right in thinking that she was attracted (then and later) to Herr K, Freud's insistence that he would regard as hysterical any girl who reacted wholly with displeasure to such an advance, even without somatic symptoms (1905e, 28), seems to be excessive, and perhaps relies on an overly mechanical model of romantic responses (what gives us pleasure is after all highly thought and context dependent). What is the proper response of a fourteen-year-old girl to what she experiences as a sexual assault, even if at the hands of someone she otherwise may be presumed to find attractive? By the time Dora turns eighteen and becomes for a brief period Freud's patient, she has developed a brooding and unappeasable sense of betrayal in response to her father having, over the years, in effect turned her over to Herr K in return for Herr K's tolerance of the father's affair with his wife. While Freud found himself unable to dispute Dora's charges against her father, he regarded her reaction as excessive and defensive (she too had colluded in maintaining this "Viennese network of infidelities"—in Erik Erikson's [1964] phrase). But Dora's reproaches were not paranoid projections, and it is difficult to know by what measure her feelings of betrayal are to be regarded as excessively intense or obsessive (1905e, 35, 54). What is an overreaction to being used as a pawn by one's own father? While Freud did not fall in with the scheme of the father when he brought his daughter to therapy in hopes of persuading her that a scene by a lake involving a proposition from Herr K (when Dora was sixteen) had been a fantasy, he does give too little weight to the intolerable nature of her circumstances. The norms governing sensitivity are subject to misreading and to argument, and conventions are rarely permanently and universally fixed. Even terms of insult as generally excoriated as "nigger" are subject to continuing controversy, both inside and outside the black community, about whether the prevailing norms do or should allow for ironic, or affectionate, or otherwise acceptable usage—at least in certain settings and by some people (Kennedy 2002).

Which brings us to our second caution. Feeling insulted is not an infallible guide to being insulted. Being and feeling need not coincide. That is (leaving aside for the moment questions of legitimacy or justification), one can be in an emotional state without being aware that one is in that state. Jealousy is a typical example—it is not at all uncommon to be the last to know, or at least acknowledge, that one is jealous. We are subject to confusion, self-deception, uncertainty, ambivalence, mixed feelings, and errors of all sorts even about our subjective states—at least when they are as complex as most emotional states are.

The situation in relation to feeling insulted and being insulted is complicated by the fact that insults involve others, and so at least two states of mind come into play: that of the insulter and that of the insulted, or of the would-be insulter and the might-be insulted. And there is a further complexity. Being insulted, unlike being jealous and more like being betrayed, is ambiguous. It may refer to either a psychological state or a social condition (which in turn one may or may not be aware of).

If being insulted depends on expecting treatment or deference of a certain kind, may one avoid insult simply by lowering expectations? But then, is to expect nothing or too little to lack self-respect (like certain allegedly submissive women who were urged by the women's movement to cultivate and express an appropriate anger and indignation—Hill 1973, Spelman 1989)? Or might immunity from insult be the sign not of diminished self-respect, but of a heightened self-esteem (accompanied by an arrogant contempt for others) or, in yet another alternative, of a special sense of what is essential to the "self" (as with Socrates, who felt assured that a good man could suffer no harm at the hands of a worse, his virtue being solely in his control and also being the only aspect of his self that really mattered)? Does the opinion of others properly count for nothing for the properly self-reliant and self-respecting individual?

Given a sufficiently cynical reading of human behavior—the notion (say) that people always (or with rare exceptions) treat each other badly—expecting little or nothing for oneself need reflect neither diminished nor heightened self-regard, but rather the view that everyone is in the same unfortunate boat. One expects little for oneself, but expects equally little for all. (One wonders whether a person holding such a view could be insulted, or at least indignant, on behalf of another.) But then, such an excessively cynical view might well be motivated by self-regarding concerns rather than simple realism. Might a similar immunity be purchased without excessive cynicism by a homogenizing view of the world and the individuals in it, of the sort a Buddhist (desiring nothing) or a Spinozist (understanding everything) might cultivate? Whatever one's view of the desires and forces at work, might an egalitarian (and so perhaps less aggrieved) reading of everyone's common situation provide some comfort? The common level need not be despairingly low. But then, even if one expects only equal treatment, couldn't one still be disappointed? What sorts of expectations and assumptions (conventional and otherwise) lie behind the experience of insult? How is one to fill in Aristotle's notion of an appropriate mean in this area?

It's all about respect. Who we think we are, at least to some extent (we must recognize that some self-evaluations are inelastic), depends on who others allow us to think we are. So far as they refuse to recognize our claims to their consideration and concern, we are denied essential elements of our moral identity. (Other aspects of our identity may also depend on various forms of recognition. Can we be "witty" if no one ever laughs at our jokes?) What we may legitimately expect of others varies with who those others are in relation to us (lovers, parents, children, friends all bear special places in our regard, and we reciprocally depend on special places in their regard), and also with how we behave toward them (reciprocal expectations may lapse when either party fails in its role). What expectations count as "legitimate" depends on social conventions, individual understandings, and structural supports at a variety of levels (there are rules of etiquette, of morality, of law). Much of our understanding of ourselves and our place in the world is contingent on these structures and on the behaviors and attitudes of those who live with us within these structures. Our responsiveness to these constraints emerges in our emotional experience in terms of embarrassment, shame, humiliation, guilt, pride, self-esteem, and self-respect as well as insult. Sometimes whole societies structure their emotional world around their particular conceptions of honor. In such a society, being shamed need not refer so much to a subjective feeling as to a public status, something done to a person, rather like being insulted in its social condition sense (Miller 1993, 119). To be insulted is, as in the hip hop usage, to be diss'd or disrespected, denied appropriate honor. Individual susceptibilities and sensitivities may distort our reactions, but we live within a web of social norms.

The relevant kinds of respect come in at least two varieties, which can be usefully distinguished in terms of self-respect and self-esteem. (See Darwall 1977; Sachs 1981; Neu 2000, 124–29.) Briefly, self-respect may be understood as a matter of basic human dignity, of which one cannot have too much (though one can have too little). Self-esteem, on the other hand, may be based on perceived merit and achievement, and, thus understood, one can have either too little or too much (i.e., think too well of oneself). Self-esteem, like esteem and admiration in general, may be a matter of desert, may be earned or merited; while self-respect is a matter of entitlement, and as a matter of one's rights and dignity as a person is non-comparative. Self-esteem may necessarily be comparative and, in some ways, competitive, and also require independent confirmation by others (and be open to independent disconfirmation). Insofar as worth and self-worth are multidimensional, insofar as there are many things we value, some will be comparative and competitive and dependent on the views of others. As a matter of self-esteem, honor cannot be totally individualistic and independent of the views of others. Certain recently popular self-help psychologies and educational theories may thus make a mistake in thinking increasing self-esteem is simply a matter of changing one's attitude rather than the more strenuous activity of changing one's life.

INSULTS AND INTENTIONS

In thinking about the relation of insults and intentions, I would start from the two striking facts already noted. First, offense is taken more often than it is meant to be given. Second, a person may have been insulted even if they fail to take offense. The first point suggests that people may make mistakes about whether they have been insulted or, where they are not mistaken, that their actually being insulted does not depend on an intention to insult. Conventions and expectations also doubtless play a role. (There is, of course, a third possibility: where the person in fact knows there has been no insult, they may nonetheless assert affront, engaging in deliberate manipulation to seize the advantages, such as they are, of claiming victimhood. But in such a case the offense would seem as much a pretense as the phantom insult to which it is a putative response.) A malicious intention can turn an otherwise innocent action or remark into an insult. But equally, thoughtlessness can wound, an insult may be unintentional and yet profoundly real. The second point, that one can be insulted without realizing it or taking offense, suggests that insult may be independent of the insulted person's knowledge as well as of the insulter's intentions. And other things may matter, for even if one is aware of an intention to insult, one need not feel the wound. The interplay of intentions and understandings and sensitivities, in both the insulter and the insulted, is complex and revealing—and further complicated and given sense by surrounding social conventions.

Is the infliction of insult up to the insulter or the insulted? What does it reveal of the character of each? John Wayne's father is reported to have taught his son that "A gentleman never insults anyone intentionally." Oscar Wilde, on the other hand, insisted "A gentleman never insults anyone unintentionally."[2] Notice that Wilde and Wayne Sr. seem to agree in presupposing that insults can be unintentional. Where they differ is in the value they attach to intention and to insults. Wayne Sr. seems to assume insults are always bad, and that we should avoid giving them whenever it is within our power. If nothing else, etiquette requires it of those who would be gentlemen. By contrast, Wilde thinks the gentleman may well find appropriate occasions to insult; the thing it is important to avoid is unintentional insults or thoughtlessness. The appropriate occasions for intentional insult might be restricted, as Jonathan Swift believed the ridicule of satire should be, to corrigible vanity and pretentiousness (chap. 9 below). Whatever may be expected of a gentleman, is the insult to be found in his intention (can it exist despite the lack of intention?), or whatever he dishes out, does its character (whatever may be said of his character) depend on how it is taken? For now, let us focus on intentional insults, though unintentional insults

2. I heard the report about John Wayne's father's teachings in a radio broadcast on the occasion of John Wayne's death in 1979. It turns out that the radio announcer was mistaken, and that the father's actual views approximated to Oscar Wilde's. In a *Playboy* interview published in May 1971, Wayne said his father's advice was "to never insult anybody unintentionally" (Riggin 1992, 59). Still, I will continue to attach the "no intentional insults" view to an imagined "Wayne Sr.," just to give it a name (bearing in mind that John Wayne's real name was Marion Michael Morrison and his father's real name was Clyde Leonard Morrison). The view is doubtless very popular, for it shares the spirit of perennial calls for restraint, such as: "If you don't have anything nice to say, don't say anything."

The attribution of the "no unintentional insults" view to Wilde also has its complications. While my memory attributes the thought to Wilde, I have been unable to find the quote in his published works. There is a compendium of quotations that makes the attribution, but it does not cite an original source (Merchey 2004, 404). In any case, I'm sure Wilde would not mind the attribution. It was a principle for him that the true artist annexes everything. James McNeill Whistler, a rival of Wilde in wit, said something clever in conversation one day and Wilde said approvingly, "How I wish I had said that." Whistler replied with the famous insult: "You will, Oscar, you will" (Ellman 1988, 133).

(as we shall see in a bit) may be especially revealing in relation to the conventions and expectations involved in insults (out and out curses are generally all too easy to understand).

When I feel insulted, whether or not I feel angry or dejected, I feel disappointed. Disappointment might therefore seem to be at the heart of insult. Disappointed expectations allow for a kind of hurt, and doubtless an insult is a kind of hurt. But one can be disappointed when one does not win a job or a prize one had (let us suppose, reasonably) counted on—without taking it personally. More is going on. Later, I shall elaborate the "more" involved in making certain kinds of disappointments amount to insults in terms of "shock" and normative (as opposed to predictive) expectations. The focus of the disappointment (in particular, concerns for attention and respect) may matter too. But for present purposes, the thing to note is that it may sometimes be that the "more" crucially depends on a particular intention being a part of the explanation for one's disappointed expectations. Natural calamities do not produce insult, whatever damage may result from them. And not every human doing of damage makes for insult either. Justice Holmes reminds us, "even a dog distinguishes between being stumbled over and being kicked" (1881, 3). While the physical harm produced by a stumble and a kick may be the same, the intention in the second adds a distinct injury. A malicious intention deepens the wound, adds insult to physical injury. An accidental slap may smart to the same degree as a deliberate one, but it is the intention behind the deliberate one (at least in certain social situations) that turns it into an insult.

We often say, in positive contexts, "It is the thought that counts," meaning that even an inadequate gift may manifest good intentions, and those are what matter. It works both ways. Intentions can transform an action into a friendly overture or into an insult. But intentions are not always easy to read. Sometimes, of course, the intention is meant to be communicated to an audience other than the insulted party—this is a frequent device in the theater, where there is necessarily an audience distinct from the parties on the stage. Sometimes the insulter is issuing the insult for the sake of others, and does not much care whether the insulted party gets the point; indeed, the point might be that the target of the insult does not get it. (See chap. 9 below.) This is one of several ways in which one may be insulted without being aware of it and so without feeling insulted.

Sometimes the intention is meant to be read by its object, but the expression is unconventional. Nonetheless, unconventional communications may succeed, and the perceived intention may well make us feel insulted. The emotional impetus behind the words, rather than their conventional meaning, may be what gives them force. This can also work in a positive direction, where conventionally insulting words are robbed of their sting by manner and context—as in certain friendly insult rituals and joking roasts. For an example of innocuous words turned into maledictions, think of Freud's Rat Man, who as a young Rat Boy was enraged with his father, but lacked the vocabulary to express his outrage. Freud describes the incident:

> When he was very small [between three and four] he had done something naughty, for which his father had given him a beating. The little boy had flown into a terrible rage and had hurled abuse at his father even while he was under his blows. But as he knew no bad language, he had called him all the names of common objects that he could think of, and had screamed: 'You lamp! You towel! You plate!' and so on. His father, shaken by such an outburst of elemental fury, had stopped beating him, and had declared: 'The child will be either a great man or a great criminal!' (1909d, 205)[3]

Manner rather than matter may sometimes be what makes for insult. The distinction between matter and manner has in fact been of central importance in the development and history of the law of blasphemy, where social class and the form taken by the expression of beliefs have sometimes been more at issue than the content of the beliefs persecuted and prosecuted. Where manner is given special prominence, it may serve either as a sign of and clue to intention or, alternatively and by contrast, as grounds for assigning intention a lesser place.

"Adding insult to injury" may sometimes simply refer to an accompanying intention. Sometimes, however, the addition is more explicit. In what must surely be the most strikingly literal example of adding insult to injury in recent years, high-profile publicist Lizzie Grubman in the summer of 2001, after a heated argument with bouncers over parking in a fire lane at a trendy nightspot in the Hamptons, got into her father's Mercedes SUV and slammed it into reverse, smashing it into the crowd that had been waiting to get in at the club entrance. She injured sixteen

---

3. Freud adds a wry footnote pointing out that the father had neglected an alternative (the one that was in fact realized in this case): a great neurotic (1909d, 205n2).

people. It is alleged she hurled an expletive and yelled out "white trash" before fleeing the scene. While Grubman subsequently pleaded guilty to some charges—a felony charge of leaving the scene of an accident and a misdemeanor assault charge—and served some time in jail, she insisted her act was an accident, that she had not been drunk at the time, and that she had not added the verbal onslaught to her vehicular assault (*New York Times* 8/24/2002). If uttered, the words certainly made explicit her intention, her sense of privilege, and her contempt.

I've said that an intention can transform an accidental injury, whether by vehicle, by slap, or by kick, into a nonaccidental insult—in certain contexts. Not in all contexts, however. Not every deprivation, not even every intentional deprivation, is an affront. The nature of the particular purposes or motives involved can matter as much as the fact of intentionality. (An act being intentional involves its being done for a reason and with awareness. The awareness is crucial. The act must be done knowingly, which is to say that the agent must be aware of what he or she is doing under a particular description [Anscombe, 1963].) Being fired in the course of a corporate downsizing might be grounds for regret without being cause for recrimination (depending, of course, on the grounds for selection of those who are downsized out—some grounds might be highly objectionable, indeed, legally actionable). Your home may be condemned by eminent domain to make room for a highway or a public housing project that will benefit many. The point may not be to hurt you, even if you suffer as a result of some intentional activity. This might be true even in more extreme situations. You might welcome the aerial bombing of an occupying army by your liberators despite the risk of injury to yourself (think of occupied Paris or Budapest during World War II). You would be wrong to feel insulted. Nonetheless, not all victims of "collateral damage"—even when the purpose of the bombing is one of which they approve—can be expected to be grateful. Even punishment, punishment aimed directly at you—so the suffering is not incidental to harm directed elsewhere—might be regarded as a benefit rather than an assault on dignity. That was certainly Socrates' view. But even punishment that aims at the improvement of the person punished, rather than simply at vengeful suffering, may be inflicted in a way that does deprive the punished of dignity. This should be a concern both for parents disciplining their children and for states seeking to reform their wayward citizens.

ON NOT FEELING INSULTED

Intentions, adequately expressed, can make all the difference. But as T. S. Eliot understood, there is many a slip between an intention and its execution, and there are more ways to fail than by weakness of will ("Between the idea / And the reality / Between the motion / And the act / Falls the Shadow" from "The Hollow Men," Eliot 1969, 85). The intention that a remark insult does not mean that the target will be hit. I have on occasion seen the ill will behind a person's remark, without feeling the sting of the remark itself. The comment sometimes is simply insufficient to its purpose—perhaps because of features of the remark, perhaps because the would-be insulter himself is beneath contempt. While an insult may typically be the expression of a certain kind of ill will, for a person to feel insulted more may be needed. The wound may arise from a certain kind of disappointment (and perhaps a particular intention, or a particular kind of inattention, must be part of the explanation), but it may be that the wound must also be to a particular part of oneself, and come from a certain type of source, and occur in a certain context.

Sometimes a context may defang what might otherwise be biting insults, as in ritual insult contests between friends. Sometimes there are signs that the words are not meant, as in joking and teasing and hyperbole. But sometimes an insult is indeed an insult, even deliberately and directly intended to be insulting, yet the victim does not feel insulted. Among other things, this may be a matter of not getting the point, of failing to see the barb attached to a remark or the intention behind a slight or inattention. You may not feel insulted simply because you do not understand, as when you are insulted in a language you do not speak.

But leaving failures to perceive and special contexts aside, an individual may recognize an insult for what it is, and yet it may fail to have its intended effect. As noted earlier, one might not feel insulted because one did not expect better. Where this sometimes might be a matter of realism (whether resigned or resentful), it might also be a matter of insufficient self-regard. A prevailing good will, between the parties or just on the part of the would-be victim, may also blunt the assault. From a different direction, a prevailing contempt, making certain persons and their attitudes beneath notice, may rob the person who would steal one's dignity of theirs, making their attack ineffective. Nietzsche's superior man, like Aristotle's grandly proud one, could not take the sting of a lowly insect personally.

To feel insulted by a boor or a buffoon might involve taking them more seriously than anyone, any sensible person, should. A wider or deeper understanding might also disarm. For example, it would be foolish for a grown-up to feel insulted at the frustrated "I hate you" of a three-year old who has not gotten what he or she wanted. Such infantile words may be meant to be manipulative as well as expressive, and it would be a gullible and insecure authority figure that fell for the maneuver.

Looking again to the boors, however, what makes one immune from their insult is an (appropriate) contempt. The poor opinion of a person whose opinion one doesn't value can hardly wound. But if contempt buys one immunity from insult, is it then insecurity and resentment that make one vulnerable to it? I would think a reasonable self-respect could be more nuanced than that. Contempt for an individual may typically come tied to indifference to their attitudes, but there is no reason to be indifferent to one's rights as a person in general or one's standing in the world in particular—and with those concerns comes vulnerability to insult. But what is reasonable here, like what expectations are legitimate, is a delicate question. Again the problem of the Aristotelian mean.

There are other types of cases where one may have all the thoughts appropriate to feeling insulted without actually feeling insulted, just as one might believe something to be dangerous without feeling afraid or believe one's lover to be unfaithful without feeling jealous. More is needed for emotion than bare thought. What more? The supplementing constituents might include affect or physiological tumult, behavior or dispositions to behavior, and the form (as opposed to the content) of the thoughts, e.g., obsessive thoughts. (See Stocker 2002; Neu 2000, 79, and 2002a, 164–68.)

If one "feels insulted," is one necessarily conscious of one's state? I've said one can be jealous without feeling jealous. Does the use of the word "feel" in describing the emotion of "feeling insulted" necessarily import awareness? Certainly there are unconscious "feelings" in the broad sense of emotions, and one could argue that sense can be given even to unconscious "feelings" in the narrow sense of sensations (Neu 2000, 265–67). I believe that, quite apart from psychoanalytic claims or special usages, a person might feel insulted, just as they might be jealous, without being aware of it, with their state being manifested and revealed especially in certain dispositions to behavior (say, inclinations to avoid or shun their unacknowledged persecutor). One may remain unaware of the significance of one's dispositions, of one's thoughts and fantasies, and even of one's internal upsets.

TRUTH HURTS

Consider now the following case: As a young boy, I don't get picked till last to be on one of the neighborhood stickball teams. Have I been insulted? Does it matter whether I am in fact the worst stickball player? Does it matter whether the choosers have other motives? Say I am an excellent stickball player, but they don't like me? Or suppose I am a middling stickball player, but they mean to insult me? If I am a poor player and the choosers are motivated only by priorities internal to the point of the game, I still may be hurt. Is it because they did not allow personal attachment and concern to override those priorities? (But didn't someone have to be picked last?) Is it because their choice forces me to recognize my inadequacies? The truth can hurt.

But can one be *insulted* by a statement of the truth? The answer, all too obviously, is yes. Calling someone fat, even if true, may be an insult. What makes it an insult? The intention to wound, to hurt and offend, may be enough. And how the truth is uttered, and in what context, may provide important clues. The manner matters. Conventional expectations (which prohibit the discussion of certain topics) may be enough. It may be a delicate matter, not to be discussed in that way. But most interestingly, the insult may be bound up with the fact that this is a truth that does not need to be told. A fat person most likely knows they are fat—calling them fat provides no new insight or illumination, and no good purpose is served.

But perhaps a good purpose may be served. What if the intention is to break through denial, to urge someone to improve their health? Even so, one must be careful when seeking to undeceive others: careful about what the truth is, about what one's own motives are, and about the actual consequences of breaking through denial or unmasking. Ibsen's *The Wild Duck* and O'Neill's *The Iceman Cometh* offer valuable cautions on these scores (Neu 2000, chap. 15, "Life Lies and Pipe Dreams"). In those plays, the would-be undeceivers are themselves grossly self-deceived, and end up doing far more harm than good. One should be humble about the limits of one's understanding. And there is other reason to be humble, for the distinction between having faith and self-deceptive commitment to illusion may be a nice one, indeed, one that may only be made in retrospect: so that we call it "having faith" when someone turns out to have been right and "self-deception" when they turn out to have been wrong. Moreover, turning out to be right, succeeding, may sometimes depend on making a leap of faith, on believing when one cannot clearly know or even when the evidence is against it. Wishful thinking (the essence of self-deception) may sometimes be the condition of success.

Nonetheless, if the various cautionary criteria are met, telling even an unwelcome truth may in fact serve a good purpose. Still, it remains true that telling the truth (at least sometimes) can be insulting: there is such a thing as insulting truth-telling, even if, given the special purposes of the law, there is no such thing as libelous truth-telling. Even where there is damage to reputation, in law, truth is a complete defense.

We have noted that telling a fat person they are fat is, in most circumstances and especially in those words, insulting. They don't need to hear it. They already know it. The truth of the statement only deepens the wound. Indeed, the truth of an insult may often make it more insulting, just as the truth of criticism may make it more difficult to bear. After all, if the criticism were unjustified, it might simply be dismissed.[4] I myself find unjustified criticism the easiest kind to take—and also, fortunately, the kind most frequently offered in my own case. (Does everyone have that thought?)

The emphasis so far on the role of intention (knowledge and desire) in insult may mislead. While it is indeed the case that the injury involved in insult may have especially to do with attitudes and underlying intentions (whether statements are true or false), attitude has other manifestations than the premeditated shooting of arrows aimed at wounding. Many if not most insults are the result of what lawyers call negligence, or what authorities on etiquette, such as Miss Manners, call "thoughtlessness."

UNINTENTIONAL INSULTS

We have seen that Oscar Wilde and Wayne Sr., despite their differences on gentlemen and intentional insults, agreed in presupposing that insults could be unintentional. One can insult both intentionally (with aware-

---

4. Katharine Hepburn, it is reported, "didn't understand stars who sued newspapers over printing lies about them. 'I never cared what anybody wrote about me,' Hepburn said, 'as long as it wasn't the truth'" (Berg 2003, 315–16).

ness, with forethought, even with malice—in the ordinary sense of ill will as motive) and unintentionally (by inadvertence, by negligence, by insensitivity, by presumption). Both can be felt as painful. Usually intentional harms are thought to be worse than negligent ones for a variety of reasons: because they involve an additional or more severe injury, or reflect a worse character, or perhaps because they are less likely to be preventable by a simple raising of awareness. The negligent driver fails to come up to societal standards of due care, and in that way is clearly at fault when he causes the death of an innocent pedestrian, but his crime seems less heinous than that of an individual who seeks out his victim and intentionally uses his vehicle as a lethal weapon—even if the harm caused in the end is the same. (Lizzie Grubman, the perpetrator of what the *New York Post* referred to as "The Horror in the Hamptons," would have us think of herself as more like the former than the latter.) The failure to care, to take one into account, to consider one's thoughts and feelings, one's rights and safety, are the faults Wilde's gentleman takes special care to avoid.

One can be insulted, feel slighted, by the fact that another is negligent in relation to one, does not, say, trouble to apologize when apology is due or to reciprocate an invitation when hospitality has been accepted and reciprocation is due. Omissions can, of course, be intentional, but the point is that they may be equally hurtful even when unintentional. We are often deeply hurt when those whom we care about and who we believe do or should care about us are thoughtless. They fail to invite us. They fail to call. They fail to inform. They disappoint our expectations.[5] Much litigation is concerned with establishing standards of due care in

---

5. The explanation for an omission and the line between the intentional and unintentional can be rather fuzzy. Alan Helms (1995) writes revealingly about standing people up during his period as a golden boyman in gay New York in the late 1950s and through the '60s. Despite feeling devastated and abandoned on those rare occasions when he was stood up, he regularly overbooked himself and so, inevitably, stood others up. Being much in demand, he generally got away with it without criticism. In his book, he attributes his deplorable practice to low self-esteem, claiming that "people of low self-esteem have a hard time realizing that they have any effect on others" (90). The more plausible explanation would seem to be a self-centered playing with power or a careless disregard for others (who might simply have ceased to exist for him when not directly in his line of sight). After all, there were so many others staring at him and making him real—making him important (the power belied by his claimed low self-esteem).

the law, with determining which expectations are legitimate and enforce-able. Too often, courts will insist that they will enforce only "reasonable" expectations, where "reasonable" expectations turn out—circularly—to be those which the court is willing to enforce. Individuals too sometimes conflate what is reasonable with what they happen to expect.

Perhaps the simplest type of unintended insult is the "overheard" insult, that is, the sort where the insulted party is not meant to be part of the audience for the remark. The actor Sir John Gielgud, according to one of his biographers, "had a legendary capacity for the accidental insult" (Brandreth 2000, 11). At a 1930s dress rehearsal for writer Emlyn Williams' *Spring 1600*, director Gielgud addressed the company with a megaphone: " 'The last act is terribly thin. We must try to make the best of it.' From the darkened stalls, Emlyn Williams' voice responded, 'We all know the last act is thin, John, but you needn't announce the fact to the entire cast. You might wait for the critics to do that' " (Brandreth, 64). While these cases are quite simple, they are also relatively unre-vealing, for in these cases the insult is in fact intentional, it is just that its victim was not intended to hear it (at least directly), that is, was pre-sumed absent. The result is perhaps embarrassment for the speaker—an embarrassment that could as well arise subsequently when the victim learns via the grapevine of the remark. It perhaps involves a special fault of carelessness (or, in some contexts, tactlessness) in not noticing the presence of the victim, but one need not plumb the depths of either the Freudian unconscious or social convention to understand what about the remark makes it insulting.[6] Of course, as in other types of Freudian slips, "not noticing" will sometimes have an explanation that involves the unconscious. A variant form of this omits the overhearing. A nega-tive, invidious, or otherwise derogatory comment is made about a group

---

6. Sometimes what is overlooked is not the presence of the insulted party, but rather some feature of that party or the situation that leaves the insulter embarrassed at his insen-sitivity. In June 2006, President George W. Bush needled a reporter for the *Los Angeles Times*, Peter Wallsten, about the sunglasses he was wearing at an outdoor press conference. As a matter of fact, "Mr. Wallsten was not wearing the sunglasses to look hip, but for health reasons. Mr. Wallsten has Stargardt's disease, a degenerative condition that causes blind-ness and can be painfully exacerbated by sunlight." When later informed, the President called to apologize (*New York Times* 6/16/06, A24).

to which the speaker is unaware a member of his (acknowledged and intended) audience belongs. Jews, gays, and members of other groups that need not exhibit visible signs of group membership are especially liable to such "unintended" insults.

Sometimes the carelessness is not a matter of failure to notice presence, but a failure to calculate risk. In another Gielgud story, this from the 1940s, the actor was handed the just-translated Danish reviews of his Elsinore *Hamlet* and started to read them out loud to the assembled company: "Suddenly, I heard myself saying, 'Miss Fay Compton has neither the looks nor the youth of Ophelia, but obviously comes from good theatrical stock.' Fay was wonderful and roared with laughter. I felt very shame-faced" (Brandreth, 60).

Other Gielgud gaffs take us closer to standard Freudian slips, where despite possible defenses of "I didn't mean to" one wishes to insist that the person in fact (at the least unconsciously) did mean to. One such story "has Gielgud being taken to lunch at The Ivy by Edward Knoblock, a minor playwright . . . 'a dear little man' (according to Sir John), noted for his dullness. A familiar figure passed by their table and Gielgud turned to his host: 'That man is the second biggest bore in London.' 'Who is the first?' asked his friend. 'Why, Eddie Knoblock, of course . . . Oh, I don't mean you, Eddie, the other Eddie Knoblock'" (Brandreth, 155). The biographer reports Gielgud was "celebrated for his apparently accidental indiscretions: 'Gielgoofs' he called them" (Brandreth, 152). Freud believed there are no accidents in the realm of the mental. (There is still much to be learned from Freud.)

What makes an unintended insult insulting is very often a presumptuous attitude or an unjustified assumption behind a remark. A tourist in the Yucatan starts telling something about the Maya to an anthropologist who has studied them for thirty years. You proudly reveal your secret recipe for borscht, having forgotten that I was the one who taught it to you. A speaker condescendingly translates a phrase in French for his interlocutor, when the speaker should know it is the interlocutor's native tongue. Someone pompously spells out obvious facts or passes a patronizing compliment (like the academic who thought she was praising her handyman when she said, "Why Walt, you are remarkably intelligent," on the occasion of his using a three-syllable word). Someone assumes a person is the janitor because of the casual way he is dressed, or perhaps worse, assumes a black person is the valet-parking attendant despite his being dressed at least as impeccably as others present (as has happened to Barack Obama). Clothing, like all signals, can be misread or ignored, sometimes willfully, sometimes presumptuously and negligently, and thus, insultingly.

Presumptions are often cultural rather than individual, and so insult may result from cross-cultural misunderstanding. In her newspaper column in the *Boston Globe* (9/30/2001, D7), shortly after the terrorist attack on the World Trade Center, Ellen Goodman reported on a meeting to promote multicultural understanding. A Muslim man spoke passionately at the meeting and a woman who had been very moved by his remarks went up to shake his hand at the end. He refused, saying that his religion did not permit him to shake the hand of a woman. Goodman reports, "it felt as if this young teacher had her extended hand slapped." Here, as elsewhere, respect for religion and the demands of secular convention can clash.

Unintentional insult may be due to unwarranted assumptions, cross-cultural differences, misunderstood social conventions, even different senses of humor. But these are not all (or always) excusing conditions. This is obvious in the case of unwarranted assumptions. But some jokes, too, may not be funny, however tickled the teller and whatever his intentions. It may sometimes be wrong to laugh (de Sousa 1987, 275–99; and chap. 9 below). The attitudes revealed, the insensitivities exhibited in racist and sexist jokes may be enough to insult the subject of the jokes even if they are not the intended audience. They need not even overhear. One may be insulted without being aware of it, just as one may be betrayed without being aware of it. And those in the intended audience who are not amused may be affronted on their behalf. One might say it is the intention of the insulter that carries the burden, but there need not be any directed, conscious, and explicit intention to insult—the underlying contemptuous and inconsiderate attitudes and lack of respect are enough. The teller of the joke cannot dissociate himself from the attitudes the joke presumes and depends upon (at least when it is the matter rather than the manner, the content rather than the envelope, that amuses).

Figures of speech may be taken as insults, even if the speaker has lost all conscious sense of the words' insulting character. A person may unthinkingly say, "The prospective buyer tried to Jew me down." (The casual use of this expression by one of his new classmates plays a crucial role in the feelings of a newly arrived, WASP-appearing, but nonetheless Jewish student at a very Protestant prep school in the film, *School Ties*, 1992.) Is the speaker's unawareness of the anti-Semitic overtones an excuse or is it grounds for further offense? Does "welshing on a bet" even still have anti-Welsh overtones? In 1995, then-President Clinton felt called upon to apologize to Americans of Welsh descent who felt his use of the expression was a slur. Does the sense of "gyp" meaning "to cheat" impugn the character of gypsies? To say someone is "hunky" is today generally a compliment, but it has its origins in turn-of-last-century hate speech for Hungarians.[7] And slurs can, and have been, appropriated and transformed by their former objects, as has happened with "queer." (In the 1990s, there emerged out of the AIDS activist group "Act Up!"—the AIDS Coalition to Unleash Power, founded by Larry Kramer in 1987—a gay political organization that called itself "Queer Nation.") Times change, things change, words change. Many people exclaim in disgust and surprise, "Jesus Christ!" when things go bad—thinking nothing of it. But sensitive Christians or Mormons may recoil and ask that the name of the Lord not be taken in vain. How considerate must we be of others in order not to insult? What is the standard of care here? Do the numbers count? Which way? (That is, must we be especially sensitive to the feelings of minorities? Or do majorities set norms for all?) Of course, there are clear cases of hypersensitivity. A man a few years ago wrote to a local paper in Santa Cruz, California to complain about the use of the phrase "Nip it in the bud"—as though it had something to do with denigrating the Japanese. And there was not so long ago a city official in Washington, DC, forced to resign for referring to a budget as "niggardly"—as though it had something to do with racial identity (Kennedy 2002, 120–23). (*The Oxford Dictionary of English Etymology* traces "niggardly" to Middle Dutch and other words for "tight" or "narrow" in the sense of "stingy.") The associations of sounds in words can lead to fantasy etymologies and phantom intentions, and so may become grounds for ill-founded offense. There are also less clear cases. After all, words can be ambiguous. In Philip Roth's *The Human Stain* (2000), Dean Coleman Silk loses his university job

7. An alternative, but equally pejorative, etymology for "hunk" traces the now positive (male) word to "a Scottish dialect word meaning 'a sluttish indolent woman,' as in 'a lazy hunk' or 'a nasty hunk,' recorded from *c*.1825" (Hughes 1998, 222).

after referring to some permanently absent students as "spooks"—meaning to refer to their ghostlike invisibility. They turn out to be black, and take offense ("spooks" also carries a racially derogatory sense), and the prevailing political correctness takes its toll. Doubling the ambiguities, Silk, it turns out, is himself a light-skinned black, "passing" for white. (Are blacks incapable of racist remarks? How about blacks who have rejected their racial identity?)

Negligence in the law has relatively explicit, even if often controversial, standards. The standard of care required may be specified as part of the obligations of a job or social position, or by legal precedent, or legislation, or contract or any number of other norm-setting mechanisms. In the less codified world of insult, the conditions that make an act or omission or statement insulting—independent of the agent's intention—are less clear. Still, if a person *could not* have known that their words or deeds were insulting, then they (by ordinary standards of negligence) have an excuse. If the slighted individual still feels insulted, it may be because of some other attitude that the otherwise excusable remark reveals (e.g., condescension). Of course different excuses may depend for their acceptability on the character and degree of the ensuing harm. There are limits. As J. L. Austin pointed out in his "A Plea for Excuses," "We may plead that we trod on the snail inadvertently: but not on a baby—you ought to look where you are putting your great feet" (1970a, 194).

IDENTITY, EXPECTATIONS, AND MORAL INSULTS

People speak naturally of feeling violated in cases of rape. They speak of feeling violated almost as readily in cases of having their home ransacked. But it would take an unusually intense form of identification to feel violated when one's car has been stolen. That is a different sort of harm, a different sort of loss. In insult too, there is a violation of the demands of respect for the integrity of one's person. Not that "feeling insulted" and "feeling violated" are the same. Talk of "violation" ups the ante. In rape, in murder, the injury is so great that any insult involved may be the least of one's concerns. We may most often associate insult with violation of the conventional norms of etiquette and with lesser harms and mere offense. Nonetheless, there may be moral insults as well, and they sometimes may come attached to great harms. Hate crimes add something to whatever other sort of harm takes place. Crimes are classified as hate crimes in virtue of their motives, the criteria for selection of a target, and their message—and they may be insulting in virtue of the same features. When Matthew Shepard was brutally murdered just outside Laramie, Wyoming in 1998 because his two assailants were unhinged by his sexual orientation, the murder was a hate crime. When extra punishment is added to an underlying offense because the crime is motivated by invidious discrimination, the extra punishment—while meant to deter those who would threaten and harm particular classes of people and also to reaffirm and express the countervailing attitudes of the wider society—is in effect for the moral insult added to the injury. Sometimes what is at stake is individual dignity, the entitlement to equal concern and respect.

Moral insults go beyond bad manners and even beyond physical harms. When the United States interned citizens of Japanese ancestry during World War II, insult was added to whatever other harms were done. The notion that people who were of foreign origin could not be trusted to be loyal to the United States was a slur on the character of those interned. But the notion involved and so the offense was even more specific and egregious, for only Japanese-Americans were in fact interned. Citizens who had their origin in Germany or in Italy, also enemy states at the time, were not interned. Xenophobia was compounded by racism.

Whether racial discrimination is always by its nature insulting is arguable. If the interning of Japanese-Americans in World War II was insulting, surely it was insulting partly because it could not be justified on the basis of military necessity.[8] If affirmative action is not insulting, it is presumably because of the existence of relevant disparities in the groups affected and because of the arguably benign purposes of taking race into account in admissions, hiring, and housing. Affirmative action

8. *Korematsu v. United States*, 323 U.S. 214 (1944). Korematsu's conviction for violating the exclusion orders was subsequently vacated by a federal district court because of the misleading character of the government's arguments in connection with military necessity—*Korematsu v. United States*, 584 F. Supp. 1406 (N.D. Cal. 1984). Congress eventually apologized and provided some restitution in the *Civil Liberties Act of 1988*, 102 Stat. 903 (codified at 50 U.S.C. § 1989 [1994]). See Irons 1983.

need not reflect invidious racial attitudes and hatred. What of racial profiling? Is it insulting, like the interning of Japanese-Americans in World War II, or is it merely sensible crime control and anti-terrorism, and so perhaps, like affirmative action, justifiable? On what does the answer depend? The purposes allegedly being served and the probabilities involved must surely be taken into account, as must the character and extent of any infringement on liberties and rights. It is conceivable that members of a particular race are no more likely to be hazardous drivers or otherwise dangerous to others than members of any other race, and that police who disproportionately stop drivers on the basis only of their race serve no good purpose. (Some states have recently outlawed the practice.) It is also conceivable that, at this time, persons of certain ethnic backgrounds boarding airplanes are more likely to be terrorists than others, and so subjecting them to special screening makes more effective use of limited resources. Again, the likelihoods involved, the seriousness of the harm to be prevented, and the extent of interference with liberty must be taken into account. (When the Justice Department permitted its fears of terrorism in the wake of 9/11 to lead to the confinement of thousands of Arabs in prisons and detention centers for lengthy and indeterminate periods, without access to counsel or judicial review, the assault on civil liberties was arguably more menacing than the danger sought to be avoided. Airport searches are one thing, indeterminate confinements another.)[9] Whatever the facts in these particular cases, certainly there might be cases where high stakes combined with comparatively limited infringements on liberty might justify profiling—without

---

9. This is not to speak of the arrest of innocent civilians and their humiliation and abuse in Afghanistan and Iraq under the authority of the U.S. Department of Defense. While Secretary of Defense Rumsfeld resisted calling such treatment "torture" (and conservative talk-show host Rush Limbaugh dismissed it as "blowing off steam"), it may properly be seen as a part of the systematic denial of civil liberties and human dignity, at home and abroad, characteristic of the administration of George W. Bush. Deaths of detainees, rendition to foreign countries for purposes of torture, warrantless wiretaps in the United States and the suspension of habeus corpus for individuals designated "enemy combatants" are further parts of the growing catalogue of outrages against law and decency. Even the notion of "moral insult" may seem too feeble when failures of respect are so systematic and so profound.

offense to anyone's dignity. Possibly extraneous motives and intentions may taint otherwise justifiable practices, but it is significant that the facts do matter and that legitimate justifications might exist.

Given that expectations and the legitimacy of expectations are crucial to the understanding and place of insults in our lives, what should we expect? What are we entitled to expect? Notice that expectations may be of a rather wide range of kinds. We have expectations that particular people will do certain things and even that the doing will be out of certain motivations rather than others. We expect, or at least hope, that our boy- or girlfriend will show up for a date because they want to, not merely out of a sense of obligation. If they show up, yet make it plain that they would rather be elsewhere, it sours the occasion almost as much as their having stood one up might have done. Equally, truth spoken from one motive may insult, while the same truth spoken from different motives might not.

Individual sensitivities and preferences also come into account. Thickness of skin is a relevant variable. And while some may be excessively sensitive and expect too much, so far as insult is a matter of assertions of or assumptions about dominance, one has to recognize that some people prefer to assume submissive positions. Does that mean that they cannot be insulted (they have no expectations of respectful treatment to be disappointed) or merely that they are welcoming sufferers of abuse? It seems that if they can in fact be insulted (they just happen to welcome and enjoy the experience, perhaps often inviting and encouraging its infliction) then feeling insulted is not necessarily a species of anger. But we should be careful here. As we have noted, being insulted and feeling insulted need not be the same. Being and feeling are not in general the same for most (if not all) emotions. And some of the complications here may be like the puzzles raised by the relation of masochism to pleasure. If masochism involves enjoying the infliction of pain on oneself (even if under very specific and stereotyped circumstances), the notion that pain is necessarily or essentially unpleasant comes into question. Does the masochist enjoy the pain or is the masochist simply willing to put up with the unpleasantness of the pain for the sake of something else? How could one tell? One of the usual measures of the unpleasantness of pain is precisely the steps taken to avoid it. Humiliation seems to be what is desired both by many masochists and many who willingly submit to insult. The moral masochist enjoys feeling insulted. It satisfies some inner need. Freud's moral masochist has a "need for punishment."

Whether due to an unconscious sense of guilt or the death instinct or something else, the moral masochist seeks out victimhood and unpleasant or humiliating situations from which they derive enjoyment, just as the sexual pleasure of the standard masochist is bound to pain. Can one have such a preference without sacrificing self-esteem and self-respect? (As noted earlier, these need not be the same. And whatever remedies low self-esteem or insufficient self-respect may call for, moral masochism raises other therapeutic issues.) It is doubtful that masochists welcome just any pain or any humiliation or insult—the conditions for such experiences bringing satisfaction are typically quite specific. We all, it would seem, have our boundaries.

If we ask again what buys immunity from and what makes for vulnerability to insult, we are confronted once more with the question of the Aristotelian mean. Being arrogant may make one invulnerable. That is, if one does not value the opinion of others, it will be difficult for those opinions (whatever they are) to wound. But such arrogance, such excessive self-regard, may unfit one for ordinary human relations and sympathy. And if expecting too much, being too sensitive, makes one constantly the subject of wounded feelings, that too may make one unfit for human relations and sympathy. Others may find it simply too difficult to deal with one's delicate sensibilities or paranoid defensiveness. The Stoic Sage runs especially the dangers of arrogance. Part of what is wrong with the Stoic Sage who seeks to be impervious to all that is not in his control (including the opinions of others) is that he is insufferable. Saying that all that is governed by chance and necessity (which many of us think is *everything*) does not matter, does not make it so. The essential self may shrink to vanishing point when so much is left out of account. While the Stoic Sage within the fortress of his self-sufficiency may never feel insulted, his constant condescension and patronizing of others will inevitably leave them feeling insulted, denigrated, and not taken seriously. Attitudes appropriate to three-year-olds may not work when applied to adults. Where is the mean?

ON HAVING ONE'S FEELINGS HURT

There is in fact a juvenile version of feeling insulted. Where adults will speak of feeling insulted, children will complain of having their feelings hurt. The word "feelings" is sometimes used to refer to all emotions, but in this context it would seem that even children are sensitive to issues of dignity and honor, of respect from their peers, and the feelings that are wounded are more specifically those involving social expectations and moral identity. (Adults will sometimes speak of taking umbrage, which is perhaps a more deliberate activity than either feeling insulted or having one's feelings hurt.)

It is a commonplace that anger consumes the angry person. But why is that so? Surely part of the answer is that it consumes his thoughts. His attention is directed at the object of his ire, and he dwells on his grievances and on thoughts of revenge. This absorption of thought is familiar in jealousy, which is in part constituted by anger. The wound in feeling insulted can be similarly consuming. Does that make feeling insulted a species of anger? Not necessarily. Remember that love too can be consuming.

I started by suggesting we needed to think about the notional object of feeling insulted (namely, insult), just as in understanding fear we need to think about danger. When we are afraid, the danger we fear is typically of injury of one form or another. Not just anything, however, can count as an "injury" (Foot 1978b). What we react to in insult is also a kind of injury, having specifically to do with expectations of attention and respect. But the concept takes one only so far. It may be helpful to remember that people can have differential reactions to or expressions of fear: some may flee, some may stand frozen to the spot. The same is true for anger. Some may shout, some may fall silent, refusing to speak with the object of their anger. Reactions to insult are at least as diverse. What brings them together (as "danger" does the expressions of fear) is the social placement of insult. (In this discussion we have introduced considerations about both the insulters and the insulted, intentions and expectations; we have been looking especially to expectations and their sources—from social practice, and law, and etiquette, to individual relations and agreements—and to the standards by which we judge expectations legitimate or, alternatively, unreasonable.) What physiological feelings are involved in emotions are typically more significant in relation to distinguishing emotions as a class from non-emotions than in distinguishing within, among, and between particular emotions. They are not what is distinctive of particular emotions. (Think of how we distinguish regret, remorse, guilt, shame and embarrassment, and other emotions in that unhappy range. It is not on the basis of peculiar sensations regularly present in one but not the others. See Neu 1977, *passim*; and Neu 2000, 11–13, 17–19, 46.) Whether one reacts to the disappointed expectations characteristic of insult with anger or dejection or some further emotion is, like the expression of fear and anger and other emotions, highly variable. I doubt that there is a unique feeling of insult, at least not the sort of physiological and neurophysiological core that may be typical of basic fear and anger. Fear and anger, in some of their forms at least, fit reasonably well the sort of affect program model favored by Paul Ekman and other evolutionarily oriented biologists and psychologists (see works cited in Ekman and Keltner, 2000). Fear and anger (I might add, unlike the more complex and social emotion of jealousy, which nonetheless includes fear and anger as components) have clear physiological syndromes, including stereotypical facial expressions, are reflex-like, pancultural, and phylogenetically ancient and do not require (indeed, may be modularly isolated from) higher cognitive processing. What has to be acknowledged, however, is that there are very different fears (from basic physiological responses, with perhaps fixed physiology, neurology, and facial expressions, to highly intellectual fears that may involve little if anything in the way of physiological upset), with variation between and at both ends in physiological feelings, dispositions to behavior, and associated thoughts. The same complexity seems to me to apply to "feeling insulted" as well, though the intellectual component (expectations, beliefs about entitlements, conventions, and the like), seems indispensable to that more complex and more social emotion in all its forms. It may feel like a "slap in the face," but the shock to the system captured in that description is more metaphorical than physiological.

In understanding feeling insulted, as with almost all emotions, we would do best to reject the notion that each individual emotion constitutes a natural kind. We are not born with a set of well-defined physiological marbles of feeling, with the problems of finding the appropriate labels for the already differentiated feelings and of communicating to others which feeling we are currently experiencing. If that were the situation, the problems might be insoluble. We might never be sure that the words we attach to these isolated inner feelings match up with those of others: our language for speaking of our inner lives might never make real communication possible. But the truth is that we enter a world with an already established language for speaking of the inner life, a social world into which we are initiated by others who take note of our circumstances and our behavior and responses. We come to divide up our inner life in accordance with the categories provided in the language we are born into, our mother tongue. (This view is elaborated and developed in Neu 2000, especially the first two essays.) It would be a mistake to think that feeling insulted must be a kind of anger or dejection or some other such fixed category. While I have tried to argue feeling insulted is essentially tied to disappointment, in order to understand the character of that disappointment much must be taken into account: the nature of norms, the varieties of things that matter to us, and the complex web of our social interactions. Here, as elsewhere, our emotional categories serve to organize and help us make sense of our chaotic inner lives in relation to our uncertain and changing place in the world. In understanding our emotional categories, we must start with that messy complexity, with the distinctive objects and conditions of emotion, rather than with imagined, fixed, basic, well-defined marbles of feeling.

Perhaps the most adequate general characterization of feeling insulted is that it is a kind of pain caused by disappointed expectations of attention and respect. The relevant expectations (as I shall elaborate in the next chapter) are normative rather than predictive, involving as they do considerations about how we *should* be thought of and treated; and the disappointment is a matter of shock rather than simple surprise. Expectations (and their legitimacy) vary individually and with the conventions that prevail within the relevant social circles (which themselves may be more or less wide). As with all emotions, the expressions and desires associated with feeling insulted also vary. The situation is further complicated by the vast range of emotions one finds regularly associated with insult, from wounded pride, to humiliation, shame, embarrassment, guilt, anger, and on indefinitely. It is not for nothing that one might equate feeling insulted with "hurt feelings." In insult, the self—one's moral identity, the core conditions of both self-respect and self-esteem—is under assault, even if the siege is the result of the indifference and negligence of others rather than their active and malicious intentions. Our place in the world is precarious. (Here I mean the social world. Our place in the natural world is equally precarious, but we are foolish if we expect anything other than indifference from that world.) Even if we strive to make our identity and sense of self-worth independent of the attitudes of others, some features of our identity necessarily depend on their reactions (can we truly be engaging and charming if no one else finds us so?) as may some of our most central desires (unrequited love may remain love, but it is difficult to sustain and such love itself rarely sustains the disappointed would-be lover). Honor and status are even more directly and obviously dependent on the attitudes of others. That we remain vulnerable to the views of others despite whatever Stoic or Emersonian strivings for self-reliance we might engage in, emerges perhaps most clearly in the experience, the all-too-common experience, the all-too-human experience, of feeling insulted.

TWO

∎ ∎ ∎

HONOR

SLAPS AND SWORDS

INSULT TYPICALLY INVOLVES SHOCK. A DISRUPTION OF EXPECTATIONS. A slap in the face. Even where one might have known better on the basis of prior experience, each new disappointment can come as a surprise. (This is the common experience of disappointed, and jealous, lovers. Each betrayal is fresh.) Feeling insulted is not just anger, not just dejection. There is a disruption of the sense of self, of one's place in the world and one's place in the heart and esteem of others. Of course, some insults do not take one by surprise. Sometimes one expects no better of others or of a particular other. But expecting and experiencing are two different things. The actual impact of an event may take one by surprise even if the event itself was expected; the impact may be fresh even where a pattern is familiar or an outcome foreseen. (Think of the impact of repeated readings of novels or viewings of movies, even suspense novels and horror movies. Think of the common experience of those associated with alcoholics. Each lapse, each repeated apology, has its own impact.) And the impact when the essential feature of an event is insult is not merely physical, it is psychological and emotional and (sometimes) moral.

Shock is not precisely the same as surprise. When the United States attacked Iraq in the spring of 2003, the air campaign that the Pentagon described in terms of "shock and awe" was hardly a surprise—the very visible buildup had been going on for months. When the Claude Rains character in the film *Casablanca* (1942) professes himself to be "shocked" that gambling is going on at Rick's place, the remark is of course overwhelmingly and comically ironic, but a part of its force stems from its play on the moral overtones in the word. (Captain Louis Renault's immortal statement doubled up on the word, yielding ironic emphasis: "I am shocked, shocked to find that gambling is going on in here!"—said as he was collecting his winnings from that very gambling.) "Shocking displays" are thought to violate norms of propriety, not simply to be unexpected. Shock, surprise, and startle, while connected, have subtly different associations and applications. The central concept in connection with insult seems to me to be shock, though the role of expectations (which are equally crucial in surprise) may obscure the picture. The situation may be clarified if we understand that there are two kinds of "expectations": one normative and the other predictive. The first is tied to shock (and when we self-consciously feel insulted, it has to do with what we believe ourselves to deserve in the way of attention, respect, and treatment). The second is tied to surprise. Both types of expectations can be disappointed. When we feel insulted, we often feel stunned and blind-sided.

We have noted that the OED emphasizes in its definition of insult that it refers to speech or behavior "intended to wound self-respect." I think we can now be more precise. We have seen that insulting behavior need not be intentional; it may be merely thoughtless or negligent. And the wound, the suffering and dejection (and even the pained anger) characteristic of feeling insulted, seems to me to essentially involve shock, a disruption in one's sense of oneself. Not that one necessarily suffers a loss of self-esteem and so thinks worse of oneself, but one comes to the recognition, the rude recognition, that others (and perhaps especially significant others) think less well of one than one had thought. Societies that place "honor" at the center of their thinking about interpersonal relations and value make this especially plain and the positional calculations become explicit and public. The nature of the inner state of feeling insulted can be illuminated by looking at its public face, the face that has been slapped.

A SLAP IN THE FACE

One of Freud's earliest patients, Frau Cäcilie M., suffered from a recurring facial neuralgia, a sensation that over a period of fifteen years had appeared suddenly two or three times a year, each time lasting for from five to ten days and then disappearing. The neuralgia had not been amenable to treatment (including the extreme and cruel treatment of having seven teeth extracted). Freud recognized the symptom as hysterical and was able to get Cäcilie to recover an originating traumatic scene which had involved a conversation with her husband in which he made a remark "which she had felt as a bitter insult. Suddenly she put her hand to her cheek, gave a loud cry of pain and said: 'It was like a slap in the face.' With this her pain and her attack were both at an end" (Freud 1895d, 178). The case (and cure by catharsis or abreaction too) is more complex than this brief summary suggests and in fact involved years of insults leading through symbolization to fresh attacks of facial neuralgia (1895d, 175–81). Cäcilie achieved other feats of symbolic conversion of thoughts into sensations: "Running parallel to the sensation of a hysterical 'aura' in the throat, when that feeling appeared after an insult, was the thought 'I shall have to swallow this'" (1895d, 180). As Freud points out, such linguistic expressions may themselves have somatic foundations.

In honor, there is great concern with saving face (or keeping face, or preserving or maintaining face). It is the face that one is concerned to save that gets slapped. The blow may be physical or metaphorical. The pain is, in either case, essentially psychological (and sometimes moral). One's identity and standing are under assault. Spitting in the face is a similar, perhaps more egregious affront, and a drink in the face (perhaps more common in the movies than in real life) conveys a similar message. What is it about the face?[1]

Wittgenstein has told us, "The human body is the best picture of the human soul" (1953, Part II, 178). I think it fair to suggest that the face gives

---

1. While some consider backslappers crudely offensive, it is interesting that, in the vernacular of interactive gestures, a slap on the back is meant to be the opposite of an affront. The friendly assault from the rear that such a slap registers is different from a similarly placed "pat." To pat on the back is to approve or console. Though a slap is sometimes a form of congratulation, it is perhaps most often meant to signify or create hearty camaraderie and commonality. The violence of a slap (again, unlike the gentleness of a pat) becomes something else when applied to the face. When the hand shifts from the back to the butt, meanings can become confused. A playful slap on the rear can be conspiratorial or seductive or—less friendly, even if equally playful—a taunt, but the rear end is also the locus for spanking. The assaultive attitude becomes naked when one talks about "kicking butt" or "beating ass." We shall return to the significances of assaults from the rear in chap. 4.

a compacted image of that soul. Orwell claimed, "At fifty, every man has the face he deserves"—a point elaborated by couturière Coco Chanel with, "Nature gives you the face you have at twenty. Life shapes the face you have at thirty. But at fifty you get the face you deserve." At all ages, we identify each other mainly through the face. In shame, one wishes to hide, especially one's face—one is shamefaced. And a shamed individual has difficulty looking anyone else in the face. It is the face through which we express (as well as conceal) our inner lives, and that thus becomes inscribed with the habitual patterns of our character and our past. Nonetheless, our social face is a construct, only contingently related to the physiological face that we are born with and that develops (indeed, the relation may in some cases be as distorted as that between Dorian Gray and his soul-reflecting portrait, as depicted in the story by Oscar Wilde). One's social face, like one's good name, is the bearer of one's reputation. The face that embodies social status and that must be kept, maintained, and preserved may have deep roots and special significance in China (Hu 1944), but every society has its own notions of social prestige and moral character and those notions very often find distinctive reflection in terms of the face. (They are almost as often expressed in terms of the head, which can be bowed or raised, covered or uncovered, touched or crowned, not to mention scalped or chopped off. See especially Onians 1951, 93–122 on the relation of head and *psyche*.) Erving Goffman is perhaps the master American sociologist of the micromanagement of self involved in projecting and saving face (see, e.g., Goffman 1967). Who we are is concentrated in our visage. Just as the king's crown can, metonymically, stand for the king, every person's face stands for them. When we save face, we protect our image, our standing in the world.

A slap in the face can also have other significances, e.g., to wake one up. But the usual sense is as an insult or as a response to insult. Unlike a fist to the face, the point is not typically to cause serious physical injury. The boundary violation is largely symbolic. It may be a response to insult, as in a woman's slap of a man who has made an unwanted and inappropriate sexual advance. It may be the formal prelude to a duel[2]—throwing down a gauntlet attenuates the slap, making the action with the gauntlet

---

2. "Montesquieu suggests, following Beaumanoir, that since knights disputed honour with their faces covered, in contrast to plebeians, the offence to the face carried the connotation of treating a knight as if he were plebeian, that is, of denying his status" (Pitt-Rivers 1966, 74n10; see Montesquieu, *The Spirit of the Laws*, Book 28 §20).

symbolic at two removes. The gauntlet toss becomes a ritual challenge to a duel—one of the many fields of honor, of the stylized theater of insult.

DUELING

The European institution of dueling had its roots in earlier practices such as medieval judicial combat, trial by ordeal, and jousts to the death (*armes à outrance*). These practices (unlike the modern duel) generally had official sanction, also

> the *pas d'armes* differed from the duel of later days in having no motive but fame, but the difference was not always great, since many duels had no cause or purpose beyond giving proof of courage. This unreasoning pugnacity was carried furthest in the duel between man and bull, perhaps of Moorish origin but taken up by Spanish cavaliers with lances. Only in Spain's time of decay, the later seventeenth century, was it abandoned to the plebeian professional, on foot, as the poor man's ladder to fame and fortune. (Kiernan 1988, 40; see also 73)

The modern duel emerged during the persistent warfare of the sixteenth and seventeenth centuries, arising first in Italy and then being taken up in France and elsewhere. While fights between individuals might break out anywhere, the formal duel was a privilege of rank and class, generally confined to the aristocracy, the military officer corps, and other groups (e.g., university students in Germany)[3] where individual honor was tied to group status. Dueling and its associated codes of honor tended to contribute to group cohesion; that is, within the hierarchies of class, the codes of dueling and the rules of *politesse* provided a rough equality. To tender a challenge is to acknowledge the offender as a peer

---

3. The *Mensur* (student duel) is still a feature of German university life as a form of sporting event (arranged dueling tournaments started to replace insult-initiated affairs in the middle of the nineteenth century). Most German universities have long-established fraternities of *Corpsstudenten* with strict rules, secret meetings, uniforms, and great prestige. In contrast to clandestine aristocratic duels, duels of "scholastic honor" were always fought with swords (rapiers), involved protective clothing that minimized injury, and were typically public events. The facial scar (dueling *Schmiss*) came to be regarded as a mark of distinction—steadfastly bearing pain was more important than finesse. (See Frevert 1995, 85–134; McAleer 1994, 119–58.)

in honor, and the true opposite of taking offense is a haughty disdain that refuses the possibility of riposte and thus humiliates. "Humiliation corresponds to disdain, and is the situation of the individual confined by his nature to an inferior position, to whom one denies the dignity of being a man to the extent of refusing to enter into a dialogue with him, even by an insult" (Bourdieu 1966, 197–98; see also Nye 1993, 128, 206). Dueling was also, like honor itself, a matter strictly for men—Italian *virtù* is explicitly an ideal of manliness (Kiernan 1988, 48). While often invoked in the protection of women, it is only men who have and lose honor, and who must duel to preserve it. (As Nye puts the point: "women's honor is primarily sexual in nature and consists first of her virginity and later her strict marital fidelity" and it is men who are charged "to oversee and protect the honor of the women in their family" [1993, 10].) The emphasis on courage, *sangfroid*, rugged combativeness, uncompromisingness, insistence on respect, and strength in notions of honor were equally marks of certain (particularly martial and heroic) male self-images. "Duelling could virtually be regarded as a test of true, unalloyed masculinity" (Frevert 1995, 27). Still, by the end of World War I, the experience of mass slaughter had put an end to the practice in those parts of Europe where it had not already died out. (The practice had been effectively ended in England in 1844 by Prime Minister Robert Peel's denial of army pensions to the widows of officers killed in duels [McAleer 1994, 95].) Arguably, what had started with Renaissance ideals of civility ended with adolescent ideals of masculinity. As Kevin McAleer puts it, "Destitute of noble values by which to live, duelists embraced a set of aristocratic guidelines for which to die: a code of honor. . . . less modern-day knights than adolescent schoolboys in the locker room snapping towels to exhibit some simple-minded and vaguely slapstick notions of masculinity" (1994, 8).

The institution has an interesting dialectical history. Initially serving to limit and control violence (preventing vendettas and feuds), it came to be discouraged and ultimately banned as it seemed to compel unwanted fights, often enough ending in unnecessary deaths. This in addition to usurping the state's monopoly on violence. The existence of the rituals came to force some people to defend their honor in situations where they (and society) would have preferred to let the matter drop or to deal with it without violence, even regimented and circumscribed violence. A point of honor can oblige one to resent, and in the world of dueling, to challenge. Some were forced to fight by the pressures of their class. The refusal of a challenge made one (in the German expression) *unsatisfaktionsfähig*—you abdicated the rights of your station and anyone could insult you without you being able to demand chivalrous satisfaction—one got reclassed a coward.

There were an extraordinary number of variations in the terms of engagement. Weaponry ranged from épées, rapiers, foils, and sabers (usually with blunted tip) to single-shot, muzzle-loaded, smoothbore pistols (notorious for their inaccuracy). Distance in pistol encounters might range from a deadly five paces to a far safer thirty-five paces (though sometimes combatants deliberately shot into the air in any case). Shots might be single or multiple, simultaneous or alternating. The duelists might move away, turn, and fire; or stand and shoot facing sideways (sometimes having to fire before the "director of combat" counted to three, thus allowing little time for aiming); or fire while moving toward each other (up to a barrier point). Seconds might be bearers of challenges, intermediaries, negotiators, referees, witnesses, and writers of official reports, or, sometimes, become actual combatants. Each combatant typically had two seconds, though the number could vary, as could the length of the obligatory waiting period between challenge and duel—usually at least twelve hours. That there was some waiting period was part of what distinguished a gentlemanly duel from a street brawl. There were also time constraints of a different sort, having the effect of hurrying things up or precipitating action: after a provocation, one generally had just twenty-four hours to challenge, and the duel itself was to take place within forty-eight hours of that. But the rules were flexible. A so-called American variant "was in essence part suicide pact and part Russian roulette, in which two men would agree to let fate harmonize their discord by drawing lots, the loser then quietly offing himself within a specified period of time" (McAleer 1994, 80). That particular variant had the merit of providing an answer to charges of murder. But in fact, while private duels were in most places and times formally prohibited, the prohibitions were rarely enforced, juries and courts often refused to convict, and where there were convictions, the penalties were generally light, and even then, violators were often pardoned. Actual outcomes of duels varied as much as format, from the generally mild cuts of French sword fights in the nineteenth century (stopping at token first blood) to the ferociously fatal German pistol encounters of the same period.

Most interesting from our point of view, however, are the "degrees of insult" that might provoke a duel and the varying remedies they allowed. There were formal codes and manuals governing such matters, from early Italian ones such as Girolamo Muzio's *Il Duello* (Venice, 1550) to the Comte de Chatauvillard's much cited, copied, and virtually official *Essai sur le Duel* (Paris, 1836). McAleer spells out the levels recognized in Germany before WW I:

> A duel was only possible where there had been an insult, of which there were three broad categories. The first classification was the simple slight (*einfache Beleidigung*), constituted by impoliteness or inconsiderate behavior. The second level of insult was cursing or attribution of shameful qualities, examples of which might be calling someone an *Esel* (jackass) or a *Schwachkopf* (imbecile). A tertiary offense was gravest and was rendered through a blow or a slap, the spectacular gauntlet-in-the-face falling under this heading, although they were rarely that hammy. To merely touch another's person qualified as a third-level offense . . . The violation of another's physical integrity was considered so reprehensible that even a threatened blow was regarded as an extreme offense, and so gentlemen would spare themselves the exertion by stating simply: 'Consider yourself slapped!' The seduction or lewd touching of one's wife, daughter, sister or other female dependent, could constitute a 'blow,' and similar actions or words that jeopardized one's entire moral being (as the phrase usually went) were also aggravated third-level insults, amenable only through bloodshed.
>
> . . . At the first level, the offended had the choice of weapons; at the second level, a choice of weaponry and style of combat; and in cases of third-level injury, the choice of arms, style, and distance.* (German-language codes recommended that all third-level insults be settled with pistols.)
>
> *An offended party could only accept an apology at the first level and still keep face—second- and third-level insults were deemed too severe for forgiveness. If, on the other hand, he rejected an apology at the first level, his right to choice of weaponry was forfeited. (McAleer 1994, 47–48, note at 222n18; and see 162 on the seduction of a wife or daughter as "a literal slap in the face.")[4]

That assault and battery should be regarded as serious offenses is hardly surprising, law everywhere generally treats them as such—though

---

4. The German codes, in this as in other matters, basically followed the Comte de Chatauvillard's canonical manual, of which Nye (1993, 144) provides a summary.

sports contexts, such as football and boxing, make for exceptions, and dueling itself might be regarded as a special context in light of the consent of both parties. Where the initiating blow was a slap, there would of course be underlying motives of varying degrees of seriousness. In any case, the injury in a slap is generally more symbolic than physical. The violation of boundaries remains.

In some places and times, verbal assaults have also been punishable as crimes. McAleer reports that was the case in Germany in the nineteenth century (however inadequate legal satisfaction might have seemed to the affronted parties): "the German penal code was a vicious weapon of retribution in cases of alleged insult, more severe than its dueling law in some ways. Almost everything could be construed as an insult under the *Beleidigung* (insult) clause, including impoliteness and cursing" (29). The legal protection from insult given in Germany at that time was stronger than that provided in France and there were no such laws (except in instances of financial loss as a result of defamation) in England. In any case, men of honor everywhere generally scorned going to law as a way of obtaining satisfaction, or were criticized if they did have recourse to the courts. Typical attitudes are reflected in the story of a French drama critic in the 1880s who sued an actor who had slapped him over a negative review and was in turn ridiculed in print by a former colleague who wrote that even after a court decision, "a man who has been slapped is still slapped." The drama critic responded this time by sending his seconds to the former colleague and was wounded in the subsequent, honor-redeeming, duel (Nye 1993, 188).

The special place given to affronts to associated females is worthy of particular attention. More than gallantry and chivalry in defense of womankind was generally at stake.

HONOR AND MASCULINITY

Achilles, at the start of the *Iliad*, got into a world-historical snit when Agamemnon took away his slave-girl prize, Briseis. His upset is misunderstood if it is thought of in terms of jealousy, at least if jealousy is taken to involve concern over lost love. The affront to Achilles' honor involved the taking of what he believed rightly his; that the prize for his previous bravery in battle was a woman and not merely gold or other valuable objects did not much affect the affront. Achilles' concern when Briseis was taken from him was not over lost love, he did not care for the concubine or her affections in particular, but over lost face, lost honor. And the loss of honor itself can be felt as emasculating.

Despite the many twists in the development of conceptions of honor, in protecting women, in many times and places, men were thought to be defending their own honor. Indeed, any insult could be taken as a sign that the other believed one powerless to retaliate, and so every insult could be taken to imply cowardice and effeminacy:

> German duelists . . . conceived of an insult—any insult, whether impinging on their family, caste, or personal honor—as testament to the secret opinion of the offender that one was powerless to retaliate; that he could injure with impunity because the object of his affront would not fight back. Thus, every *insult* implied the supreme insult among men of honor: imputation of physical cowardice—an imputation tied to notions of effeminacy. The duel was, therefore, an ostensible measure of courage, a litmus test of manhood that pretended to overturn the implicit emasculation entailed in every indignity. (McAleer, 44–45)

This was not a hidden aspect of the undergirding attitudes. "Maximilian Beseler, the Prussian minister of justice, noted in 1907 'that in Germany, a duel is not solely occasioned by the fact that someone's honour is besmirched, but also indirectly by the fact that the masculinity of the offended party is attacked, and that he subsequently seeks to restore his impugned masculinity in a duel'" (Frevert 1995, 179–80). Nor was the attitude confined to Germany or even just to countries with formal institutions of dueling (though it was certainly prevalent in such countries). The sexualization of honor is just as, if not more, typical of Mediterranean cultures and other warmer climes. As David Gilmore explains:

> Honor and shame are reciprocal moral values representing primordial integration of individual to "group." They reflect, respectively, the conferral of public esteem upon the person and the sensitivity to public opinion upon which the former depends. Since all face-to-face societies are moral communities where public opinion arbitrates reputation, all such societies may be said to have some form of honor and shame. However, what seems descriptively outstanding about the Mediterranean variant is the relationship to sexuality and

gender distinctions . . . Honor is everywhere "closely associated with sex." . . . Its basic currency and measurement is the "shame" of women, by which Mediterraneanists mean female sexual chastity. Throughout the Mediterranean area, male honor derives from the struggle to maintain intact the shame of kinswomen; and this renders male reputation insecurely dependent upon female sexual conduct. Men are responsible for the shame of their women. . . . (Gilmore 1987, 3–4)

It appears that men can be, indirectly, raped of their honor. This could occur even where a kinswoman's loss of chastity was consensual. In cases of actual rape, in Turkey and Pakistan and elsewhere, there have been countless "honor killings" where the victims of rape are made victims a second time—by their families—for the dishonor they are imagined to have brought to their families. The practice is, of course, an unconscionable distortion and displacement of responsibility onto the woman victim and away from the rapist and from the male family members who were supposed to protect her. Their male honor is supposed somehow to require the forfeit of the woman's life with her chastity—a striking devaluation of female life.

Concerns over chastity were no doubt tied to inheritance practices and other social and economic realities, as well as to conceptions of manhood. But affronts to women and womanhood might readily serve as "a pretext for the struggle between the two men" (Nye 1993, 29, quote 179, cf. 201). Indeed, chivalrous masculine ideals went with a concomitant denigration and subjugation of the women those ideals claimed to serve. "Contempt for women went hand in gauntlet with their elevation . . . a woman was an object of worship *and* an object of scorn. And for this reason she was the exquisite object of a duel, which pretended to save her honor but really pronounced her shame and fastened her yoke." Women were not taken seriously: a woman could not insult a man directly, could not directly provoke a duel. Seduction of dependent women by male rivals, which could and did regularly provoke duels, had an indirect object. "The intimation of a 'sexual insult' was that its male object once-removed was incapable of redress and by equation a moral eunuch"—was, in effect, a woman (McAleer 1994, 160–64, and 177–78).

As we shall explore further in chapter 4, in many societies, especially small, face-to-face communities of the Mediterranean type, honor is strongly male and strongly sexualized, often tied to the chastity of one's women—and, symbolically—to the inviolability of one's own (male) rear. This goes back at least to the ancient Greeks. But again, the relevant attitudes are not confined to Mediterranean cultures or dueling societies, or even to small, face-to-face communities. Aspects of honor culture persist in the modern American South, and can be seen in the penchant for violence of the Southern white male. Nisbett and Cohen (1996) argue that in the American South, as in many of the world's cultures, male violence is strongly related to the importance attached to a reputation for strength and toughness, which in turn has its roots in the realities of herding economies where animals are always vulnerable to predation (the South, having been settled by herdsmen from the fringes of Britain, remained a low-population, and relatively lawless, frontier region until well into the nineteenth century). Using a remarkably wide range of evidence—anecdotal and historical data, archival homicide data, survey and experimental data, the attitudes manifested in legal and social policy—Nisbett and Cohen argue that the disproportional violence in the American South is tied to a sense of honor in which a perceived willingness to fight for what is one's own, and so to defend one's honor, is linked to social status, economic well-being, and life itself. Honor here is a matter of status and power rather than moral virtue or probity of character (honesty and integrity), hence the forceful response to insults. "When someone allows himself to be insulted, he risks giving the impression that he lacks the strength to protect what is his. Thus the individual must respond with violence or the threat of violence to any affront" (Nisbett and Cohen 1996, xv).

More specifically, given their culture of honor, Southern white males tend to take insults personally, rather than thinking they reflect most on the insulter (52), and they tend to approve more of violence in response to insults (28). The result of feeling diminished is that the affronted southerner may respond with aggressive or domineering behavior. As Nisbett and Cohen elaborate, "A key aspect of the culture of honor is the importance placed on the insult and the necessity to respond to it. An insult implies that the target is weak enough to be bullied. Since a reputation for strength is of the essence in the culture of honor, the individual who insults someone must be forced to retract; if the instigator refuses, he must be punished—with violence or even death. A particularly important kind of insult is one directed at female members of a man's family" (5).

HONOR AND ETIQUETTE

The attitudes of a culture of honor do not, however, depend on a shepherding past, where a reputation for defending one's own might have been economically crucial. Nor do they pertain only to violence. They in fact persist very widely in modern societies, perhaps especially in the expectations of etiquette. One must remember that while in one of its senses honor is a matter of virtue, moral character, honesty and integrity, in the sense in play in dueling and the matters we have been discussing, it is more a matter of status and precedence. This could, in some times and places, turn to some degree on inner virtue, but more often is a matter of birth, wealth, social position, and other aspects of reputation. Certainly that was the way in ancient times. The punctilios of the early dueling codes, and even more primitive mores, are not far from the demands of our less bloody modern forms of etiquette. They are all sources of the standards, norms, and expectations that govern, guide, and adjudicate our feelings of offense, and thus provide the social context of domination and due deference that structures the world of insult. It does not much matter that these days we talk in terms of self-esteem rather than honor (and low self-esteem rather than shame).[5]

William Ian Miller focuses a good deal of attention in his book, *Humiliation*, on the Icelandic sagas. He points out that like the people of the Icelandic sagas, we are in many respects ourselves still an honor society: "we, like the saga people, are not strangers to the nervousness and tensions that necessarily accompany caring about what others think about us. Like those ancient heroes, we care about honor, about how we stack up against all those with whom we are competing for approbation" (1993, ix–x). He especially emphasizes the ties of honor to the idea of reciprocity: "Much of the substance of honor is still rooted in a desire to pay back what we owe, both the good and the evil" (x). He brings out the ways in which we may compete even in expenditure on the apparently selfless gifts we bestow, and how the receipt of a gift can be felt as a

---

5. It does matter, however, when talk of low self-esteem trivializes shame into a matter of not feeling good about oneself and so leaves out the social dimension and questions of real value and achievement. It can come to seem that all that matters is thinking well of oneself—independent of whether one merits such self-approval. (See Miller 1993, 135.)

burden, imposing the obligation of an appropriate reciprocal gift. Even the unwanted gift must be requited. Birthdays and Valentine's Day and other occasions for gifts can create anxiety over the appropriately measured gesture, and there are fairly precise social expectations in relations to gifts of money, wedding registries, and the like. Gifts aren't quite free and unconstrained. Miller discourses on the subtleties of refusing dinner invitations and on Valentine's Day embarrassments, playing Miss Manners as he sketches our conventional expectations. (Here and elsewhere he is following in the sociological footsteps of Erving Goffman, examining the detailed ways in which we continue to live in the comparative, outer-directed world described by David Riesman [1950].) As Miller concludes, "our gift-exchange practices share features with the game of honor, albeit with stakes considerably smaller than they were when Egil and Einar [Viking figures] played the game. Gift exchanges cannot avoid the adjustment of status and dominance between the parties to the exchange and occasionally among third parties as well" (47).

While Miller is doubtless right that aspects of traditional honor societies persist in our more sophisticated sphere, especially manifesting themselves in the relevant constellation of emotions (particularly including shame, humiliation, and embarrassment—the dark side of pride), things have changed. As he acknowledges, things have toned down since Egil was prepared to hunt down and kill Einar for an extravagant shield that seemed to impose on Egil, the unwilling recipient, demands for poetic reciprocity. For one thing, gifts play less of a role in our economy (21). For another, as he says, we have "criminalized vengeance and decriminalized debt: the law of the talion gave way to the law of bankruptcy" (50). The ideology of the free gift works to mask the continuing and underlying demands of reciprocity. "There may be an intimate connection between our official denial of the dark, obliging, and importuning side of gifts and the official illegitimacy of revenge" (5–6). Many of our desires for vengeance get displaced onto movies and into subtle exchanges; we generally prefer to avoid direct confrontations (whether over gifts, or priority of seating, or unwanted invitations). The refusal of a dinner invitation can be a particularly delicate matter. We avoid confrontation by such strategies as referring vaguely to "prior engagements" rather than directly declining, a reference that gracious inviters know not to probe or question. It is important to avoid offense and to allow others to save face.

The more traditional attitudes may persist more visibly on the fields of combat in schoolyards and the workplace, but the exchanges of gifts and meals also bear their marks. "Giving forces us to make a visible sign of our preferences among the people we know and as such it has the capacity to insult, to create envy, to honor, and to dishonor" (Miller, 48). The norm of reciprocity "along with the inevitable ranking of others inherent in giving, gives the gift its aggressive aspect, its capacity for annoying and offending" (49). Despite these illuminating excursions into the honor stakes of everyday life, where we must pay back what we owe, Miller perhaps underemphasizes the ways in which we desire specifically to be honored, to be recognized.[6] That, surely, was the aspect of honor that concerned Achilles at the start of the *Iliad*. The *Iliad* is a tale of, among other things, honor. Achilles felt entitled to the slave-girl Briseis as his due reward for valor in the service of the Greek cause against Troy. He was mightily insulted when Agamemnon took away his prize. And that is the aspect of honor most prominent today when we feel insulted by the failures of people to pay us due attention. People want to be treated with care and respect. What counts as care and respect, of course, varies over time and place. It may also vary with subject-matter. (In chap. 8, we shall consider what "respect" for another's religion requires.)

As we have seen, some insults are breaches of etiquette. Miss Manners (Judith Martin) points out in her discussion of "Heavy Etiquette Theory" that etiquette is designed to protect people's feelings, that social conventions provide "nonprovocative ways of performing common tasks," and conformity can be a way of showing respect for the community and consideration for others. Social conventions also, she points out, can serve to give order to the erratic feelings that may attend milestone occasions such as weddings and funerals (1990, 15). As Miller puts it, "Manners help us negotiate social encounter without giving offense; they include practices that allow others to maintain their self-respect even as we deny them what they want . . . They provide us with ways of signaling respect and inclusion even as they are used to distance us from others" (30). The other side of these positive contributions is that social rules can occasion discomfort, and our commitment to good manners and sensitivity to the feelings of others can force us into unwanted situations—including

---

6. We see it illustrated, for example, in a threatening encounter over precedence in seating arrangements between one Gudmund and one Ofeig (Miller 1993, 85–86).

accepting unwanted invitations when no adequate and face-saving covering excuse can be generated. And, as Miss Manners points out, people
can take advantage of the good manners of others (Martin 1990, 12; see
the dramatic outcome of one such instance in Miller's tale of "Burning a
Witch" with which he opens his book [1993, 1–5]). While the rules of etiquette may give the well-intentioned-but-unsure needed guidance when
navigating uncertain territory (e.g., whether to invite former spouses to
second and third weddings), they may provide the ill-intentioned new
forms of effrontery and trip up the well-intentioned-but-ill-informed.
While thoughtlessness may always be a kind of insult, evolving etiquette
may establish new occasions requiring thought.

Etiquette in its best forms may ease and facilitate human interaction and smooth relations, but at its stilted worst it may create new forms
of insult and traps for the unwary. One may even wonder whether etiquette is designed to avoid pre-existing grounds of offense or to create
new ones: to prevent hurt feelings or create new occasions for such hurt.
Things may in fact work both ways, and even, in particular cases, shift
over time from one to the other.

We have already noted that the duel was started to limit violence
but led in time to unwanted fights. The *point d'honneur* is at the bor-
derland of etiquette—taking matters to an often bloody extreme. But
etiquette shares the dialectical potential of the duel. Etiquette provides
ways to avoid offense (simply follow accepted practice), but also offers
new ways to give offense by laying down rules in what might previously
have been unregulated territory. It also offers the possibility of new forms
of humiliation.

THE UNIVERSAL AND THE LOCAL

It is essential to etiquette that it varies from place to place and changes
over time. It reflects conventional understandings and expectations. That
social conventions in general vary and change might make them seem
less significant. Some might conclude that they do not matter. But, first,
they might actually change less than one thinks. For many of the underlying concerns—wanting generosity acknowledged and showing respect
for the dead and for the feelings of their survivors—persist. Nonetheless,
when chivalry came to demand that the strong yield to the weak, this was

a fundamental change from the heroic ideals of the past. When Socrates and Jesus urged that one never repay evil with evil (indeed when Jesus urged that one love everyone), this was a fundamental change from the expectations of their worlds, expectations that demanded that one help one's friends and harm one's enemies (the simple reciprocity of honor). Even in cases of such radical change, however, people often need guidance on how such fundamental moral attitudes should play out in ordinary day-to-day interactions. There is a need for norms, and that some are clearly conventional does not make them less significant. It is a mistake to think that etiquette has only to do with using the right salad fork. If, as Miss Manners argues, etiquette aims to avoid hurt feelings and to enable people to show consideration for others, then it may, sometimes at least, be an important business. (Complicated by the question of whether feelings sometimes may be hurt only because of conventional—contingent, changeable, and perhaps unnecessary—expectations.)

We have seen in our earlier discussion of hate crimes, of the internment of Japanese-Americans during WW II, and of contemporary issues of racial profiling, that there may be moral insults. Some think that the difference between morality and etiquette is that etiquette is simply conventional and changing, whereas morality is not. But many think morality too is conventional, not universal and unchanging. The point of etiquette might be thought to be less important than the points served by the constraints of morality. But again, etiquette is not only about the right salad fork. Manners and decency provide rules of behavior in polite (and ordinary) society. The point may sometimes be reciprocity, nonprovocation, giving order to erratic feelings, showing consideration to others, preventing offense, saving face. Sensitivity to such matters need not be trivial, even if the forms of showing sensitivity are contingent and not eternal. Erving Goffman goes further in his discussion of "The Nature of Deference and Demeanor." He argues that etiquette and our less formal rules of personal interaction provide what he calls the "ceremonial grounds of selfhood" (1967, 93), and so may be an essential business.

Jurisprudence distinguishes between offenses that are *malum in se* (wrong in themselves) and *malum prohibitum* (wrong because prohibited). Murder is an example of the first. Driving on the left side of the road is an example of the second. There is nothing inherently wrong with driving on the left side of the road. Indeed, there are many countries, including England, India, Australia, and Japan, where that is the rule of the road.

While it may be arbitrary which side of the road is chosen, it is important that there be just one (however local the mandate) consistent rule of the road. Without such normative guides, crashes would be massively multiplied. That other locales may have other prevailing norms does not make the enforcement of the local conventional norm any less important. That some legal norms (say the one prohibiting murder) may be universal, and that others (say the rule of the road) may vary and change, does not make the variable norm less significant. There is a bumper sticker one sometimes sees in California asserting that "skateboarding is not a crime." Well, it isn't and it is. It is not a crime on the order of assault or robbery. It is not prohibited by God's law, or nature's law, or the moral law, or any other would-be universal standard. It is not *malum in se*. But it is, in many places, *malum prohibitum*. And where there is a posted warning that skateboarding is prohibited in the parking lot or on the sidewalk, and there is a local statute enforcing such prohibitions, it is indeed a crime. (Not paying income tax was also not a crime until statutes were passed requiring the paying of income tax.) One may argue about whether the social good to be gained or the social harm to be averted is great enough to warrant such a restriction on liberty, but if the appropriate legal norm-creating procedures have been followed, skateboarding is indeed a crime. There is further room for argument about what sort of penalties should be attached to such offenses (supposing it should be outlawed, should it be treated as a minor violation, a misdemeanor, or a felony?), but the mere fact that something is not regarded as an offense everywhere and always or that some may believe it should never be regarded as an offense anywhere, does not make the setting of the norm or its enforcement pointless or arbitrary. In the matter of manners and submitting to the (varying) demands of local custom, as Miss Manners points out, "The idea that each person can develop his or her own language of behavior without worrying about its being comprehensible to others just doesn't work" (1990, 6). Of course, customs do change, and even Miss Manners acknowledges one must keep up with the contemporary expressions of expectations, e.g., "That previous generations had offensive habits, such as treating certain adults as children or all ladies as socially available, does not excuse doing so when this has been widely identified as insulting. Ignorance of society's reforms is no excuse unless you are in a line of work where you don't mind having it known that you are oblivious and insensitive—not a description of anyone who ought to be in a position to pass judgment" (1990, 10). Of course, the situation may be complicated by the difficulty sometimes of distinguishing violating a convention and attempting to change it—perhaps by breaking it. Surely that is how standards in dress regularly evolve.

A similar point about importance can be made in terms of the sociological distinction between substantive and ceremonial rules of conduct. Even the conventional and apparently merely symbolic can, in certain contexts, be significant. As Erving Goffman illustrates:

> An interesting limiting case of the ceremonial component of activity can be found in the phenomenon of "gallantry," as when a man calmly steps aside to let a strange lady precede him into a lifeboat, or when a swordsman, fighting a duel, courteously picks up his opponent's fallen weapon and proffers it to him.[7] Here an act that is usually a ceremonial gesture of insignificant substantive value is performed under conditions where it is known to have unexpectedly great substantive value. (Goffman 1967, 54n5)

GIVING THE LIE

In the days of judicial combat, the process typically started with an accusation, followed by the accused, in denying the charges against him, "giving the lie" to his accuser. "Giving the lie" became a pervasive as well as a profound charge. "It was from the term *calumnia*, for false accusation, that the fourteenth-century word 'challenge' was derived" (Kiernan 1988, 33). Giving the lie became the fundamental way of questioning a man's status as a gentleman (Peltonen 2003, 60). "The word *mentita* (giving the lie) figures in the Italian codes of honour as the formal provocation which cannot easily be refused" (Pitt-Rivers 1966, 32). According to the earliest codes of honor, "The two gravest transgressions were a blow, and an accusation of lying. . . . A charge of mendacity might be direct or

---

7. There are related customs in professional bicycle racing. When the overall lead rider in the *Tour de France* crashes or has a flat tire (or needs to pee), his rivals will not attack and take advantage—typically they will slow to give him time to recover. One is impressed by such sportsmanship (a kind of gallantry) that seems to go beyond the call of duty and may be costly.

indirect (anything up to thirty-two species could be reckoned), and the reply might be a 'retort courteous' or any one of a graduated ruder series" (Kiernan 1988, 48). Of course, some of the finer distinctions became the object of ridicule by many, including Shakespeare. Touchstone in *As You Like It* mocks the degrees of cause and retort, spelling out seven:

> *Touchstone.* O sir, we quarrel in print, by the book, as you have books for good manners. I will name you the degrees. The first, the Retort Courteous; the second, the Quip Modest; the third, the Reply Churlish; the fourth, the Reproof Valiant; the fifth, the Countercheck Quarrelsome; the sixth, the Lie with Circumstance; the seventh, the Lie Direct. All these you may avoid but the Lie Direct, and you may avoid that too, with an If. . . . Your If is the only peacemaker. Much virtue in If. (*As You Like It*, V.4.85–97)

Shakespeare also makes mock of the jargon of punctilio elsewhere (e.g., *Love's Labor's Lost*, V.2.683–704).

Nonetheless, there is something profoundly offensive about being lied to, and consequently about being accused of lying. We shall explore the significance of truth in greater detail when we come to the law of libel and slander, but Bernard Williams, by focusing on the person who has been deceived, brings out the particular wound, the humiliation, the blow to honor, involved in being lied to:

> In allowing himself to accept the other's belief as his own, and taking it that he has been given the truth through the speaker's assertion, he will feel that he has come as close to the real thing as anyone in his situation could do. When he realizes that he has been betrayed, there is a complete reversal: the speaker's will was entirely out of the picture, but now the picture is nothing but a product of that will. The victim recognizes the bare-faced lie as a pure and direct exercise of power over him, with nothing at all to be said for it from his point of view, and this is an archetypal cause of resentment: not just disappointment and rage, but humiliation and the recognition that in the most literal sense he has been made a fool of. (Williams 2002, 119)

Given Williams' plausible account of why lying is such an insult (and especially his recognition of the role of domination, a will to power, in the insult), we can perhaps see why an accusation of lying, of lack of honor in one's words, should be such a provocation. That being called a liar should be the most serious affront (along with a physical blow, and—one should add—being accused of cowardice, and so having one's masculinity questioned) is, however, a bit of a paradox in a world of civility in which politeness required insincerity and lying.[8] Markku Peltonen spells out the problem in relation to the English theory of courtesy and dueling: "On the one hand, it directed people to use complimentary lies in their daily conversation. On the other hand, the very same theory prescribed that giving the lie was to hurl the most vicious insult. The paradox was of course that a duel arose from speaking the truth" (Peltonen 2003, 129). The conflict was not lost on Walter Ralegh (also spelled Raleigh) in his seventeenth-century arguments against dueling:

> To accept the theory of civil courtesy and thus to take trifling incidents as serious insults was ridiculous enough, but to take a lie given as the most serious insult of all was downright ludicrous. Ralegh pointed out that on the one hand, he who gives the lie to a man who had actually lied 'doth him no wrong at all, neither ought it to be more heinously taken, than to tell him, that he hath broken any promise which he hath otherwise made.' If, on the other hand, there had been no lie, and yet the lie is given, then giver 'doth therein give the lie directly to himself.' To feel deeply insulted in such a situation was utterly ridiculous. . . . Of course, Ralegh acknowledged, 'it is an extreme rudeness to tax any man in public with an untruth . . . but all that is rude ought not to be civilized with death.' (Peltonen, 127)

APOLOGY

"Giving the lie" actually has a double significance in the context of dueling. On the one hand, it is the grievous insult of accusing someone of being a liar. On the other hand, the point of a duel (perhaps provoked by an accusation of lying) was to give the lie to one's enemy's insult and the imputation of cowardice presumed to stand behind it and any insult, behind the manifest willingness to insult openly and as it were with impunity.

---

8. Intentions can complicate the paradox. Pitt-Rivers invokes the role of intentions to explain at great length how "on the one hand honour demands keeping faith and to break one's word or to lie is the most dishonourable conduct, yet in fact a man is permitted to lie and to deceive without forfeiting his honour" (1966, 32ff).

The point was not simply revenge—after all, the offended party could lose and even a loser's honor was thought to be vindicated. The aim was to prove one's manhood and give the lie to the offender's imputations of cowardice. The aim of dueling was "satisfaction" of an impersonal concept of honor, not revenge. "Satisfaction for German duelists was not achieved by seeing an enemy sprawled lifeless but through having him personally witness one's worth while performing with aplomb when the chips were down . . . The German duelist redeemed his honor by removing the blemish to it, not the source of that blemish" (McAleer 79, 81; cf. Kiernan 1988, 147). Some present nonlethal apology as providing a different kind of satisfaction, a way of evening humiliation—rough justice.[9] We shall see that is not necessarily the case. The game of honor is not the only game in town. Often, an apology can take the form of a simple denial of intention, which can allow all concerned to save face. There can be a more subtle play and interplay of attitudes. (See chapter 10.)

Within the world of honor, we can see how an abject apology by one who has insulted or humiliated a person might restore lost status. Of course, the submissive posture is crucial to the effect. As Miller says, "If an apology does not look somewhat humiliating to the wronged person or to third parties, then it isn't one and it would be utterly ineffective in accomplishing the remedial work it is supposed to do. We have all given, witnessed, and received surly apologies that are intended and received as new affronts requiring more apology" (1993, 163). Third parties can be crucial. The restoration of status, where status is a matter of public reputation, may require public acknowledgement. Witnesses, after all, may make an insult especially damning, and an audience may play a vital role in all sorts of contexts (as we shall see in the insult rituals discussed in the next chapter and in the role of the collusive audience for tendentious jokes discussed in the later chapter on insult humor). Some emotions, such as embarrassment, may require an actual audience, while in others,

---

9. Miller sometimes tends to such oversimplification, though he generally recognizes that the Christian world of conscience, confession, and forgiveness, and other worlds where self-evaluation is prominent, is different from the saga world of public reputation. Honor is a zero-sum game of public status (Miller 1993, 116). In such a world, apology is basically a ritual of humiliation (Miller 1993, 163). Miller gives a fuller and more subtle account of apology in *Faking It* (2003, 77–95). A fuller account still can be found in Murphy (2003) and Lazare (2004). See also Pitt-Rivers (1966, 26).

such as shame, judgment by an inner or an imagined audience may be enough. How one is viewed is crucial in any case. (A person without honor may also be said to be shameless.) The self-esteem involved in honor is comparative, and competitive, and dependent on the views of others, and so in need of independent confirmation. It may also be seen as literally zero-sum. As Pitt-Rivers notes, "The victor in any competition for honour finds his reputation enhanced by the humiliation of the vanquished. . . . It was believed at one time in Italy by the common people that one who gave an insult thereby took to himself the reputation of which he deprived the other" (1966, 24). This competitive honor is, once again, not to be confused with the sort of moral virtue which is in theory limitless in its plenty. What is at stake is a kind of comparative pride, in which society accords to one the high opinion one might wish to accord to oneself while denying it to others. It can become a kind of power play.

THREE

■ ■ ■

INSULT IN PLAY AND RITUAL

THE PRACTICE OF FRIENDLY TEASING IN THE FORM OF PLAYFUL RITUAL INSULT is remarkably widespread. It goes by a variety of names, from medieval flyting to modern sounding, signifying, ranking, woofing, screaming, cutting, capping, chopping, and playing the dozens. The practice is especially common among adolescent males from the black urban ghettoes of America to the rural villages of Turkey. The interchange is often quite structured, requiring an audience of a certain sort and even formal properties such as rhyme. The content of permissible insults is also structured. What is of special interest, in terms of understanding the nature and various functions of the insults, is what precisely marks the difference between an acceptable insult within the ritual and words that amount to an actual assault, that get taken personally, despite the cover of the conventions. When does the playful interchange get transformed into an actual fight, as it often does? Of course, sometimes a fight emerges simply because one of the contestants runs out of clever retorts. In such instances, the one who resorts to blows is typically regarded as the loser. There is a story, perhaps apocryphal,[1] of an exchange between long-feuding

---

1. I say "perhaps apocryphal" because while I am quite sure I heard the story on TV many years ago from what seemed at the time a reliable source (could it have been Gore Vidal himself?), a careful search of the available biographies and autobiographies (including Vidal's own) has yielded the details of the party and the punch, but not, unfortunately, the punch line (which, after all, is the point of the story here).

authors Gore Vidal and Norman Mailer at a party. Vidal made some clever gibe directed at Mailer's most recent book and Mailer in response lashed out with his fist, decking Vidal. Rising from the floor, Vidal had the presence of mind to continue, "Once again, words have failed Norman." While one could argue that Mailer had won the fight, Vidal had clearly triumphed in the larger contest. Words are what matter—and that remains true even when the combatants are not famous writers.

A DRIVE TO INSULT

It has been argued that human beings have a basic instinct for play and contest. It is hardly surprising, if there is such an instinct or basic drive, that it should find expression through insult as well as through other means. But one could as well argue that what is more basic is a drive to insult and that it is that drive that expresses itself in play and contest (as well as through other means). Given the centrality of themes of domination in the message of insult, and recognizing the significance of domination in human life, such a shift in emphasis, priority, and perhaps even causation would seem highly plausible. There may be, even at the root of much playful behavior, a drive to dominate—what Nietzsche spoke of as a "will to power."

Johan Huizinga argues in *Homo Ludens* (1950) that widespread phenomena of group play (including contests, performances, exhibitions, challenges, showings-off) make compelling the hypothesis of an instinct for play inherent in the species. Such activities are typically devoid of standard utilitarian purpose, but nonetheless "there is something at stake" (49). What matters is not the material result; rather success is measured by internal rules and when achieved leads to social approval and self-approbation. What is at stake is honor and esteem. Huizinga distinguishes the sort of superiority marked by winning in such games from power or domination, claiming that what is primary is "the desire to excel others, to be first and to be honored for that" (50). Intrinsically valuable prizes (like the stakes in some card games) or contests in which winning is supposed to influence nature (e.g., improving the yield of crops) mark the limits of play, the material benefits standing extraneous to the goal of victory in the contest itself. Huizinga's model for the sort of play that is crucial to the emergence of culture (agonistic play) is the potlatch, a ritual squandering of goods in a competitive giving and destroying of valuable objects, practiced by a number of Indian tribes in British

Columbia (and, with variations, in Melanesia and elsewhere). While I think one can question the ultimate separability of issues of honor and esteem from issues of power and domination (Huizinga himself notes that the potlatch "hinges on winning, on being superior, on glory, prestige and, last but not least, revenge" 59), it enables Huizinga to see that "the potlatch spirit is akin to the thoughts and feelings of the adolescent" (60). This will be crucial to understanding the insult rituals that are the focus of this chapter. They are ultimately adolescent contests for honor.

As described by Huizinga, the arena of the potlatch is "the world of honour, pomp, braggadocio and challenge" as opposed to "the ordinary world of toil and care" (60). Leaving aside questions of magical and religious belief, it is the world of modern boyhood, of dares and boasts and visions of heroism; and the evidence of anthropology suggests that "playing for honour and glory" may be a fundamental human need (62–63). It is familiar in western ideals of virtue, where "doing something well means doing it better than others," where excellence is a matter of superiority (63). Huizinga points out that the need finds expression in words ("bragging and scoffing matches") as well as in potlatch "squandering-matches," practices that are widespread throughout the world from the Trobriand Islands, to pre-Islamic Arabia, ancient Greece, the world of the Icelandic Sagas, and on indefinitely (65–66). (Though one wonders whether nonmacho societies, perhaps certain Asian ones, would recognize what Huizinga calls the "virile ideal of virtue": virtue as a manly fitness to fight and command, typical of archaic communities based on the tribal life of warriors and nobles [64]. Still, even in ancient China — perhaps especially there — one would find "courtesy-matches," inverted contests in politeness [66].) The anthropological and linguistic data suggest that "the agonistic factor," contest and competition, is universal (71). Certainly it is present in the insult rituals that we will now explore.

THE DOZENS

The dozens is a practice, common especially among urban African-American adolescent boys, of aggressive, joking exchanges of patterned insults. John Dollard provides a useful early sociological account in "The Dozens: Dialectic of Insult" (1939). He describes the practice as exhibiting some variations across different regions and in differently sized communities, within different classes and genders, and among different age groups. He reports that while the joking regularly touches on forbidden matters (incest, sex with the other's mother, passive homosexuality, and personal defects), some themes are strictly excluded (menstruation, castration, and dead relatives in particular). Speaking of an analogous joking relationship between two friends, Dollard notes "an unconscious perception and agreement" that the joking "does not touch upon actual weaknesses"—that would be going too far (4). As we shall see, others have suggested that it is precisely when charges come too close to being true that ritual insult becomes transformed into personal insult and that a fight may ensue (Labov, 335, 341). Dollard gives many examples from the dozens where, despite the risk, an opponent's actual weak point is attacked (e.g., gibing about crossed eyes, a father in jail, or a sister pregnant with an illegitimate child [5, 8–9]). Sexual themes are most common (often focusing on female relatives of the opponent), notably including homosexuality (in one example, a boy is attacked for getting the "next dish" [better food] at camp by "giving some of his behind" [8]). A distinction is sometimes drawn between the clean dozens and the "dirty" dozens, with jeers concerning inferiority, stupidity, cowardice, and the like dominant in the former and sexual accusations dominant in the latter.

Dollard notes an audience is essential, that players often use rhymes to express the forbidden themes (a point of interest in relation to modern rap music), and that in at least one traditional variant of the game there is a pattern of 12 obscene rhymes (which may be the origin of the name, "the dozens").[2] One example (from a big Southern city) that focuses on the opponent's mother goes:

> I saw your ma
> At Tulane and Broad;
> She was coming out
> Of the red light yawd. (7)

The evolution of the dozens into modern rap music is nicely illustrated in the Eminem movie 8 *Mile* (2002), in which the white rap-

---

2. While "the dozens" can be used interchangeably with "signifying," it also can be understood as a subspecies of signification (Gates 1988, 99). Signifying is a rhetorical strategy with a wide variety of modes and uses in African-American literature, richly elaborated by Henry Louis Gates in his *The Signifying Monkey* (1988).

per battles for status in a rap competition with black rivals. It is really an insult contest. Unlike the traditional dozens, however, speaking the truth seems a criterion for success rather than an act outside the ritual constraints. In the movie rap battle, the insults aim at truth, indeed aim to wound through their accuracy—as well as through superior flair of statement and originality of rhyme. There are also some interesting twists on what counts as an insult (e.g., Eminem accuses a would-be urban rapper of being suburban, in particular of coming from an intact family with happily married mother and father).[3]

In the dozens, the two protagonists are typically egged on by the crowd, and the approbation of the crowd is the reward (providing the "honor" emphasized by Huizinga). Dollard also reports that when the dozens is played with out-group members it generally ends in physical fighting. This factor may be as important as jests coming too close to fact in turning a joking encounter into a serious one, though in this case (exchanges with out-group members) the presumptions of friendship, good intentions, and a playful attitude may already be weakened or absent. Dollard suggests that there may be less fighting in-group because an individual would lose status if he were not able to take the playful

3. In the culminating rap battle in 8 *Mile*, Rabbit (Eminem), self-described "fuckin white trash," comes at his rival, Papa Doc, like a sophisticated lawyer—first making his opponent's best arguments and then defiantly topping them:

This guy aint a mother-fuckin MC,
I know everything he's got to say against me,
I am white, I am a fuckin bum, I do live in a trailer with my mom,
My boy future is an uncle tom. . . .

But I know something about you,
You went to CRANBROOK, thats a private school,
Whats the matter dawg you embarrased?
This guys a gangster?
His real name's Clearance.

And Clearance lives at home with both parents,
And Clearance's parents have a real good marriage,
this guy dont wanna battle, hes shook, . . .
He's scared to look in his fuckin yearbook, fuck CRANBROOK.

abuse. One could add: taking a jest seriously might risk turning it into a plausible charge.

Dollard regards the dozens as adaptive, a way of coping with aggression generated by frustration in an economically and socially disadvantaged group. Because the play is confined within caste, that is, among blacks, Dollard concludes that the dozens serves as "a valve for aggression in a depressed group" (22). It is not clear how this would fit with Huizinga's data suggesting universality. Dollard himself points to analogous friendly (typically obscene) joking practices in other societies, including the Manus, the Tikopia, and Aleutian and Greenland Eskimos (18–19). While aggression is no doubt present in all these cases, it is not clear that it is confined to economically depressed (or oppressed) groups. (It should be acknowledged, however, that at the time of Dollard's studies, if not now as well, African Americans of all classes suffered from discrimination.) Dollard was famous in mid-century American psychology for his broad frustration-aggression hypothesis, but one should not assume that frustration is the only source of aggression. And contests for honor may have independent motives.

When Dollard tries to draw distinctions within his data groupings, the lines sometimes become muddy. For example, he suggests that mobile middle-class boys are quicker to fight (as they were in his Northern big city sample [17]) because they are more strongly repressed and suffer from more anxiety when forbidden topics are touched upon (23); but Dollard himself notes that lower-class boys in his Southern small city sample were quicker to fight than their middle and upper-class counterparts (15).

Venting the aggression of a depressed/repressed/oppressed group cannot be the whole psychological story. Dollard says that "Negroes . . . have obviously the same taboos on incestuous behavior, homosexuality, adulterous activities and possession of extreme negroid characteristics which whites have" (24–25). Dollard means to be emphasizing the shared humanity (including the shared repressions) of blacks and whites, but "extreme negroid characteristics" as a subject for ritual insults among blacks invites more complex interpretation. One approach might suggest that criticizing an opponent for a characteristic the attacker shares might involve self-hatred using the oppressor's values. But it also might involve defanging criticism by appropriating it or, in the context of the game, showing the insult is not meant to be real or personal. (An "appro-

priation" interpretation might require the use of irony of the sort sometimes employed by blacks who call each other "nigger" or gays who call
each other "queer" or "fag.") Or it might simply be an effort to differentiate oneself from one's opponent and deny that (from certain perspectives) one could be seen to share the despised characteristic. This sort of
denial might bring us back to universal mechanisms of repression that
regularly make use of projection and aggression. What one should not
assume is that the values invoked are universal.

While values may not be universal, underlying anxieties may be.
The data examined by Dollard suggest that part of what goes on in the
dozens (and perhaps in related rituals as well) is "exposure of the other
person's unconscious wishes" (e.g., incestuous and homosexual), which
may bear an uneasy relationship to one's own (22). The aggression that
is expressed in insult rituals such as the dozens takes a particular controlled—but pointed—form.

Roger D. Abrahams (1962) builds on Dollard's study; using observations of black adolescents "Playing the Dozens" in a lower-class South
Philadelphia neighborhood, he develops a more nuanced psychological
account of the forces at play. Agreeing with Dollard that the dozens
serves as a release mechanism for the anxieties of black youth, Abrahams
adds a speculative suggestion and a valuable insight. The suggestion has
to do with the special place of matriarchy in black society. The insight is
about how an insult aimed at another's mother may serve as a proxy for
an attack on one's own. The objects of our attacks may be deeply and
subtly entangled with the objects of our anxieties.

In some examples from younger combatants, there is a reversal of
roles, "with the mother playing the male role," as Abrahams says, "a
realization of a basic fact of lower class Negro family life" (210). Thus,
e.g.:

> I hear your mother plays third base for the Phillies.
> Your mother is a bricklayer, and stronger than your father.

Older boys tend to vilify each other's mothers in more directly sexual
terms. The slanging match might include short punning jabs:

> Least my mother ain't no cake; everybody get a piece.
> At least my mother ain't no doorknob, everybody gets a turn.

It might also include more elaborate rhyming assaults:

> I hate to talk about your mother,
> She's a good old soul.
> She's got a ten-ton pussy
> And a rubber asshole.
> She got hair on her pussy
> That sweep the floor.
> She got knobs on her titties
> That open the door.

And,

> I fucked your mother on an electric wire.
> I made her pussy rise higher and higher.

And,

> I fucked your mother on a ten-ton truck.
> She said, "God damn, baby, you sure can fuck."
> (210–11, 216—with Abrahams' discreet blanks filled in)

The point to note is that among both younger and older boys, the other's mother is a special target, as is homosexuality in a father or brother (e.g., "Least my brother ain't no store; he takes meat in the back" [211]). These twin targets suggest particular anxieties.

In neighborhoods where the dozens is popular, which is to say poor black neighborhoods, stable adult male figures tend to be fleeting presences. As a result, as Abrahams emphasizes, women "are not only the dispensers of love and care, but also of discipline and authority" (213). It is not surprising then that they should become the objects of resistance and rebellion, and ultimately of vituperation. Adolescent lower-class black males grow up in families dominated by the mother, in a matriarchy. This places special burdens on such youths when it comes time to separate and individuate, to develop an independent identity. The same forces that leave women largely alone to raise and support their families (whether through work or welfare) contribute to a pervasive distrust of each sex by the other. Boys in particular ("when they reach puberty, they must eminently be rejected as men by the women in the matriarchy"

[213]) must turn outside the family to find their positive ideals of masculinity, and not uncommonly they turn to groups of other boys, to gangs.

The end result of the circumstances that lead to matriarchy (and they are multiple), and the character of that matriarchy (including its distinctive distrust and contempt for men and their pathologies — "men are dogs" as they say on the afternoon TV talk shows), is that for gang-oriented boys "femininity and weakness become the core of the despicable" (Abrahams, 214). The countervailing ideals of virility and manliness that prevail within gangs come naturally tied to insecurities about that very insistently expressed masculinity, including concerns about being a momma's boy and about homosexuality (the twin targets of the ritual insults of the dozens).

While the place of matriarchy in certain black communities may give the dozens a special content and significance, the existence of analogous practices in all sorts of rather different communities suggests that matriarchy is not essential to the practice — even where mothers may regularly serve as objects of attack (after all, incest taboos may be universal and, a related but separate point, mothers may be universally sacred and therefore especially suitable objects when one is in the business of smashing icons, one of the standard techniques if not points of insults). Indeed, while Abrahams' work in South Philadelphia was doubtless in neighborhoods dominated by matriarchies, we know from Dollard's more geographically and socially diverse sample that the dozens is practiced in very different African-American communities — this without looking to analogous practices outside the United States. The expressive issues may have more to do with the general problems of adolescent males emerging into manhood than the special problems that may arise when that transition takes place under a matriarchy. Matriarchy may accentuate certain problems without being necessary to their arising in the first place. Abrahams himself, in a later book (*Deep Down in the Jungle*), softens his views on the importance of matriarchy, what he in that book derisively refers to as the "Mammy Family" argument (1970, 2).

Nonetheless, it is in connection with his speculation about the special significance of matriarchy that Abrahams brings forward what seems to me a profound insight (with importance well beyond the special features of the dozens, whatever they may be). He suggests that the shift from mother-oriented to gang-oriented values is eased through the dozens providing a surreptitious means for an attack on the mother, the ambivalently beloved mother, that the boy is in the process of rejecting.

He must in some way exorcize her influence. He therefore creates a playground which enables him to attack some other person's mother, in full knowledge that that person must come back and insult his own. Thus someone else is doing the job for him, and between them they are castigating all that is feminine, frail, unmanly. (This is why the implications of homosexuality are also invoked.) (Abrahams 1962, 214)

The attack on the other's mother as a way of arranging a proxy attack on one's own may serve as a model both for our uneasy relations to our own unconscious wishes and for our clever, if insulting and devious, techniques for giving voice to our ambivalences.

Dollard, despite his awareness of analogous practices in societies outside the United States, writes as though ritual patterns like the dozens were confined (within the United States) to African Americans. One reason he gives is that the aggression generated by their frustrations can be tolerated when expressed within the subgroup. He writes, "Negro society constitutes a frontier area of relative lawlessness within white society, where the social punishment for aggressive expressions is diminished much below our standard practice. Such a circumstance makes it immediately plausible why a pattern such as the Dozens can appear"—so long, of course, as the violence is confined within the subgroup/caste (Dollard 1939, 22). While historically particular social contexts might shape practices like the dozens, the psychological processes at play (including aggression, repression, and anxiety) are simply too widespread to think insult rituals could be confined to subgroups. Indeed, an instinct for aggression is at least as plausible as Huizinga's instinct for play; certainly such instincts are not confined to particular social classes. (Dollard's particular reading of the tolerance level of subgroups for aggression within themselves and within other subgroups is, of course, itself questionable.) A study by Millicent R. Ayoub and Stephen A. Barnett, "Ritualized Verbal Insult in White High School Culture" (1965), amply documents the existence of such practices even within the white society that Dollard (stereotypically? naively? wishfully?) believed could not tolerate such "lawlessness."[4]

---

4. On white sounds, see also Labov 1972, 321–22. Labov describes the white material as relatively limited in content as well as form and quantity, often with fixed "snappy answer" sequencing, e.g., "A: Got a match? B: My ass against your face."

Ayoub and Barnett further use different aspects of their data to challenge other features of Dollard's, and also Abrahams', account. Where Dollard emphasizes the role of the dozens in coping with aggressive impulses and Abrahams focuses on the difficulties of establishing a masculine identity in a matriarchy (the tensions of moving from a woman's world to a man's), Ayoub and Barnett attach special importance to adolescent peer group culture. Their data come from middle- and upper-class fifteen-year-old white high school students in an Ohio town who engage in verbal rituals of sounding, burning, ranking, dusting, icing, putting down, cutting down, and tearing down—terms which Ayoub and Barnett take as equivalent to "playing the dozens" (338). In this context, race (black) and class (lower) do not seem to have the significance they were given in the earlier studies. Nonetheless, as with the black dozens, "victory is reckoned when either competitor is unable to supply a fitting retort or when the excellence of one boy's response evokes loud laughter and jeers from the necessary audience" (338). Of particular interest are their observations concerning "mother-sounds," scurrilous references to an opponent's mother. As in Abrahams' material, younger boys tend to impute a male role—"Your mother wears combat boots"—while older boys move on to attribute various forms of sexual misconduct, most often promiscuity. Mother-sounds are apparently confined to in-group boys, the prestigious athletic types. Members of the chess club refuse to mother-sound. Indeed, it is partly the willingness to engage in mother-sounds and other taboo-breaking that helps define the boundary of the in-group. Accepting the inevitable attacks on one's own mother yields status within the group, and it is suggested that such sounding weakens family bonds and creates shared in-group guilt, thus contributing to peer-bonding. (This is connected with the more general point that which group you are a part of is a matter of whom you can freely insult. While joking relationships in some cultures may be kin-based, in ours they typically exist between friends. In either case, they exist between those who are otherwise and in other ways close.) Ayoub and Barnett conclude, "Sounding, especially Mother-Sounding, demonstrates the second place given to the mother-son bond in comparison to the primary place assigned the clique and defines the in-group's boundaries by fostering a shared sense of guilt" (343). This form of peer-bonding seems actually rather close to Abrahams' views concerning the shift from mother-oriented to gang-oriented values (as Ayoub and

Barnett acknowledge, 341). Ayoub and Barnett, despite the absence of matriarchy in their sample population, do not seem to me to undermine Abrahams' account. Indeed, their emphasis on peer groups may be seen as just another version of the conditions for masculine identity emphasized by Abrahams in terms of gang membership. Peer groups provide the audience essential to affirming the honor and status that take the place of the childhood search for parental approval. Adolescents achieve identity partly by revolting against adult authority.[5] The dozens and sounding provide (among other things) a structured and controlled

5. Ayoub and Barnett report that girls do not engage in sounding (342–43). The reasons they suggest for this are of uneven plausibility. First, they claim girls simply don't have similar peer groups. Boys flock in large groups, while girls only need two or three close confederates and don't form cliques. But this image of high school social structure seems simply false; certainly it fails to correspond to my unsystematic observations. Their second suggestion seems more persuasive. They point out that while it is socially acceptable to be a Daddy's Girl, it is not similarly okay to be a Momma's Boy. There is less pressure on girls to break links with home. This observation fits well with theoretical discussions of differential separation-individuation issues and processes in relation to boys and girls (see, e.g., Chodorow 1978).

Dollard and Abrahams report sounding among girls in their study samples as only a very occasional phenomenon. To his report that "'sounding' occurs only in crowds of boys" (1962, 209), Abrahams adds the following note:

> One will occasionally find girls making dozens-type remarks, but for the most part not in the organized fashion of the boys. The boys do not generally play in front of girls, except where one boy is trying to put another down. In this case the game can lead to a physical fight. Dollard seems to have encountered more girl "players" than I have. It certainly could not perform any similar psychosocial function among females, but the mechanism does exist as an expression of potential hostility by either sex. (Abrahams 1962, 219n3)

For comment on the general neglect of women's voices in such early language studies, see Marcyliena Morgan, "When Women Speak: How and Why We Enter" (2002, chap. 4, 84–110). Morgan explains that for African-American girls "instigating" seems more central than signifying games in battles over social face. They worry about the rumors instigated when a girl talks about another girl behind her back, and elaborate interrogations and confrontations can ensue. (See also Goodwin 1990.)

context for that revolt, a context in which they can achieve their independence in collusion with other adolescents.

WHEN DO WORDS COME TO BLOWS?

Unpleasant words are sometimes a provocation to other words. This is especially so when there is a custom allowing for the ritual exchange of insults and there is a crowd to be pleased by and to egg on the participants. Sometimes what is provoked is a fight. On occasion, this may be because the crowd desires such a conclusion. But there are many other reasons. One of the participants may run out of verbal retorts and so fall back on physical blows. More interestingly, sometimes a line is crossed. The boundaries of the game are breached and honor demands satisfaction. When does this occur? It depends on the boundaries of the game—as well as, of course, the inclinations, sensibilities, and sensitivities of the participants.

How does one know when an insult is not meant? How does one know one is engaged in a game or ritual? It is complicated by the fact that fanciful play may also constitute a real power struggle. But the marks of ritual and play may offer a relatively, however tentatively and penetrably, secure buffer. Entry into the permissive and protected game context is sometimes initiated by contrived witticisms. We have already seen one typical opening: "I hate to talk about your mother, she's a good old soul / She got a ten-ton pussy and a rubber asshole" (cited also in Labov 1972, 307). Formulaic patterns (like "least my mother/brother ain't no . . ."), rhyme, and special speech rhythms are among the linguistic devices that signal the context of contest (Abrahams 1962, 211; Labov 1972, 319–20). Of course, there may also be a direct challenge to "play the dozens" or a threat of one boy to another to "put him in" the dozens. Then the contest is clearly on, and it is clear that it is a contest. (With some adults, however, the mere challenge may be enough to provoke a physical response.) In general, the various framing devices work to attenuate the shock and surprise characteristic of personal—which is to say, serious—insults.

The use of rhyme has special advantages. Traditional rhymed couplets tend to be less threatening, and so provide one of several techniques for controlling and limiting the aggression in sounding contests.

The fact that rhyming has roots in and harks back to various childhood activities may itself have a soothing influence. Martha Wolfenstein provides a plausible account of why rhyming should have a disarming effect in her discussion of childhood taunts, the ancestor of dozens rhymes:

> What is the function of rhymes in these joking attacks? I would suggest that the first rhyming word has the effect of compelling the utterance of the second, thus reducing the speaker's responsibility. . . . There is a further reduction of responsibility in the use of a rhymed formula: the words are not my own. Moreover the rhyme is apt to induce other children to take it up; the attacker will cease to be alone. It should be added that rhymes are often in themselves funny to young children. Children of three, for instance, may laugh simply at finding two words that rhyme or a word that rhymes with a name. Thus the rhyme affords a façade of harmless joking to facilitate the expression of hostility in the rhymed insult. (*Children's Humor*, Free Press, 1954, 182—quoted in Abrahams 1970, 50–51)

Perhaps the surest mark that an insult is not meant to be taken seriously is its absurdity. William Labov, in his "Rules for Ritual Insults," cites many apparently absurd ritual insults; for one: "Your mother's a duck" (1972, 305). As with all communication, ritual insults depend on shared conventions and shared assumptions, shared knowledge and shared understandings. The "duck" sound is an example of perhaps the simplest of all sound forms, a comparison or identification of the mother with something old, ugly, or bizarre. Other examples equate her with Flipper, a Milk Dud, James Bond, a butcher, and an iceman (309). The simple absurdity may sometimes be the result of deleting an attribute being criticized (which all involved may understand), thus "Your mother look like Flipper" may be what remains from "Your mother is so ugly that she looks like Flipper" (336). The elided criticism might even be based on truth. Alternatively, a derisive truth may be spoken, but an absurdity be appended in order to defang what might otherwise be a biting assault. (A version of this is what is going on in the "duck" example. In context, the ludicrous equation of mother and duck followed and defused what might otherwise have been taken as a serious challenge to a gang leader's authority. Had the gang leader continued to insist on taking the situation seriously after the playful ritual insult, he would in effect have been saying that it could be true that his mother was a duck [351–53].) Similarly, where matters of fact may be unclear, an appended absurdity may help make it clear that no personal insult is meant. Using a dozens rhyme, Labov explains, "Among young adults, to say I *fucked your mother* is not to say something obviously untrue. But it is obviously untrue that 'I fucked your mother from tree to tree / Your father said, "Now fuck me!"'" (340). Blatant untruth can be a way of forestalling overt aggressive responses.

Truth bites. Even the intention to attack using the truth, where one may actually be mistaken, may be enough to turn a ritual insult into a personal insult and so a game into a fight. It can be very important to clarify intentions. Absurdity and blatant untruth can clarify intentions. Unbelievability can be a good indication that a statement is not meant to be believed. No one need feel insulted. It is all in fun.

That the boundaries of the game have been felt to be breached may be revealed in the response to a would-be ritual insult. Playful insults are responded to in kind, not denied. If one denies it, one has taken it as a serious charge. Since ritual insults are not intended as factual statements, since it should be a matter of general knowledge that they are obviously untrue, direct and simple refutation is out of place. To take a sound seriously, as though it were perhaps true, is to turn the situation into something else, a serious confrontation in which symbolic distance is lost. In one of Labov's transcriptions of exchanges between members of a gang, one participant says, "I went in Junior house 'n' sat in a chair that caved in." Junior responds, "You's a damn liar, 'n' you was eatin' in my house, right?" (317). House-sounds, which are directed against the poverty of a household, tend to be taken personally (for all that members of the audience may know, they might be true). In this instance, the response adds to denial a countercharge of hunger and poverty ("You was eatin' in my house"—which, incidentally, while charging ingratitude, seems indirectly to concede that there was an occasion when a chair caved in [347]). In another exchange between gang members, a critique of a father's real stuttering ("at least my father don't be up there talking uh-uh-uh-uh-uh-uh!") leads to an equally personal counterattack ("at least my father ain't got a gray head!") and devolves into strident argument between the no-longer merely playing participants (332–34). The traditional and correct response to "Your momma drink pee" is "Your father eat shit," *not* "That's a lie!" Sounds are answered by other sounds. As Labov concludes, "a personal insult is answered by a denial, excuse, or mitigation," but it "is an invariant rule: sounds are not denied" (335).

Just as shared conventions and assumptions put boundaries around ritual insults, those boundaries may be broken when shared understandings fail. Gregory Bateson points out that play, ritual, and other human activities involve metacommunicative messages that have evolved over time and are present in other species as well, as in the play fighting of monkeys and the playful nips of puppies. Thus the frame, "This is play" expands into something like, "these actions in which we now engage do not denote what those actions for which they stand would denote." In the case of puppies, "the playful nip denotes the bite, but it does not denote what would be denoted by the bite" (1972, 180). There are, of course, risks that such frames may shift. Bateson writes:

> In the Andaman Islands, peace is concluded after each side has been given ceremonial freedom to strike the other. This example, however, also illustrates the labile nature of the frame "This is play," or "This is ritual." The discrimination between map and territory is always liable to break down, and the ritual blows of peace-making are always liable to be mistaken for the "real" blows of combat. In this event, the peace-making ceremony becomes a battle. (182)

Other shifts are possible too. Even when an image does not denote what it might in other contexts denote, and we understand this, we may have genuine fear of fictional and fantasy objects (183). We have already noted the complication generated by the fact that fanciful play may also or ambiguously constitute a real power struggle.

In some places, the ritual vying for superiority is given a formal juridical role, with the outcome depending on the quality of the performances rather than the merits of the underlying dispute (a kind of trial by verbal combat), as among the Greenland Eskimos:

> When two men quarrel, a preferred way of resolving the difference is (or was) through an institutionalized contest in ridicule, invective, and satirical abuse known as the drum match or song duel. The two enemies face each other before the assembled tribe, who look on the affair as a festive occasion and are delighted with the lampoons, the obscene scurrilities, the mockery and jibing and flouting which the two contestants hurl at each other, each accompanying himself on a drum. Along with the duel in song may go complicated physical gyrations, such as snorting in an opponent's face, butting him, and tying him to the tent pole—indignities which the performers try to

bear with surface impassivity. The match may continue at intervals over a long time, even years, and the opponents' ingenuity in abuse is likely to be stretched, even though they may recite well-known drum songs (or parts of them) that have been handed down by oral tradition. But finally the tribe makes a decision in the matter at issue (it often concerns a woman) in favor of one of the contestants. Then the two may become reconciled, or the match may end in blows or, rarely, even death. Loss of the decision is an extremely painful affair; for the loser not only has had publicly to bear the devastating mockery of his enemy, but at the end finds himself alone, against all the others, a laughing-stock. Occasionally, he may go into voluntary exile. (Elliott 1960, 70)

We have seen that insult matches can serve a number of functions, from venting aggression, to expressing anxieties about the repressed, to establishing a male (and adult) identity. Why, however, should these purposes be pursued through insults? Huizinga suggests it may start with the substitution of verbal boasting for heroic deeds. He suggests competitive boasting develops into competitive insult rituals, both being ways of pursuing honor and distinction. After all, both boasting and contumely are ways of claiming superiority: one by exalting the self, the other by lowering competitors:

The nobleman demonstrates his "virtue" by feats of strength, skill, courage, wit, wisdom, wealth or liberality. For want of these he may yet excel in a contest of words, that is to say, he may either himself praise the virtues in which he wishes to excel his rivals, or have them praised for him by a poet or a herald. This boosting of one's own virtue as a form of contest slips over quite naturally into contumely of one's adversary, and this in its turn becomes a contest in its own right. It is remarkable how large a place these bragging and scoffing matches occupy in the most diverse civilizations. (Huizinga, 65)

DISPLACED AGGRESSION: BRIGA

Sometimes the game, if it is a game, is not meant to lead to a volley of insults. The practice, the temperaments, the social context may make blows inevitable. Indeed, that may be the point. What satisfies honor is not clever retorts. The passions in play demand a different sort of expression and a different sort of satisfaction—and this may be independent of whether there is a crowd to set standards, appreciate cleverness and deft moves, and recognize superiority. Abrahams reports that, among the people he studied, when derogatory reference is made to members of another's family by an adult, it rarely leads to a playful exchange (1962, 210–11). In the army, in prisons, in bars and poolrooms, it almost invariably ends in a fight. Instead of a safe release of aggressions and repressed instincts as among adolescents, the stylized insults when used by adults are generally a prelude to, often a deliberate provocation of, a fight. Consider the Brazilian practice of *briga*, where the raw passions at stake are in plain, often bloody, view.

As described by Daniel Touro Linger in his *Dangerous Encounters* (1992), the structure is minimal. There is a "provocation" (a challenge to honor), followed by a "connection" (accepting the challenge), followed by a fight. *Briga* is essentially a street fight, typically the result of challenge and response but often enough the result of challenge and failure to respond. With all provocations, even ambiguous ones, one risks either humiliation (by not connecting) or *briga* (by connecting). Some will insist on *briga* whatever the response. The need for "*desabafo*" (discharge) pushes both provocations and responses. What counts as a "provocation" is highly variable and subjective. It may be as little as an accidental bump or an innocent question. It may also be a deliberately challenging insult. In a life overflowing with petty frustrations, myriad tensions, felt exploitation, and suppressed anger, there emerges a pattern of expectations—often shaped, distorted, and obscured with the help of alcohol—that leads one person to physically assault another in response to what is taken to be an affront. While there is something ritualistic about this, there is nothing playful about it—it can, and sometimes does, end in death. Such rituals of self-assertion over nothing in particular are perhaps sharpest in certain macho societies such as Brazil's, where underclass males, having little and with little to hope for, seek to assert some sort of superiority or at least dignity. That this is done in such grossly "undignified" forms as drunken knife fights may appall outsiders (and terrify insiders), but the impulses do not seem so alien. Every ghetto and barrio and barroom has its charges of "looking at me the wrong way" and associated threats and reprisals. Sometimes they are simply matters of someone looking for a fight and cooking up a pretext, much of *briga* surely takes that form, but even a pretext may perhaps be read as a text.

Linger (105–9) tells the story of a drunken man, a stevedore or fisherman, high on marijuana, who approaches a group of people waiting for a bus late on a Saturday night and announces to no one in particular, "I'm really stoned." A young fellow, sitting on the sidewalk with his girlfriend, responds, "Stoned, huh?" The drunk becomes infuriated, kicks the fellow's leg and makes some threats, even threatening to pull out a nonexistent revolver. But the boy does not give the drunk the further attention, the excuse to fight, he hoped for (the girlfriend had been pleading with the boy not to) and the confrontation dissipates after the intervention of a nearby guard. By kicking the boy, the drunk had retrospectively revealed that his initial apparently innocuous venting was meant as a provocation and that the boy's repetition of his remark had been interpreted, constructed or reconstructed, as a connection. Anonymous confrontations between strangers generally require connecting, acknowledgment of the provocation, before a fight can ensue. How much of a connection, like how much of a provocation, is needed may depend on how driven the participants are, how fraught the situation is. The initial (likely innocent) repetition of "stoned" in this case apparently did not, by itself, make it over the threshold to provide the needed permission.

Provocation in *briga*, where someone is looking for a fight, bears some resemblance to the reflexive proxy mechanism invoked by Abrahams in his account of the dozens. Abrahams described how insulting the other's mother may serve as a way of arranging (provoking) a proxy assault on one's own. (In relation to Brazilian *briga* among boys, Linger mentions a third party might instigate a fight with the line, "Whoever rubs out this line is rubbing out the other one's mother" [109]. Mothers are apparently flashpoints in many places.) Here, of course, the mechanism is crudely short-circuited. The opponent is being used, but the provocateur is looking for a fight, not by proxy or through collusion like the dozens player who provokes a verbal assault on his own mother, but directly with his opponent and in directly physical form. The opponent is as likely as not a stranger. What remains displaced is the object of aggression.

Briga fits Dollard's model of aggression in an economically depressed group, though unlike verbal insult contests, *briga* is not a harmless safety valve. It is rather a stark expression of aggression, notably directed at other individuals rather than the presumed real object of anger, the frustrating economic and social system, which in its pervasiveness is not open to direct physical attack. (Versions of the practice are familiar in barrooms around the world, where even the nondisadvantaged may act out their personal frustrations by unleashing their demons on whoever happens to be unluckily to hand.) *Briga* is unlike the controlled environment of insult rituals. While these permit the exploration of otherwise forbidden themes, they also limit and control that exploration and its consequences. And unlike the dozens and similar rituals, an audience is not essential to *briga*. In *briga*, an audience's awareness of a confrontation may increase the stakes and make it more difficult for one party to back down, but the drama may be largely confined to the parties involved. Given the centrality of peer-bonding and peer-ranking in adolescent verbal duels, an audience is essential. The assertion of masculinity and adulthood by uncertain adolescents is best achieved in the presence of an affirming and confirming crowd. Related adult practices may make the venting (whether harmlessly or not-so-harmlessly) of aggression a more central function, and an audience may be less central to that. Though where trial-by-verbal-combat or professional entertainment is part of what is going on, a jury/audience may indeed be crucial.

In many of its instances, *briga* is an extreme of aggression, involving looking for excuses to fight and attack. A perceived provocation (like insults in general according to Aristotle) calls for vengeance, despite the risks. Brazilian machismo is characterized by a hair-trigger readiness to fight, sexual bravado, and hypersensitivity to insult. One is compelled to respond to perceived assaults on one's virility and to defend the boundaries of the self. Linger suggests that machismo may actually provide a form of power to the powerless, however crudely and brutally physical: "Personal force becomes his illusionary measure of power; slights to his masculinity become symbolic of his daily diet of indignities" (110). Economic and social disadvantage, reinforced by the cultural milieu, helps create the conditions and attitudes that result in *briga*. That these conditions become enmeshed and entangled with sexuality and masculinity has some significance, as we shall see in the next chapter, in connection with insults in general.

There is no doubt that the poverty and social dislocation characteristic of Brazilian slums plays a role in generating the aggression displayed in *briga* as well as other practices. But if we are to describe that aggression as "displaced," a question arises about the object from which it is displaced. Causes and objects are often, but not always, distinguishable and distinct. I may be hyper and irritable because I have had too much coffee to drink, and as a result lash out at you. You are the object of my anger. The excess caffeine, however, is its cause. On the other hand, cause and object may sometimes come together. Your insensitive and insulting remark may (all by itself, without the help of excessive caffeine or other stimulants) be both source and object of my anger. (The object of an emotion is perhaps most often its *believed* cause, which in a particular case may or may not correspond with its actual cause.) Thus, while social conditions are doubtless a cause of the anger and aggression behind many a *briga* attack on some innocent, are we to say those conditions are the *real* object of the aggression, while the innocent is the *displaced* object of the emotions and the attack? Perhaps the innocent is similarly downtrodden. But perhaps the innocent is a member of one of the better-off classes (in which case a question may arise whether the innocent is perhaps a beneficiary and so not simply a bystander in the system of injustice, and so perhaps not so innocent after all). Is the real object a pervasive set of social conditions, an oppressing social class, an individual or set of competitors within one's own class? Couldn't it be all three? After all, aggression may have multiple causes.

A parallel issue arises within the dozens. Abrahams says of Dollard that "he sees the game as a displaced aggression against the Negro's own group instead of against the real enemy, the whites, a reading which I find untenable not because it is wholly wrong, but because it is too easy" (Abrahams 1962, 213). Dollard had argued that the aggression within the dozens is socially tolerated because it is kept within the under-caste. Certainly even merely verbal assaults against whites in the period of Dollard's studies (the 1930s) would not have been (and when they occurred, were not) so readily tolerated. But that does not settle the question of what causes the aggression, and so of what might be called its "real" object. It is aimed in the dozens at a particular challenger. But, as Abrahams suggests, it may have its source in underlying emotions directed both against "the Negro's own group" and against "the real enemy, the whites." The situation is complicated by the fact that "the Negro man from the lower class is confronted with a number of social and psychological impediments. Not only is he a black man in a white man's world, but he is a male in a matriarchy" (Abrahams 1962, 213). It is in this difficult context that boys must make the transition to manhood, and Abrahams emphasizes how the dozens (and gang affiliations) may function to help in making that transition. Clues as to the "real" object of aggression (given the multiple sources of frustration) may sometimes be found in the content of the particular insults exchanged. As already suggested, they point to underlying anxieties of particular sorts. The sexualized forms of the insults may, as we shall see in the next chapter, provide particularly revealing clues. The links of sex and aggression, of concerns for honor and issues of domination and submission, and of the active and passive aspects of sadomasochism may play out in particularly legible form in certain localized versions of ritual insults.

LOOKING AT SOMEONE
"THE WRONG WAY"

Going back to the concept of a "provocation," I've suggested it can be as little as a glance, as insubstantial as looking at someone the wrong way. I do not think there is any single "right way" of describing what amounts to "the wrong way" of looking at someone. Sometimes looking the wrong way might amount to merely looking at all. Even a peasant or a cat may look at a king—sometimes. In Japan, peasants were *never* supposed to gaze at the emperor. And in Europe, Mandeville wrote that in early dueling manuals notions of honor were so refined "that barely looking upon a Man was often taken for an Affront" (1732, 64).

   Sometimes a look is a caress. We can look lovingly. Sometimes it is the challenge of recognition or the birth of self-consciousness, as in Sartre's keyhole story (to which I will return shortly). The look may perhaps sometimes have elements of disrespect, even of contempt, perhaps it verges on staring. But sometimes the look may be a mere glance, not even a furtive or a sinister glance. But the object sees in the look a challenge, and the counter-challenge may take the form of asking, "What are you looking at?" (Recall Travis Bickle, the unnerving De Niro character in *Taxi Driver*, all alone, talking to the mirror: "You talkin' to me?") The person may have been thinking nothing in particular and intending no challenge whatsoever, but the counter-challenge forces a confrontation that must either be met or somehow backed away from. Even denying an intent to challenge may be taken as engagement by a person intent on fighting. That is part of the story of *briga*.

In other contexts, we may disrespect people by *not* looking at them, or if we should look in their direction, by carefully not seeing. The British have the highly cultivated practice of "cutting," sometimes described more fully as "cutting someone dead." You see the enemy, say walking on the street, they see you seeing them but you give no acknowledgment, no sign of noticing. We can insult people by willfully ignoring them.

The significance of looks and looking in our interactions with others can be metaphysically subtle. Acknowledgment and recognition by others may be important to our consciousness of self, perhaps to our very existence, as suggested by Sartre in his story of the "keyhole" in the section on "The Look" in *Being and Nothingness* (1956, 259–61). Imagine you are in a corridor, on bended knee, looking through a keyhole. Imagine further that the scene is gripping (if you wish, imagine it is the "primal scene" of parental intercourse), and so your consciousness is full of nothing but the scene at the other side of the keyhole. You are a disembodied mind, unaware of yourself. But then . . . you hear footsteps coming down the corridor. All of a sudden, *everything* changes. From being aware of nothing but the scene, you become aware of the existence of another and of the other's point of view, and you realize that from that point of view *you* are an object of perception—you become aware of your body and aware of yourself. You become embodied, conscious, conscious of yourself, self-conscious (in both the psychologically uneasy and ontological senses), embarrassed and ashamed. Our existence, our consciousness and self-consciousness, depends on our being embodied and on the existence of others and of their consciousnesses, of external points of view from which we can be seen. (Kant provides a more elaborate argument for this in his "Transcendental Deduction of the Categories" in the *Critique of Pure Reason*, but Sartre's anecdotes may sometimes be sufficiently compelling.) Of course, for Sartre, the mere existence of others can also be a challenge to our freedom. But that is another story—though we have already seen a version of it in Linger's drunk at the bus stop. And, of course, there are many other ways in which who we are and what we can imagine ourselves as being depend on recognition by others (recall our earlier questions: could someone be "witty" if no one ever laughed at their jokes? "charming" if no one were ever charmed?). Abstract issues of identity and awareness, of acknowledgment and challenge, of being looked at and being seen, will have to be given place in our understanding of the stakes in insults.

But things need not be subtle. A look may itself be an accusation, a blow. A comic routine by one of the men in Abrahams' Camingerly Philadelphia neighborhood begins:

> "Man, why you want to look at me like that?"
> "'Cause you ugly."
> "I'm ugly? You got the nerve to call me ugly?"
> "Yeah, you ugly."
> "No, I ain't."
> "Look, boy, you so ugly that the stork that brought you here should be locked up by the F.B.I."
> "Look here, man, you was so ugly when you was a baby that your mother had to put a sheet on your face so sleep could creep up on you."
> (Abrahams 1970, 57)

In this case, the words spell out the meaning of the look, but its significance is perceived before the verbal gloss is offered. And no gloss is needed for the terrorizing evil looks that are sometimes used as weapons in the provocations and connections of *briga* (Linger, 111–14).

Staring is one "wrong way" of looking. The fixed and unchanging gaze of a stare generally (but, significantly, not always) has sinister implications. While eye contact can in certain circumstances be inviting, a relentless, unexplained, and unwanted stare is generally perceived as a threat. There have been social psychology experiments that confirm this for humans, and the evidence of ethology is suggestive of evolutionary roots. As Phoebe Ellsworth and her colleagues summarize some of the evidence: "One of the most frequently reported components of agonistic or threat displays in primates is a steady, direct gaze at the object of aggression. This type of gaze is characteristic of the aggressive behavior of chimpanzees . . ., gorillas . . ., and a wide variety of monkeys. . . ." And in humans, "staring is a salient stimulus which forcibly involves the subject in an interpersonal encounter and demands a response" (Ellsworth et al., 1972, 302, 311, citations omitted). The valence of a particular instance of staring may depend on the particular context; whether a look is the "wrong way" may depend on available contextual explanations.

Eyes are expressive. There is the familiar description, "looking daggers" at someone (the eyes may in various ways be armed); and there is the more localized aggressive practice of "mad-dogging," which involves relentless, hostile staring. "Glaring" comes in a variety of forms, from darkly menacing to withering. But while "ogling" can be invasive, it can also strike imploring, charming, and comic notes. The standard meaning of "making eyes" at someone is flirtatious and seductive. Eye-contact in humans can signal both friendly engagement and hostile intentions (Ellsworth and Carlsmith 1968; and Ellsworth and Langer 1976). As noted, the ethologists tell us that direct eye-contact may serve as a challenge among our simian relatives, including the baboons. At the other end of things, among the baboons, the ritual presentation of the behind is a sign of submission, presumably evolved from the female invitation to mate (Zuckerman 1932; Lorenz 1966, 116–17; and Vanggaard 1972, 71). This is of some significance in understanding the sort of challenge presented by the play for status and honor in insults, whether we speak through our eyes or other organs and orifices.

Alan Dundes and his colleagues provide an extensive sociolinguistic report on "The Strategy of Turkish Boys' Verbal Dueling Rhymes" (1972). Turkish boys from age eight to fourteen indulge in attempts to verbally put each other down via "parrying phallic thrusts": "One of the most important goals is to force one's opponent into a female, passive role" (Dundes, 135). This may be by a direct "my-penis-up-your-anus strategy" (153), or via disparagements or threats to the opponent's female extensions, his mother or sister. Male honor in Turkey, as in many Mediterranean and other societies, is identified with the inviolability of mothers and sisters. It is particularly humiliating for the man himself to serve as a sexual receptacle, thus being unmanned and feminized. While there is nothing insulting about being an active homosexual, in the Turkish as in other traditions, it is wholly debilitating to play the passive role in a homosexual encounter. As in the dozens, insults (raps) are followed by replies (caps), challenges by structured responses. In the context of the tradition, one boy might begin with "*Hiyar*" (meaning, literally, "you cucumber" and, figuratively, "you prick") and be responded to with "*Götüne uyar*" ("it fits your ass") (137). That "*hiyar*" rhymes with "*uyar*" is no accident, just as sodomy sets the theme for the exchanges, and rhyme sets a formal constraint on the successful combatant (135). Both challenge and retort are fixed in tradition, the dexterity required is less originality than memory and acuity in drawing on the available store of thrusts and parries.

The Turkish boys' ritual can be understood, like the dozens, as facilitating one route to manhood. It is one of the rites of passage from boyhood to the world of responsibility, authority, and power. As Dundes and colleagues put it: "Turkish male verbal dueling serves in part as a kind of extended rite of passage. Like most if not all puberty initiation rites, the ritual allows the young boy to repudiate the female world with its passive sexual role and to affirm the male world with its active sexual role" (159). These attitudes may be complicated and colored by the Turkish practice of circumcision at age four to eight (just before the start of participation in the verbal dueling tradition), which tends to be experienced as an aggressive attack and as symbolic castration, and to be blamed on mothers as betrayal (157–58). The crucial point is that "to belong to the world of men in Turkish culture, a boy needs to prove that he is a man, not a woman, and one of the ways of proving this is to demonstrate through act and symbolic words that one has a powerful, aggressive phallus" (158).

FOUR

■ ■ ■

ASSAULT FROM THE REAR

WHILE A LOOK CAN BE MENACING, AN INABILITY TO SEE CAN BE frightening. Danger lurks in the rear. This is partly an artifact of physiology: we don't have eyes in the backs of our heads. So, when threatened, we need someone to "get our backs." Gangsters (and intelligence officers) often sit with their backs to the wall in restaurants and other exposed places, so that they can see their enemies as they approach. We are especially vulnerable from the rear. But other factors have contributed to the construction of a need for a rearguard. The rear is also the region of excretion, and the orifice that serves that end may also serve as an entry point. Developmentally, it becomes the troubled center for issues of (in Erik Erikson's [1963, 52, 82] terminology) "holding on and letting go." The anus is an early locus of sexual pleasure, and for many (if not all) it continues to have sexual significance of one kind and degree or another. We all start polymorphously perverse, capable of deriving sexual pleasure from many regions of the body. The genital locus for sexual pleasure is a late development. Freud's classic psycho-sexual developmental scheme has us move from the oral to the anal stage, and only later to a genital focus. The mouth is the first erotogenic zone—in connection with the infant's original need for taking nourishment it readily develops independent satisfaction in sensual sucking (Freud 1905d, 182). With greater sphincter control, better-formed feces, and the pressure for the mother to wean created by teething, the forces that move one forward on the erotogenic developmental path are at least partly biological. The early stages, nonetheless, persist in foreplay (the mouth continues to function as a zone of sexual pleasure in kissing, licking, sucking, etc. as well as in oral intercourse), in perversions,[1] and—in displaced form—neuroses and character. Some are disturbed by that persistence. Aside from the multiplication of functions (but recall that the genitals, both the penis and vagina, also have excretion among their functions), some individuals and societies find perverse and passive sexual activity disturbing. Passivity is of special interest. Its association with femininity gives the social valuation (or disvaluation), the distaste, for passive homosexuality in many societies a misogynist cast. The phallus becomes the fantasy form of power, active penetration the image of domination, and sadomasochism and sodomy the sexual theaters of insult.

Roger D. Abrahams, in his book *Deep Down in the Jungle* (1970), suggests that the source as well as the content of black verbal "sounding" contests, teasing or boasting sessions, is sexual:

> The terms in which the arguments are waged indicate that the word battles derive their impetus from sexual matters. A verbal attack is called "mounting" or "getting above"; that is, placing the other in the female position. Getting the best of someone is called "putting him down," a similar sexual slur. Winning such a battle not only proves the masculinity of the victor; it conclusively feminizes the other. (46)

The rejection of the feminine is important. "Motherfucker" is the most common obscenity among the men and can be used alternatively to praise or damn (32), matching the ambivalence about mothers. Some of the examples of sounding Abrahams gives show an explicit presence of thoughts about sodomy, the feminine position to be avoided in oneself and imposed on the other, in the pool hall and the barbershop: "Suck my ass . . . Sucking ass is out of style, button your lipper, suck my

---

1. "Perversions are sexual activities which either (a) extend, in an anatomical sense, beyond the regions of the body that are designed for sexual union, or (b) linger over the intermediate relations to the sexual object which should normally be traversed rapidly on the path towards the final sexual aim" (Freud 1905d, 150; see also Neu 2000, chap. 9, "Freud and Perversion").

---

dick awhile. . . . Sucking dicks ain't no trick. Button your ↑ ing mouth up my asshole, nuts and dick" (45). Of course informant says of such sounding, "It's just passing speech mean no harm; they just saying it" (46). The teasing cont sive and protective. If it were meant, or thought to be ↑ would likely ensue. But even words which are not serious have meaning and their expression be meaningful. Consc is not the only form of significance.

TURKISH BOYS' RHYMING INSU RITUALS

With Turkish boys' insult rituals, as with ritual insult ↑ (including the dozens), it is an interesting fact that ↑ possibility of truth in an assertion that can serve to otherwise be one in a series of playful ritual insults ↑ personal insult, often leading to physical fighting. It playful, let alone good, intentions behind the direct ↑ come and defaming truths. It is interesting, too, tha insult rituals (like the traditional dozens, like conten involve rhyming and the presence of a vitally impo most interesting of all, the insults involved in the ⌐ are all about sodomy—as are certain relevant pract ancient Greece and elsewhere. Those we shall turn

---

2. Gangsta rap is also notable for its literally feminizing Dogg raps: "I got a little message, don't try to see Snoop / I'↑ her name, it's Luke" (in the song "Tha Shiznit" on his 199? Cent disses several of his rivals with: "I smell pussy. Is that y↑ you Ja? / I smell pussy. Is that you Black? / I smell pussy. I is pussy. . . . / You niggas get so emotional / You remind m↑ Smell Pussy" on his 2002 album *50 Cent Is the Future*). A in Dr. Dre's conflict with fellow ex-N.W.A. member Eaz ain't another ho that I gots ta fuck with / Gap teeth in ya m And I'ma snatch your ass from the backside / To show yo who-ride" (in the song "Fuck Wit Dre Day" on his 1992 ↑ to Dan Shulman-Means.)

A similar verbal dueling tradition, with formal constraints and focused content, exists among the Chamula of Chiapas, southern Mexico. Instead of rhyme, the formal requirement is "a minimum sound shift from word to word or phrase to phrase combined with a maximum derogatory or obscene attack on the opponent" (Gossen 1976, 129). While the Chamula themselves describe such verbal dueling as "truly frivolous talk," the verbal parries, as with the Turkish boys, can be interpreted as "a drama of phallic attack and submission" (146).

Opening gambits are standardized formulas (as with "Yo momma . . ." in versions of the dozens); "Look at me" is one. In a long example of a couple of hundred exchanges that Gary H. Gossen (1976, 131–37) cites, there is lots of talk of penises (one gets pulled out and displayed at one point), including "your cigar" (an invitation to the opponent to put the exhibited penis in his mouth), erections ("You are getting excited" followed by "Your pants are already ripping"—in the native Tzotzil "ta šabat" followed by "ta ša šhat aveš"), and imputations of femininity to the other speaker ("The hole is very big"). The business concludes with an exchange of sexual directions. Whether "they are male/male instructions or male/female instructions is not entirely clear. Rapid sexual role reversal between the two players, however, appears throughout" (138). In one passage "the players 'one-up' each other by adopting the female role when chastising the male opponent for his inadequate sexual performance" (139).

There is a special joking relationship that participants in the verbal duel must have in order to be able to play.

> These joking relationships also entail much public physical contact. Boys and men between twelve and thirty-five years of age typically hold hands, in couples, and dance embraced together at fiestas. They also engage publicly in playful grabs at one another's genitals and rub and stroke each other's shoulders, legs, and groins. Such familiar behavior frequently accompanies verbal dueling as well. Furthermore, the homosexual nuances of this behavior carry over into the themes of the exchanges. When not accusing each other's female relatives of being promiscuous or male relatives of being stupid, the duelers tend to impute femininity and passivity to each other. (Gossen 1976, 129)

In this nonserious setting, serious anxieties about male social and sexual immaturity can get played with and laughed about. The problems shared by adolescents and young married men are verbalized.

"Although competitive on the surface, verbal dueling also expresses solidarity in this male age-mate group. Never in the life cycle are men more *equal* in status and influence, or lack thereof, than at this stage. Joking expresses this solidarity" (138). As we have seen before, a friend is someone you can insult freely. The assumptions of good intentions can mark the boundary between in-group and out-group. A friend is also someone who will get your back, and whom you can trust not to take advantage of a position to the rear or behind.

ACTIVITY/PASSIVITY AND MASCULINITY/FEMININITY

In terms of societal attitudes, the problem is positional. The problem is not homosexuality, but the receptivity of the bottom, that is to say, passive homosexuality. Since anxiety also attaches to the passive partner in homosexual fellatio (though it might seem puzzling that a person who actively sucks is regarded as passive), it might be considered more broadly as the problem of organs and orifices, the horror of the hole (made ontological by Sartre—1956, 612–15). Penetration gets seen as violation, and personal integrity as a bodily boundary that must be defended for honor to be maintained. The physical postures and entanglements become the embodiment of a metaphysical concern over domination and submission. The attitudes are not just those of Turkey and Mexico, the Mediterranean and Brazil, and other regions we have discussed.[3] We see them in modern prisons in America, they go back to ancient Greece, and extend to more northerly climes.

Jack Abbott, the habitual criminal (championed as a writer by Norman Mailer and briefly released with fatal consequences for a waiter who had a minor altercation with him), reports from a lifetime in prison:

---

3. T. E. Lawrence was brought up in the world of the English public school, but achieved fame as Lawrence of Arabia. Having adopted Arab attitudes, he famously lamented the irrecoverable loss of his "bodily integrity" and became undone after being taken prisoner at Deraa in 1917. Legend has it that he was there tortured and sodomized by Hajim Bey, the Turkish governor of the occupied territory, and that he felt himself permanently humiliated after the incident ("unclean, unclean!"—as he wrote in a letter—Vanggaard 1972, 105–7).

In prison, if I take a punk, *she is mine.* He is like a slave, a chattel slave. It is the custom that no one addresses her directly. He cleans my cell, my clothing and runs errands for me. Anything I tell him to do, he must do—exactly the way a wife is perceived in some marriages even today. But I can sell her or lend her out or give her away at any time. Another prisoner can take her from me if he can dominate me.

... The majority of prisoners I have known—something like ninety percent—express sexual interest in their own sex. I hesitate to call this "homosexual" because American society recognizes *only* the passive homosexual—the one who plays the female role—as being a "homosexual." So it is really the same outside as in prison, but open in prison.

So you can see already how this distorts a lot of meanings and can fuel a lot of violence, both physical and psychological. Because no prisoner really respects a homosexual, and yet—as I said—almost all have these desires themselves. It is the same as in the society of men outside prison. (1982, 94–95)[4]

While one may doubt Abbott's understanding of attitudes outside of prison, he certainly understands prison mentality; it is his mentality. And he sees the misogyny behind the mentality, perhaps most clearly here: "when a man sodomizes another to express his *contempt,* it demonstrates only his contempt for woman, not man. The normal attitude among men

---

There is evidence in that other celebrated English Lawrence (D. H., the novelist) of a special horror attached to anal intercourse, even when its object is a woman. Even that champion of obscene words and plain speaking about sex seemed reticent when it came to that act. Geoffrey Hughes points out that "at the most crucial union in" *Lady Chatterley's Lover* (the unexpurgated Penguin edition of which was the subject of an important English obscenity trial in 1960), Lawrence "writes symbolically of 'Burning out the shames, the deepest, oldest shames, in the most secret places,' of 'the sensual flame [that] pressed through her bowels and breast' to 'the core of the physical jungle, the last and deepest recess of organic shame. The phallus alone could explore it.' Furthermore, 'She had to be a passive, consenting thing, like a slave, a physical slave'" (Penguin *Lady Chatterley's Lover* 1960, 258–59, quoted in Hughes 1998, 194). Hughes cites the arguments of John Sparrow, Frank Kermode, and others that the passage is about buggery, *penetratio per anum,* as is the climactic sexual act in *Women in Love,* which is also described in (florid) terms of shame (Hughes 1998, 194).

4. In the gay enclaves of San Francisco and elsewhere, there are tee shirts with the self-refuting and self-mocking slogan: "I'm Not Gay, But My Boyfriend Is."

in society is that it is a great shame and dishonor to have experienced what it feels like to be a woman" (1982, 92–93). (Poor Tiresias!)

The attitudes go back at least to ancient Greece. While much homosexual activity was acceptable, even idealized, passive anal penetration was not. We get some of the picture from Plato's *Symposium*. In that feast of speeches in praise of love, not only are the exemplars of love discussed most often homosexual, they are exemplars of a very special socially sanctioned form of pederasty, characteristic of Plato's time and class. (See Neu 2000, chap. 8, "Plato's Homoerotic *Symposium*.") In Pausanias's speech, the ideal love relationship is between an older man and an adolescent youth, with the youth offering his beauty and sensual satisfaction, while the older man is supposed to provide moral instruction and spiritual and intellectual guidance. But there are strict limits on the forms of sensual satisfaction. The conventional attitude was that the youth was expected not to enjoy the physical intimacy as such, and the range of physical interaction (at least in conventional depictions, as on vases) was rather limited. The assuming of what to the ancient Greeks as to many modern "macho" cultures would appear a passive and so womanly sexual role was problematic and was supposed to be a passing phase (the youth eventually becoming *erastes* to another youth and husband to a wife)—the gratifications involved were supposed to be nonsexual. A strong statement of the view is attributed to Socrates in Xenophon's *Symposium* (8.21): "the boy does not share in the man's pleasure in intercourse, as a woman does; cold sober, he looks upon the other drunk with sexual desire." Of course, depictions of cultural expectations should not be mistaken for accounts of actual practice and experience.

Kenneth J. Dover in his authoritative work, *Greek Homosexuality*, notes the prevalence of intercrural frottage (between-the-thighs rubbsies), as opposed to other physical interactions, and the absence of erections in the *eromenoi* ("even in circumstances to which one would expect the penis of any healthy adolescent to respond willy-nilly") in depictions on vases (1978, 91–109). And as illustrated in the case of Timarkhos, the general societal view was that by willingly "assimilating himself to a woman in the sexual act . . . the submissive male rejects his role as a male citizen" and can be disbarred from later service in political office (103). Michel Foucault describes the asymmetry in terms of a

> principle of isomorphism between sexual relations and social relations.
> What this means is that sexual relations—always conceived in terms of
> the model act of penetration, assuming a polarity that opposed activity
> and passivity—were seen as being of the same type as the relationship

between a superior and a subordinate, an individual who dominates and one who is dominated, one who commands and one who complies, one who vanquishes and one who is vanquished. . . . this suggests that in sexual behavior there was one role that was intrinsically honorable and valorized without question: the one that consisted in being active, in dominating, in penetrating, in asserting one's superiority.

. . . When one played the role of subordinate partner in the game of pleasure relations, one could not be truly dominant in the game of civil and political activity." (Foucault 1986, 215, 220)

The recognition of analogies between sexual relations and social relations goes back at least to Plato's *Symposium*, where Pausanias draws a direct link between sexual repression and political repression (an idea now familiar from the work of Marcuse and many others). Pausanias explains that: "The Persian empire is absolute; that is why it condemns love as well as philosophy and sport. It is no good for rulers if the people they rule cherish ambitions for themselves, or form strong bonds of friendship with one another. . . . plain condemnation of Love reveals lust for power in the rulers and cowardice in the ruled" (182B–182D, trans. Nehamas and Woodruff).

There emerged in ancient Greece a complex etiquette of wooing. As on the Victorian model for young ladies, the desired youth was expected to be at first coy and to avoid giving in too soon or for base motives (as would be suspected were he to give in to a rich or famous person who could not offer a suitable long-term mentor relationship in pursuit of virtue and excellence). The mix of attitudes toward homosexuality and passivity produced what Foucault calls the "antinomy of the boy": "On the one hand young men were recognized as objects of pleasure . . . no one would ever reproach a man for loving a boy . . . But on the other hand, the boy, whose youth must be a training for manhood, could not and must not identify with that role" (Foucault, 221).

The antinomy of the boy rests ultimately on the problem of the female position, the assimilation of passivity to subordination: "the difficulty caused, in this society that accepted sexual relations between men, by the juxtaposition of an ethos of male superiority and a conception of all sexual intercourse in terms of the schema of penetration and male domination. The consequence of this was that on the one hand the 'active' and dominant role was always assigned positive values, but on the other hand it was necessary to attribute to one of the partners in the sexual act the passive, dominated, and inferior position. And while this was no problem when it involved a woman or a slave, the case was altered when it involved a man" (220).

Whatever the complications in ancient Greece, as we have seen, the equation of activity and dominance is widespread. Linger, in the course of discussing machismo in the Brazilian practice of *briga*, notes the symbolic link of masculinity and power and the view of penetration as domination (linguistically, to penetrate is to "*comer*" in the sense of eat, conquer, vanquish, possess, own, while the passive partner submits or gives, "*dar*"). Maleness is identified with activity and only the passive male partner is regarded as homosexual (Linger 1992, 110–11), as in Abbott's world of prison. We have earlier discussed the gendering of honor as male and notions of masculinity, typical of the Mediterranean and other regions, that identify male honor with the sexual purity of women family members. As David Gilmore develops the point, "Sexuality itself is perceived through a competitive idiom by which men jockey for control over women as objects to achieve narcissistic gratifications and dominance over other men. Sexuality is a form of social power" (1987, 4). Honor can be seen as a power play and dominance is both sexual and sexualized. Honor is related to many things, including wealth, but women may themselves be regarded as a form of property, and sexual control of them as a form of dominance—not just over them, but over other men. Sexual dominance can be achieved through the maintenance of female chastity and fidelity. Honor involves the "defense of a beleaguered 'manliness'" (Gilmore 1987, 10), and the manliness that is so precarious and at risk may require public demonstrations of virility (as through one's wife's pregnancy) along with control over one's women. At the same time, being a "real" man involves emphatic contrast with being a woman, with being effeminate or effete or impotent. This can find psychological realization through fears of being feminized, of homoerotic penetration. As Gilmore puts it, it appears

> that sexual access in the Mediterranean area often involves an indirect threat to the masculine integrity of another man. This amounts to a symbolic "penetration" in rape or seduction . . . the stress on virility seems to belie a defensive or prophylactic strategy. This strategy is institutionalized in the particularly aggressive Mediterranean ethnomasculinities with the relentless, almost obsessive manliness—a feature found from the *machismo* of Spain and *maschio* of Sicily to the *rajula* of North Africa to cognate forms in the Balkans. (Gilmore 1987, 10–11, citations omitted)

Looking to more northerly climes, we are told: "it was disgraceful for a man in ancient Scandinavia to be another man's underdog and to be used sexually as a woman by him. On the other hand, it was not considered in the least shameful to be able to force another man into that position—on the contrary, it was something to brag about" (Vanggaard 1972, 77). And the point is linguistically encoded: *argr* is "the crudest term of abuse in old Norse. Applied to a man it indicated not only that he was effeminate, but also that he submitted himself to being used sexually as a woman" (Martin Larsen quoted in Vanggaard 1972, 76).

William Ian Miller's book, *Humiliation*, drawing on the Icelandic sagas, elaborates on and is very helpful in understanding the eroticization of honor and shame. As discussed previously, he brings out ways in which in our rituals and practices modern society remains an honor society, bound by the compelling requirements of reciprocity to requite insults and even gifts, enmeshed in competition for status. We remain in some ways like the people of the Icelandic sagas, who lived in "a world of shame and envy, the emotions of status, not of guilt and remorse, the emotions of conscience" (123). He notes important differences in honor and shame in the saga world and in the Mediterranean region. In particular, in the saga world, honor and shame "were not obsessively focused on the condition of the female genitalia and did not lead to an ideal or a reality of female sequestration" (118). Nonetheless, honor and shame were clearly gendered and the status anxieties often played out in eroticized forms. "In the Norse world the language of challenge at its most vulgar and most provocative made sure to suggest the effeminacy of the insultee. The coward was the man who was penetrated by other men, no different from a woman. But the actions that were shameful and the shames that could be done the honorable man involved the reputation of his women only occasionally" (118–19).

Miller points out that in violence, even today, victimizers tend to be male and victims tend to be gendered female, as Miller puts it, "A male victim is a feminized male" (55). He suggests: "Our root notion of violence as boundary-breaking, the fist-meets-face view of violence, has a seductive essentiality to it" (65). Of course, our views on violence are in fact heavily context-dependent. Nonetheless, destroying the external integrity of the body is generally taken as a particular mark of violence (poisoning seems less violent than murder by gun or knife, an axe that mutilates more violent than a bullet, 68), and that may provide us a hint about the link between bodily integrity and integrity as virtue, a step toward understanding the horror of the passively female. What is it to take an insult? Is it somehow passively female? Miller tells us, "Neither Jews nor women instill fear by being marked as violent. Both Jews and women (of course) are feminized. They are violated, they do not violate" (63). Miller tells us that "humiliation is also richly gendered as feminine" and he interestingly speculates

> The gendering of humiliation as feminine is intimately connected to vulgar views of the sexual act. In this view, men poke, prod, pierce, penetrate; their actions rely heavily on verbs that cause deflation. And what is being deflated if not the pretension of women to moral equivalence with men? Women are on the bottom, on the *humus*; they are brought low, done dirt, subjected to a host of metaphors which capture the root sense of humiliate. In this view of sex, a view held by some feminists [n. 64 cites MacKinnon, *Feminism Unmodified*], the sexual act can only humiliate women in the eyes of men and often in their own eyes as well. (168–69)

As we have seen, the assault in insult is typically not directly physical, but the dominance assumed or asserted is meant or taken to put the other down, to disrespect and humiliate. The play of gender can be seen in the complex imaginative identifications in fantasy and in sadomasochism (to which we will return). Vulgar—and one might add, infantile—views of sex and sexuality need to be questioned, and so far as they inform normative expectations, they need to be rejected. But the surface of rituals, manifest meanings, may help reveal subterranean significances.

Freud interprets many slips of the tongue in terms of interfering intentions, and in one exemplary interpretation the interfering intention suggests that an insult is something one does to a woman. The instance involves a young man who approached a lady he did not know on the street, saying he wished to "*begleit-digen*" her. The nonsensical word is a composite of "*begleiten* [to accompany]" and "*beleidigen* [to insult]" (Freud 1916–17, 33, 42, 172).

Most immediately, there is the interesting question of why men should be so threatened by passivity, and the perhaps prior question of the meaning of "passivity"—is it simply anatomical?

ISOMORPHISM: THE SEXUALIZATION OF THE SOCIAL

We concluded at the end of the first chapter that feeling insulted may be usefully characterized as a kind of pain caused by disappointed expecta-

FOUR

■ ■ ■

ASSAULT FROM THE REAR

WHILE A LOOK CAN BE MENACING, AN INABILITY TO SEE CAN BE frightening. Danger lurks in the rear. This is partly an artifact of physiology: we don't have eyes in the backs of our heads. So, when threatened, we need someone to "get our backs." Gangsters (and intelligence officers) often sit with their backs to the wall in restaurants and other exposed places, so that they can see their enemies as they approach. We are especially vulnerable from the rear. But other factors have contributed to the construction of a need for a rearguard. The rear is also the region of excretion, and the orifice that serves that end may also serve as an entry point. Developmentally, it becomes the troubled center for issues of (in Erik Erikson's [1963, 52, 82] terminology) "holding on and letting go." The anus is an early locus of sexual pleasure, and for many (if not all) it continues to have sexual significance of one kind and degree or another. We all start polymorphously perverse, capable of deriving sexual pleasure from many regions of the body. The genital locus for sexual pleasure is a late development. Freud's classic psychosexual developmental scheme has us move from the oral to the anal stage, and only later to a genital focus. The mouth is the first erotogenic zone — in connection with the infant's original need for taking nourishment it readily develops independent satisfaction in sensual sucking (Freud 1905d, 182). With greater sphincter control, better-formed feces, and the pressure for the mother to wean created by teething, the

83

forces that move one forward on the erotogenic developmental path are at least partly biological. The early stages, nonetheless, persist in foreplay (the mouth continues to function as a zone of sexual pleasure in kissing, licking, sucking, etc. as well as in oral intercourse), in perversions,[1] and — in displaced form — neuroses and character. Some are disturbed by that persistence. Aside from the multiplication of functions (but recall that the genitals, both the penis and vagina, also have excretion among their functions), some individuals and societies find perverse and passive sexual activity disturbing. Passivity is of special interest. Its association with femininity gives the social valuation (or disvaluation), the distaste, for passive homosexuality in many societies a misogynist cast. The phallus becomes the fantasy form of power, active penetration the image of domination, and sadomasochism and sodomy the sexual theaters of insult.

Roger D. Abrahams, in his book *Deep Down in the Jungle* (1970), suggests that the source as well as the content of black verbal "sounding" contests, teasing or boasting sessions, is sexual:

> The terms in which the arguments are waged indicate that the word battles derive their impetus from sexual matters. A verbal attack is called "mounting" or "getting above"; that is, placing the other in the female position. Getting the best of someone is called "putting him down," a similar sexual slur. Winning such a battle not only proves the masculinity of the victor; it conclusively feminizes the other. (46)

The rejection of the feminine is important. "Motherfucker" is the most common obscenity among the men and can be used alternatively to praise or damn (32), matching the ambivalence about mothers. Some of the examples of sounding Abrahams gives show an explicit presence of thoughts about sodomy, the feminine position to be avoided in oneself and imposed on the other, in the pool hall and the barbershop: "Suck my ass . . . Sucking ass is out of style, button your lipper, suck my

---

1. "Perversions are sexual activities which either (a) extend, in an anatomical sense, beyond the regions of the body that are designed for sexual union, or (b) linger over the intermediate relations to the sexual object which should normally be traversed rapidly on the path towards the final sexual aim" (Freud 1905d, 150; see also Neu 2000, chap. 9, "Freud and Perversion").

dick awhile. . . . Sucking dicks ain't no trick. Button your motherfuck-
ing mouth up my asshole, nuts and dick" (45). Of course, Abrahams'
informant says of such sounding, "It's just passing speech. Guys don't
mean no harm; they just saying it" (46). The teasing context is permissive and protective. If it were meant, or thought to be meant, blows
would likely ensue. But even words which are not seriously meant can
have meaning and their expression be meaningful. Conscious intention
is not the only form of significance.

TURKISH BOYS' RHYMING INSULT RITUALS

With Turkish boys' insult rituals, as with ritual insult games elsewhere
(including the dozens), it is an interesting fact that it is precisely the
possibility of truth in an assertion that can serve to shift what might
otherwise be one in a series of playful ritual insults into an aggressive
personal insult, often leading to physical fighting. It is difficult to see
playful, let alone good, intentions behind the direct assertion of unwelcome and defaming truths. It is interesting, too, that the Turkish boys'
insult rituals (like the traditional dozens, like contemporary rap music)[2]
involve rhyming and the presence of a vitally important audience. But
most interesting of all, the insults involved in the Turkish boys' rituals
are all about sodomy—as are certain relevant practices and attitudes in
ancient Greece and elsewhere. Those we shall turn to later.

2. Gangsta rap is also notable for its literally feminizing insults. E.g., Snoop Doggy
Dogg raps: "I got a little message, don't try to see Snoop / I'm fin to fuck a bitch, what's
her name, it's Luke" (in the song "Tha Shiznit" on his 1993 album *Doggystyle*); and 50
Cent disses several of his rivals with: "I smell pussy. Is that you Irv? / I smell pussy. Is that
you Ja? / I smell pussy. Is that you Black? / I smell pussy. Is that you Tah? / Y'all niggas
is pussy. . . . / You niggas get so emotional / You remind me of my bitch" (in the song "I
Smell Pussy" on his 2002 album *50 Cent Is the Future*). An early example can be found
in Dr. Dre's conflict with fellow ex-N.W.A. member Eazy-E, when Dr. Dre raps: "If it
ain't another ho that I gots ta fuck with / Gap teeth in ya mouth so my dick's gots to fit /. . .
And I'ma snatch your ass from the backside / To show you how Death Row pull off that
who-ride" (in the song "Fuck Wit Dre Day" on his 1992 album *The Chronic*). (Point due
to Dan Shulman-Means.)

Alan Dundes and his colleagues provide an extensive sociolinguistic report on "The Strategy of Turkish Boys' Verbal Dueling Rhymes" (1972). Turkish boys from age eight to fourteen indulge in attempts to verbally put each other down via "parrying phallic thrusts": "One of the most important goals is to force one's opponent into a female, passive role" (Dundes, 135). This may be by a direct "my-penis-up-your-anus strategy" (153), or via disparagements or threats to the opponent's female extensions, his mother or sister. Male honor in Turkey, as in many Mediterranean and other societies, is identified with the inviolability of mothers and sisters. It is particularly humiliating for the man himself to serve as a sexual receptacle, thus being unmanned and feminized. While there is nothing insulting about being an active homosexual, in the Turkish as in other traditions, it is wholly debilitating to play the passive role in a homosexual encounter. As in the dozens, insults (raps) are followed by replies (caps), challenges by structured responses. In the context of the tradition, one boy might begin with "*Hiyar*" (meaning, literally, "you cucumber" and, figuratively, "you prick") and be responded to with "*Götüne uyar*" ("it fits your ass") (137). That "*hiyar*" rhymes with "*uyar*" is no accident, just as sodomy sets the theme for the exchanges, end rhyme sets a formal constraint on the successful combatant (135). Both challenge and retort are fixed in tradition, the dexterity required is less originality than memory and acuity in drawing on the available store of thrusts and parries.

The Turkish boys' ritual can be understood, like the dozens, as facilitating one route to manhood. It is one of the rites of passage from boyhood to the world of responsibility, authority, and power. As Dundes and his colleagues put it: "Turkish male verbal dueling serves in part as a kind of extended rite of passage. Like most if not all puberty initiation rites, the duel allows the young boy to repudiate the female world with its passive sexual role and to affirm the male world with its active sexual role" (159). The attitudes may be complicated and colored by the Turkish practice of circumcision at age four to eight (just before the start of participation in the verbal dueling tradition), which tends to be experienced as an aggressive attack and as symbolic castration, and to be blamed on mothers as a betrayal (157–58). The crucial point is that "to belong to the world of men in Turkish culture, a boy needs to prove that he is a man, not a woman, and one of the ways of proving this is to demonstrate through act or symbolic words that one has a powerful, aggressive phallus" (158).

sidered in the least shameful to be able to force another man into that position—on the contrary, it was something to brag about" (Vanggaard 1972, 77). And the point is linguistically encoded: *argr* is "the crudest term of abuse in old Norse. Applied to a man it indicated not only that he was effeminate, but also that he submitted himself to being used sexually as a woman" (Martin Larsen quoted in Vanggaard 1972, 76).

William Ian Miller's book, *Humiliation*, drawing on the Icelandic sagas, elaborates on and is very helpful in understanding the eroticization of honor and shame. As discussed previously, he brings out ways in which in our rituals and practices modern society remains an honor society, bound by the compelling requirements of reciprocity to requite insults and even gifts, enmeshed in competition for status. We remain in some ways like the people of the Icelandic sagas, who lived in "a world of shame and envy, the emotions of status, not of guilt and remorse, the emotions of conscience" (123). He notes important differences in honor and shame in the saga world and in the Mediterranean region. In particular, in the saga world, honor and shame "were not obsessively focused on the condition of the female genitalia and did not lead to an ideal or a reality of female sequestration" (118). Nonetheless, honor and shame were clearly gendered and the status anxieties often played out in eroticized forms. "In the Norse world the language of challenge at its most vulgar and most provocative made sure to suggest the effeminacy of the insultee. The coward was the man who was penetrated by other men, no different from a woman. But the actions that were shameful and the shames that could be done the honorable man involved the reputation of his women only occasionally" (118–19).

Miller points out that in violence, even today, victimizers tend to be male and victims tend to be gendered female, as Miller puts it, "A male victim is a feminized male" (55). He suggests: "Our root notion of violence as boundary-breaking, the fist-meets-face view of violence, has a seductive essentiality to it" (65). Of course, our views on violence are in fact heavily context-dependent. Nonetheless, destroying the external integrity of the body is generally taken as a particular mark of violence (poisoning seems less violent than murder by gun or knife, an axe that mutilates more violent than a bullet, 68), and that may provide us a hint about the link between bodily integrity and integrity as virtue, a step toward understanding the horror of the passively female. What is it to take an insult? Is it somehow passively female? Miller tells us, "Neither Jews nor women instill fear by being marked as violent. Both Jews and women (of course) are feminized. They are violated, they do not violate" (63). Miller tells us that "humiliation is also richly gendered as feminine" and he interestingly speculates

> The gendering of humiliation as feminine is intimately connected to vulgar views of the sexual act. In this view, men poke, prod, pierce, penetrate; their actions rely heavily on verbs that cause deflation. And what is being deflated if not the pretension of women to moral equivalence with men? Women are on the bottom, on the *humus;* they are brought low, done dirt, subjected to a host of metaphors which capture the root sense of humiliate. In this view of sex, a view held by some feminists [n. 64 cites MacKinnon, *Feminism Unmodified*], the sexual act can only humiliate women in the eyes of men and often in their own eyes as well. (168–69)

As we have seen, the assault in insult is typically not directly physical, but the dominance assumed or asserted is meant or taken to put the other down, to disrespect and humiliate. The play of gender can be seen in the complex imaginative identifications in fantasy and in sadomasochism (to which we will return). Vulgar—and one might add, infantile—views of sex and sexuality need to be questioned, and so far as they inform normative expectations, they need to be rejected. But the surface of rituals, manifest meanings, may help reveal subterranean significances.

Freud interprets many slips of the tongue in terms of interfering intentions, and in one exemplary interpretation the interfering intention suggests that an insult is something one does to a woman. The instance involves a young man who approached a lady he did not know on the street, saying he wished to "*begleit-digen*" her. The nonsensical word is a composite of "*begleiten* [to accompany]" and "*beleidigen* [to insult]" (Freud 1916–17, 33, 42, 172).

Most immediately, there is the interesting question of why men should be so threatened by passivity, and the perhaps prior question of the meaning of "passivity"—is it simply anatomical?

ISOMORPHISM: THE SEXUALIZATION OF THE SOCIAL

We concluded at the end of the first chapter that feeling insulted may be usefully characterized as a kind of pain caused by disappointed expectations of attention and respect. Given the understanding of normative expectations that we have developed, and remembering that insults can be unintentional, it would appear that all insults involve assertions or assumptions of dominance. In understanding the forces that lead people to "put down" each other, to abuse, neglect, and in other ways disappoint expectations of attention and respect, we can look to Hegelian understandings of the master-slave relation (how dependence becomes interdependence and we become enmeshed in a battle for status and recognition). Further, we can learn from Freudian explorations of the sexual origins of character traits (why do we describe some people as "tight-assed"?) and the sources of aggression (which, once again, clearly go beyond Dollard's psychology of aggression as a response to frustration). There may be simpler explanations in those instances where, as Oscar Wilde would have it, insults are deserved, where the disappointed expectations are presumptuous, and insulting is a proper putting of someone in their place, a puncturing of pretensions. The place to start here, however, is with a different kind of puncturing or penetration, where the aggressive aspects of insult are to the fore. Let us start with the widespread visions of honor that we have been discussing, visions that invoke recurring patterns that align sexual and social positions, the "isomorphism" that Foucault discerns in the normative expectations of ancient Greece. Once again:

> sexual relations—always conceived in terms of the model act of penetration, assuming a polarity that opposed activity and passivity—were seen as being of the same type as the relationship between a superior and a subordinate, an individual who dominates and one who is dominated, one who commands and one who complies, one who vanquishes and one who is vanquished. . . . this suggests that in sexual behavior there was one role that was intrinsically honorable and valorized without question: the one that consisted in being active, in dominating, in penetrating, in asserting one's superiority. (Foucault 1986, 215)

In ancient Greece, in modern prisons, in *briga* Brazil, from the boyish insults of Turkey to the pride-filled sagas of Iceland, and throughout the world, dominance is understood in sexual terms and passivity is denigrated. Why should this be so and is it inevitable? Is "passivity" an anatomical category and a social destiny? Over and over we have seen evidence of societal attitudes relatively untroubled by homosexuality but deeply distressed at

the position of the passive partner, the "bottom." It is an image of emascu-
lation, femininization, of being unmanned. Is misogyny thus the hidden
secret of the isomorphism of sexual and social relations?

Are women just tokens in the duels of honor, incapable of a dignity of their own? (As noted earlier, in certain cultures there are "honor
killings" where the victims of rape are made victims a second time, by
their families, for the dishonor they are imagined to have brought their
families.) When bodily integrity is violated, what boundary has been
crossed, whose body and whose honor has been undone? Is the struggle
for honor given expression in terms of fear of the female position, or is it
that fear that leads to the struggle for honor?

If we start with anatomical facts, we do not get very far. One might
equate activity with having a penis and passivity with having a vagina,
but it would seem that such meanings and valuations are reversible.
What appears as penetration from one perspective might be seen from
another as enveloping. The enveloping could be regarded as welcoming
and comforting or as frightening and destructive (that is the perspective
of the devouring "*vagina dentata*" of fevered fantasy). Perhaps motion is
supposed to be what makes the difference. But which body more actively
moves is a matter of positions and preferences. The person with the vagina
may do more moving. In fellatio, the person providing the mouth is said
to be passive, though there may be less thrusting and more sucking. In
cunnilingus (not to mention rimming), the tongue is active. Does that
make it, and the mouth it is located in (whatever the owner's gender),
a penis? If so, the person with the active tongue in homosexual fellatio
should perhaps not be thought of as the passive/feminized partner.

If we start with the conditions for social-sexual development, we
may find clues to differentiating valuations. The dominance of women
in child-rearing may help explain the male need to see power in masculinity. We have seen Abrahams' ghetto youths seeking support in gangs in
an attempt to break free from disapproving, controlling, and disciplining
mothers. We have seen Turkish boys blaming "castration" on their mothers, the women who raised them, even when it is men, the associates of
the psychologically distant fathers, that do the actual cutting in circumcision. There may be general issues of separation/individuation for boys
raised by mothers that are less troubling for the daughters raised by those
same mothers, for the daughters share the mothers' gender. Penetration
becomes the marker of differentiation. The masculine insistence on

power and independence may stem precisely from developmental conditions of dependence on "passive" women. The societal valuation of activity becomes a search for male self-reassurance.

Perhaps the isomorphism of the sexual and the social, the gendering of penetration as positive and a source of honor, takes its start in widespread patriarchy and male social dominance of females. If we start historically with patriarchy, with males holding power, that they prefer to maintain power is not very surprising. Why would they want to change places with the powerless females? The explanation of why males held power initially might appeal to their greater physical strength and the special value of that strength in the conditions of the time. As times have changed, and physical strength has become less important, the continued greater power of the males might follow simply from the advantages of incumbency. Sociology recapitulates biology. The valorization of penetration and the rejection of passivity would then just be a metaphor for an independently achieved, desired, and sustained power.

But then, where did the baboons pick up the metaphor? Does it all stem from biology? In baboon troops, weaker males present their rears like a female in heat to signal their submission. And the sexualizing of power relations is not limited to relations between males. "Mounting and presentation are used as signals among baboons, regardless of sex. For instance, a young male may present to an older and stronger female, and she may mount him. Among the females presentation and mounting are used in the same way" (Vanggaard 1972, 72). But the meaning of the gesture does not seem biologically necessary. For every baboon presenting his or her buttocks in submission, there is an American teenager mooning in defiance. Putting the point in words, saying "Kiss my ass" (what Freud describes delicately in his essay on "Character and Anal Erotism" as "an invitation to a caress of the anal zone"—1908b, 173) is, and has been since ancient times, an expression of defiance. This reversal of the baboon submission symbolism may be a part of the ambiguous meaning of many signs,[5] but the human significance of mooning in particular as defiance seems connected to the general social

---

5. Freud writes of "The Antithetical Meaning of Primal Words" (1910e). Even nature has its variants. The female spotted hyena is unusual both in having a penis and in having the erect penis serve as a signal of submission within the female dominance hierarchy (Roughgarden 2004, 38).

constraint that requires the covering of the buttocks—a restriction that applies to humans but not baboons, so uncovering and displaying the buttocks, even if in a bent-over posture, is in and of itself an act of defiance. The result, once more, is that meanings seem reversible.

READING THE BODY

The anal zone speaks eloquently. In addition to anal erotism signaling submission through the presentation of the behind, dominance and defiance may be signaled through mooning, in which the dominant butt is the one that becomes visible. Exposure may have multiple meanings, but "covering one's ass" is presumably always aimed at protecting it from assault. In the realm of character traits, there are a plethora of disagreeable "ass holes," and it is not for nothing that "suck-ups" are also described as "ass-kissers," "ass-lickers," "brown-nosers," and the like. The Freudian trilogy of anal character traits, orderliness, parsimony, and obstinacy, are connected in the vernacular under the rubric of being "tight-assed." A theory of anal erotism and the source of character traits in psychosexual stages seem built into our ordinary vocabulary.

Freud laid down "a formula for the way in which character in its final shape is formed out of the constituent instincts: the permanent character-traits are either unchanged prolongations of the original instincts, or sublimations of those instincts, or reaction-formations against them" (1908b, 175). Each of these types of connection requires its own appropriate type of evidence. For example, to show that miserliness can be understood in terms of sublimation, one needs to show the psychological equivalence of money and feces so that the hoarding of money can be seen as involving a displacement of the instinctual object (and perhaps a deflection in aim as well). It is equation of the substance (as shown by evidence from mythology, literature, and ordinary language),[6] along with similarities of activity (infantile hoarding, retaining feces as a source of gratification—treating excrement as the body's property), that allows one to see the persisting similarities that establish the connection between the adult character trait and the infantile erotic interest. Establishing cleanliness as the product of reaction-formation

---

6. Among other instances, Freud cites the unconscious equation of money with excrement when we describe wealthy people as "filthy rich," or a spendthrift as a "Dukatenscheisser" ("shitter of ducats") (1908b, 9:173–74).

requires a different sort of evidence, of the sort that enables us to see the truth of what is denied when one says "the lady doth protest too much." A fuller understanding of Freud's view of sexuality and of the nature of psychoanalytic explanation would be needed to make his account of the sources of adult character traits in infantile sexuality persuasive. (See Neu 2000, chap. 9 "Freud and Perversion" and chap. 14 "Getting Behind the Demons.") For now, I propose that we continue to use his insights in our efforts to understand the isomorphism of sexual relations and social relations. They offer hope of unifying a very diverse array of phenomena, including the fact that the nether regions are so often taken as the locus of invasive concerns, that may in turn help us understand what kind of assault and what kind of shock provide the psychological underlayment of insult.

Images of anal penetration often remain on an unconscious level—e.g., in threats to "whip (or whup) your ass" (or variants such as "kick your ass," "beat your ass," or—perhaps most tellingly—"your ass is mine"). Any actual violence is more likely to in fact be visited on the face or torso, shins or groin, why is the "ass" the mentioned target? The anus, as Freud teaches, is an erotogenic zone, and so the threat bears a sexual meaning that is not too hard to plumb. An assertion of dominance via a sexualized assault to the opponent's ass seems rather explicitly to imply anal penetration—though it may be repressed from the conscious level, so it seems a threat of physical assault and nothing more. The common prison activity is simply an overt expression of what is unconsciously asserted in regular insults.

We say "Fuck you!" and "Up yours!," making the male other into a passive homosexual, while leaving the agent of the action unmentioned and so the agent's implied sexuality out of account. ("Up yours" in particular seems always directed at the anus, whatever the gender of the insulter or the insultee.) Carl Sagan ties the locution to the facts of ethology. He tells us that squirrel monkeys bare their teeth in greeting and

> lift their legs to exhibit an erect penis. While such behavior would border on impoliteness at many contemporary human social gatherings, it is a fairly elaborate act and serves to maintain dominance hierarchies in squirrel-monkey communities.
>
> The connection between sexual display and position in a dominance hierarchy can be found frequently among the primates. Among Japanese macaques, social class is maintained and reinforced by daily mounting: males of lower caste adopt the characteristic submissive

sexual posture of the female in oestrus and are briefly and ceremonially mounted by higher-caste males. These mountings are both common and perfunctory. They seem to have little sexual content but rather serve as-easily understood symbols of who is who in a complex society. . . .

The behavioral as well as neuroanatomical connections between sex, aggression and dominance are borne out in a variety of studies. The mating rituals of great cats and many other animals are barely distinguishable, in their early stages, from fighting. . . . Consider the peculiar circumstance that the most common two-word verbal aggression in English, and in many other languages, refers to an act of surpassing physical pleasure; the English form probably comes from a Germanic and Middle Dutch verb *fokken*, meaning "to strike." This otherwise puzzling usage can be understood as a verbal equivalent of macaque symbolic language, with the initial word "I" unstated but understood by both parties. It and many similar expressions seem to be human ceremonial mountings. (Sagan 1977, 52–54)

Kenneth Dover reminds us that "vulgar idiom in many languages uses 'buggered' or 'fucked' in the sense 'defeated,' 'worsted'" (1978, 105).[7] Following Sagan's treatment of "fuck you" as an anachronistic survival from our pre-human past, Joel Feinberg groups the locution with various other "symbolic dominance claims." Clearly the expression does not get its force from offense at the underlying referent, though there is a word taboo connected with societal attitudes and ambivalences toward sex (Feinberg 1985, 224, 206–8). Historical practices and historical meanings do persist, sometimes unconsciously.

When it comes to words, the past is the future. Which is not to say that new meanings do not emerge over time. They certainly do. But old meanings often lurk and resonate, come trailing along; and, more important for our present concerns, meanings don't change simply because an

---

7. There is a story that Khrushchev, after a confrontation with Harold Macmillan, told an associate that he had "fucked [the British Prime Minister] with a telephone pole" (*The New Yorker*, Mar 31, 2003, 100).

Sodomy can also be by proxy, as in this Afrikaans taunt: "*Sit jou kop is die koei se kont en wag tot die bul jou kom holnaai.*" Which, translated, means "Put your head in a cow's vagina and wait until a bull penetrates your anus" (*The Alternative Afrikaans Dictionary*, http://www.notam02.no/~hcholm/altlang/pdf/Afrikaans.pdf).

Also noteworthy, an out of the way place is sometimes referred to as "bumfuck."

individual speaker forgets or fails to think of old referents. Of course people say things like "fuck you" without a thought to the literal meaning of the expression. But the sexual significance does not disappear just because the speaker does not intend to include it. The meanings of our words are not limited by what we intend them to mean. That was Humpty Dumpty's error in *Through the Looking-Glass* when he insisted to Alice that "glory" meant "a nice knock-down argument." His view of language was that he was the "master": "'When I use a word,' Humpty Dumpty said, in rather a scornful tone, 'it means just what I choose it to mean—neither more nor less'" (Carroll 1965, 268–69). But we speak a public language and its sense is publicly fixed, we cannot make words mean whatever we happen to want them to mean at the moment, at least not if we hope to communicate with others. Humpty Dumpty cannot have his way with words.

Try Wittgenstein's experiment of saying "cold" meaning "hot" (1953, §510). His invitation to attempt to invert meanings is part of his larger critique of private languages and of the empiricist notion that the meanings of our words are to be found in associated ideas in our heads. Our public words have public meanings independent of the speaker's thoughts of the moment, and a speaker cannot change the meanings of the words he uses by invoking private associations (though such associations may indeed add special connotations to the words for him). Our words depend on public criteria. Communication and mutual understanding require it. Some might think that "fuck you" has become such a formulaic interjection that it has lost its sexual significance. But again, one need not be consciously thinking of intercourse in order for the words to retain their sexual significance. Our words carry their public meanings and their etymological histories in their train. Equally, giving the finger (or any of a myriad of comparable Neapolitan gestures) carries a fixed social and sexual significance. Saying "kiss my ass" or mooning have significance in terms of anal erotism independent of what is going on in the mind of the speaker or hearer, agent or spectator, at the moment. Though, as those examples should remind us, symbolic significances are reversible. Anatomy, etymology, and even evolutionary origins do not create an unalterable destiny.

"A CHILD IS BEING BEATEN"

There is a further complication which must be considered, the fact that even a conscious fantasy may have a hidden significance: like a manifest night dream it may be an expression of unconscious thoughts, unconscious fantasies, unconscious wishes. Freud, in one of his discussions of the psychological roots of sadomasochism, gives a very layered account of the wishes and desires involved in fantasies that "a child is being beaten" (1919e). He traces such fantasies to the early life of his patients, not later than the fifth or sixth year. While memories of actual beatings at home, at school, or read of in literature such as *Uncle Tom's Cabin* doubtless play a role, Freud unravels stages and layers of meaning in such childhood sadomasochistic fantasies. In girls, the fantasizer in the first stage typically sees her father beating another child, a rival; in the second stage (typically not consciously remembered) the fantasizer herself is being beaten by her father; and in the third a father-substitute such as a teacher is beating children, typically boys, with the fantasizer present as a spectator (as in the first stage). Freud suggests the beating fantasy ultimately can be traced to genital love for the father with punishment for her incestuous wishes attached in a form that provides a regressive (anal) substitute for the genital satisfactions. ("This being beaten is now a convergence of the sense of guilt and sexual love. It is not only the punishment for the forbidden genital relation, but also the regressive substitute for that relation" 1919e, 189.) Under the imaginative scenario of "a child is being beaten," what starts as a largely nonsexual fantasy motivated by jealousy and aggression emerges in the end as a consciously sadomasochistic fantasy resulting in masturbatory activity, but the underlying unconscious fantasy and wish is masochistic. Guilt plays a dominant role in transforming sadism into masochism in this account, but the sexualization of beating fantasies is at least partly influenced by the sadistic theory of intercourse, that is, the notion that during intercourse the father beats up the mother, a theory common among children (1908c)[8]—given that theory, beating fantasies can serve as an expression of the almost universal desire to be loved sexually by the father.[9] Freud notes elsewhere that beating

---

8. And, as William Ian Miller suggests in the passage quoted earlier (1993, 168–69), among the vulgar and some feminists.

9. The two-stage male version of "a child is being beaten" has a preliminary unconscious stage in which the father (who as with the girl is the object of an incestuous attachment) does the beating of the fantasizer, and it gets transformed in the end to a conscious fantasy of the mother (or other women) beating him.

fantasies can serve as confessions of masturbation as well as occasions for masturbation (1925j, 254). He also notes "if one has an opportunity of studying cases in which the masochistic phantasies have been especially richly elaborated, one quickly discovers that they place the subject in a characteristically female situation; they signify, that is, being castrated, or copulated with, or giving birth to a baby" (1924c, 162).

The moral of this excursion into Freud's analysis of childhood beating fantasies is that one should not assume that conscious fantasies, whether daydreams or masturbation fantasies or fantasies embedded in the language of domination, are transparent, providing a clear window into the underlying desires or wishes. A conscious masturbation fantasy may be like the manifest content of a night dream, with an unconscious fantasy behind it. In Freud's account of the beating fantasies had by young girls, the consciously exciting fantasy is of some boy being beaten by some authority figure. But that is the third stage in the development of the scenario. According to Freud it is a transformation of the second stage, an unconscious layer, where the general rubric "a child is being beaten" is filled in by a particular fantasy of the fantasizer being beaten by her father in fulfillment of and as punishment for incestuous desires. There are layers of meaning. There is a similar peeling back of layers in Freud's interpretation of Dora's cough, an hysterical symptom with multiple meanings, including a sexual one—analyzed in terms of an unconscious fantasy of fellatio with her father (1905e, 47–52). A conscious fantasy, a daydream, like a manifest night dream or a symptom, conceals while expressing underlying desires. Fantasies, like dreams and symptoms, may require interpretation.

There is another moral. The functioning of the imagination is more complex than might be thought. The problems with a simple Cartesian view of the imagination as "forming images" that are brought out in Wittgensteinian critiques are not the only problems. A Freudian appreciation of fantasy wish-fulfillment makes clear that an imagined scene, say "a child is being beaten," may have a variety of rather different contents when the details are filled in (is the beater the father, a teacher, the fantasizer, another?), may invite rather different identifications (the beating scene may be ambiguously masochistic or sadistic, depending on whether the fantasizer identifies with the agent or the subject of the beating), and may be imagined from rather different perspectives (for example, either from outside or, as Richard Wollheim [1979] puts it, "centrally," that is, from within). It is these complexities in the interpretation and the layering of fantasy that should help make intelligible the reversibility of symbolic significances. (For a fuller consideration of the workings of fantasy, see Neu 2000, chap. 11, "Fantasy and Memory"; and Neu 2002c, "An Ethics of Fantasy?")

DOMINATION AND SUBMISSION

Let's return to butt kicking. In addition to resonances of invasive sodomy, our excursus into childhood beating fantasies should alert us to the fact that there may be an infantilizing element in threats of violence that take aim at the butt. In an actual fight, of course, the ass is unlikely to be the target of blows. As noted, fists typically fly toward faces, stomachs, and other parts of the torso. The butt is typically the target for more humiliating blows, as in the supposedly pedagogical spanking of children. To address one's violence to an adult's rear is to infantilize and so demean them. Our figures of speech seem to capture the thought. To elaborate: beating someone's ass is rarely what literally happens. Behinds tend to get spanked, but those are typically juvenile behinds and that is a part of discipline rather than a fight, discipline which is inherently humiliating. To beat someone's ass is not simply to defeat them, but to humiliate them. The ass is the locus of humiliation. Beating an ass, like beating or spanking a behind, is putting them in their place, an exercise in humiliation. (It would appear that normally only children, not adults, are described as having a "behind," just as "poop" is an infantile word—e.g., "get your behind over here, boy.")

When "putting my ass on the line," why is it that the "ass" is the metonymical stand-in for the person? How is it that our identity gets located in our rear? The rear (with its cheeks) sometimes stands for the whole person (just as the face, with its cheeks, does when we talk of "saving face"). There appears to be displacement down. We have already spoken of the sexual stakes, but once again we may see a kind of wisdom in Wittgenstein's dictum that "the human body is the best picture of the human soul" (1953, Part II, 178), even if he had a more prosaic behaviorist point in mind.

The sexual stakes help us appreciate the isomorphism we have been considering; what gets sexualized is the invasive shock of insult. There is an assault on one's dignity, a disruption of one's sense of self. A loss of bodily integrity seems an appropriate image. The bodily violation seems to provide an analogue in terms of bodily injury to the personal, moral and psychological, injury of insult where there is a crossing of normative boundaries by disappointed expectations of attention and respect. Anal erotism provides both the language of many of our psychological categories and the bodily locus of the sadomasochism that is the psychology of insult writ large.

Whence the need to "put down" others? It may be seen as a route to achieving self-regard, both self-respect and self-esteem. Lowering others can be a means to raising the self—at least it can appear that way. There are many theories of aggression and of the Nietzschean "will to power." It has its metaphysical roots traced in Hegel's master-slave dialectic, which Hegel conceives as a fight to the death for recognition. We have already seen hints of the dependence of our self-consciousness on others in Sartre's keyhole scenario. Hegel's drama of master and slave, a dialectic of the development of self-consciousness and individual identity, is also the dialectic of our more mundane struggles for status and recognition—and even for love. At least that is the story Sartre tells in *Being and Nothingness* (1956, part 3, chap. 3). It is a story of the inherent futility of love. Aiming at the full possession of a free being, our desire must fail as possession insofar as the other is free, and it must fail in terms of freedom insofar as the other is possessed. Thus Sartre speaks of "the impossible ideal of desire" (394), "the lover's perpetual dissatisfaction" (377) and "the lover's perpetual insecurity" (377). Love falls into masochism and sadism. In Sartre's account, these have little to do with pleasure and pain, and much to do with freedom and control. Love is embedded in conflict, a war for recognition, in which Sartre concludes "it is indifferent whether we hate the Other's transcendence through what we empirically call his vices or his virtues . . . The occasion which arouses hate is simply an act by the Other which puts me in the state of *being subject* to his freedom" (411).

While Sartre's somewhat overheated metaphysics of sadomasochism is oddly detached from action and real interaction, and while it imagines a peculiar transcendent freedom too much always at issue, it nonetheless fruitfully explores in other terms the intricacies of identification, of introjection and projection; and the prosaic but important truth emerges and remains that the lover wants to be loved. Whatever may be the case for putative selfless loves on the one hand, or pure physical cravings on the other hand, it is true for erotic love that the lover wants to be loved. And this has consequences.

Love brings with it dependence and vulnerability. And these are fertile grounds for hatred. The more dependent an individual is on another, whether for freely given love or for other things, the more opportunities there will be for disappointment. But possibility does not amount to actuality. Why should hatred be inevitable? No reason so far has been given unless dependence is in itself hateful. Is it? While men are often ready to assume that it is, that may be a gendered assumption. It may be that men in our society reject dependence as hateful while women accept it as a desirable aspect of relationships, and that their differing assumptions have to do with current and local conditions of psychological development. It has been argued that "for boys and men, separation and individuation are critically tied to gender identity since separation from the mother is essential for the development of masculinity. For girls and women, issues of femininity or feminine identity do not depend on the achievement of separation from the mother or on the progress of individuation. Since masculinity is defined through separation while femininity is defined through attachment, male gender identity is threatened by intimacy while female gender identity is threatened by separation" (Gilligan 1982, 8; see also Chodorow 1978). Is the attitude toward dependence, whatever the facts of our particular society, in general socially formed and therefore variable? Why should dependence, especially interdependence, be experienced as a danger? Help can be found by going back to Hegel.[10] Sartre's sadomasochistic pessimism about love is ultimately derived from the "impasse" of the master in Hegel's account, who, even when he achieves recognition from the slave, must be disappointed, for what was sought was recognition from an independent equal. What is the worth of approval from those for whom one has nothing but contempt? The development of self-consciousness and individual identity is in tension with the reciprocal need for definition and recognition in other individuals—and also groups.

10. "Ironically," as Jessica Benjamin puts it, "the ideal of freedom carries within it the seeds of domination—freedom *means* fleeing or subjugating the other; autonomy means an escape from dependency. . . . Perhaps the most fateful paradox is the one posed by our simultaneous need for recognition and independence: that the other subject is outside our control and yet we need him" (Benjamin 1988, 221).

Parts of the discussion above are extracted from Neu 2000, chap. 5, "*Odi et Amo:* On Hating the Ones We Love"; and parts of the discussion below are extracted from Neu 2000, chap. 7, "Pride and Identity."

THE NARCISSISM OF MINOR DIFFERENCES

Freud observes that groups of individuals characteristically direct their greatest hostility toward those who, from a wider perspective, are in fact most similar to them. What is the source of this "narcissism of minor differences"? Is it an interesting but accidental sociological fact? Or is it somehow rooted in features of human psychology and the conditions for identity-formation; does it bespeak a natural polarity in thought?

Freud introduces the concept in his discussion of "The Taboo of Virginity" (1918a). There the topic is male hostility to and fear of women, and is complicated by the castration complex, but Freud is already prepared to take a point about individual separation and isolation ("that it is precisely the minor differences in people who are otherwise alike that form the basis of feelings of strangeness and hostility between them") and see in it "the hostility which in every human relation we see fighting successfully against feelings of fellowship and overpowering the commandment that all men should love one another" (199). When he turns to *Group Psychology* a few years later, he returns to the idea, there tying it to wider ambivalences as well as to narcissism (1921c, 101). He develops the idea most fully in *Civilization and Its Discontents* where he discusses it in terms of aggression, which in this form serves "cohesion between the members of the community" against outsiders (1930a, chap. 5, esp. 114). It is this final link, to what Freud regards as instinctual aggression, which may help clarify what may also be understood as a conceptual condition of identity formation. It makes conflict our normal state—and if we seek in our pride to raise ourselves and those we identify with by denigrating and insulting others, this may be at least part of the explanation.

There is an old logical principle that holds "all determination is negation" (*Omnis determinatio est negatio*), and both individuals and communities often define themselves by opposition, by contrast, that is, in terms of what they reject. Stuart Hampshire elaborates the point in relation to incompatible conceptions of the good:

> Most influential conceptions of the good have defined themselves as rejections of their rivals: for instance, some of the ideals of monasticism were a rejection of the splendors and hierarchies of the Church,

and this rejection was part of the original sense and purpose of the monastic ideal. Some forms of fundamentalism, both Christian and others, define themselves as a principled rejection of secular, liberal, and permissive moralities. Fundamentalism is the negation of any deviance in moral opinion, and of the very notion of opinion in ethics. (Hampshire 2000, 34–35)

People are who they are at least partly (and sometimes self-consciously) in terms of who and what they are not. The logical point is developed in Hegel and in F. H. Bradley. It is taken even further along a metaphysical dimension by Spinoza. As Hampshire puts Spinoza's vision: "Men and women are naturally driven to resist any external force that tends to repress their typical activities or to limit their freedom . . . It is a natural necessity for each distinct entity to try to preserve its distinctiveness for as long as it can, and for this reason conflicts are at all times to be expected in the history of individuals, of social groups, and of nations, as their paths intersect" (38–39).

In psychoanalytical terms, the individual ego (and more specifically, the ego-ideal) is formed out of identifications and introjections, the other side of which is the rejection—typically a violent spitting out—of those characteristics one does not wish to incorporate. "At the very beginning, it seems, the external world, objects, and what is hated are identical. If later on an object turns out to be a source of pleasure, it is loved, but it is also incorporated into the ego" (Freud 1915c, 136). As Norman O. Brown puts it, "The distinction between self and not-self is made by the childish decision to claim all that the ego likes as 'mine,' and to repudiate all that the ego dislikes as 'not-mine'" (1966, 142). The move from individual to group identity is explored in Freud's volume on *Group Psychology and the Analysis of the Ego* (1921c), where his central concern is with groups, such as churches and armies, characterized by identification with a leader. The important role of unconscious mechanisms of identification via incorporation should make clear that socially imposed identities are not the only alternative to consciously chosen identities. With unconscious mechanisms, ambivalence and aggression come to the fore. Others reject us, we reject others, and we project out "bad" and undesired aspects of ourselves while at the same time introjecting the desirable aspects of others.

Perhaps the "will to power" is not so much about domination as about identity. The need is less to dominate than to distinguish and differentiate. What gives this an aggressive twist is that these ends are achieved by rejection. Group pride is built on the rejection of an out-group, often enough reinforced by discrimination against and denigration of that out-group. The self is identified by contrast and exclusion, what it (insultingly) rejects.

Belonging to a group is tied to rejection of outsiders. Freud writes, "a religion, even if it calls itself the religion of love, must be hard and unloving to those who do not belong to it. Fundamentally indeed every religion is in this same way a religion of love for all those whom it embraces; while cruelty and intolerance towards those who do not belong to it are natural to every religion" (1921c, 98). One might think that toleration and the embracing of diversity should provide a ready alternative, but history suggests vast impediments to such an alternative, and psychoanalysis sees aggression in the very mechanisms that serve to create a distinctive self or group. Freud's skepticism about demands to "love thy neighbour" and even "thine enemies" is tied to his belief in fundamental instincts of aggression (1930a, chap. 5). The sources of division and ambivalence run deep, perhaps deeper even than any putative aggressive instincts. All determination is negation. An embraced identity entails a rejected identity. Even the very languages that help define the identity of certain individuals and communities (not all Frenchmen need live in France) isolate and separate at the very time they unite (the story of Quebec is but one of many, very many, examples; see Ignatieff 1993 for more). The ambiguity that some see in pride (arrogance vs. self-respect) may have behind it a deeper ambiguity in self-love and in identity itself (rejection and isolation vs. affirmation and community). The ambiguities and ambivalences inevitably play themselves out in identity politics and in insulting attitudes (expressed, among other ways, in insult humor).

ANGER AND DEJECTION

The complex psychology of identity and identification even colors our subjective experience of disappointed expectations. We may find in Freud's analysis of "Mourning and Melancholia" (1917e) a clue to understanding the observation that we started this book with: that we sometimes react to insult with anger, sometimes dejection. The difference may ultimately depend on our prior emotional relationship with the insulter: so that where an insult comes from someone we love or care about, the tendency is to feel dejected, while an insult from someone unloved or indifferent is more likely to lead to anger. Freud's analysis of melancholia (or in more modern terms, depression) invokes mechanisms of identification and appeals to underlying currents of ambivalence to understand the disorder, but similar mechanisms and forces may well be in play in our more fleeting and less dramatic emotional reactions.

Like mourning, depression (at least reactive depression) takes its start with the loss of a loved object, though in the case of depression the significance of the loss may be unconscious. The most striking clinical feature of depression in Freud's account is the emergence of self-reproaches, self-reproaches that do not lead the sufferer to seek to hide in shame, but rather loudly announce themselves:

> The melancholic displays . . . an extraordinary diminution in his self-regard, an impoverishment of his ego on a grand scale. In mourning it is the world which has become poor and empty; in melancholia it is the ego itself. The patient represents his ego to us as worthless, incapable of any achievement and morally despicable; he reproaches himself, vilifies himself and expects to be cast out and punished. . . . it must strike us that after all the melancholic does not behave in quite the same way as a person who is crushed by remorse and self-reproach in a normal fashion. Feelings of shame in front of other people, which would more than anything characterize this latter condition, are lacking in the melancholic, or at least they are not prominent in him. One might emphasize the presence in him of an almost opposite trait of insistent communicativeness which finds satisfaction in self-exposure. (1917e, 246–47)

The unbridled self-criticism reflects a split in the ego, with an observing and judging aspect (which Freud will later speak of as the superego) setting itself against the rest of the ego. But the key to understanding the clinical picture is to be found once "we perceive that the self-reproaches are reproaches against a loved object which have been shifted away from it on to the patient's own ego" (248). The real target of the criticisms is an incorporated other, the abandoned and abandoning object. The criticized ego is one that has been altered by identification: "the shadow of the object fell upon the ego" (249). Freud offers much evidence to support this insight, including the fact that the depressed person's loud complaining does not reflect "the attitude of humility and submissiveness that would alone befit such worthless people. On the contrary, they make the greatest nuisance of themselves, and always seem as though they felt slighted and had been treated with great injustice" (248). Starting with an insult from a beloved, the love relation is simultaneously preserved and distorted through identification by incorporation, and the ambivalences that characterize all love relations come to the fore, with hatred now finding expression in self-tormenting and self-punishment. Freud summarizes the process:

> In melancholia, the occasions which give rise to the illness extend for the most part beyond the clear case of a loss by death, and include all those situations of being slighted, neglected or disappointed, which can import opposed feelings of love and hate into the relationship or reinforce an already existing ambivalence. . . . If the love for the object—a love which cannot be given up though the object itself is given up—takes refuge in narcissistic identification, then the hate comes into operation on this substitutive object, abusing it, debasing it, making it suffer and deriving sadistic satisfaction from its suffering. The self-tormenting in melancholia, which is without doubt enjoyable, signifies, just like the corresponding phenomenon in obsessional neurosis, a satisfaction of trends of sadism and hate which relate to an object, and which have been turned round upon the subject's own self . . . In both disorders the patients usually still succeed, by the circuitous path of self-punishment, in taking revenge on the original object and in tormenting their loved one through their illness, having resorted to it in order to avoid the need to express their hostility to him openly. (251)

Following this model, our early contrast between feeling insulted as anger and as dejection may line up with the distinction between insult from a hated or indifferent source and insult from a loved source. This gives the shock of a "slap in the face" an added depth. And it gives the anal issues of humiliation and sadism an added dimension with the internalization (identification with) the external, ambivalently loved, source of the insult. One becomes the double victim of humiliation, from the external insulter and from the internal self-punisher (complicated by the "self" that is being punished sometimes having incorporated aspects of the other). This is in keeping with the layers of identification we have discerned in "a child is being beaten" fantasies.

Others are central in our self-understanding and in (insulting) shocks to that self-understanding. We want each other's recognition and approval, and we want (and perhaps need) it most from those who are closest to us. That differing initial relationships to an insulting other should have implications for how we emotionally respond to our disappointed expectations seems natural enough. It also seems unsurprising that our unprotected rear flanks should be especially vulnerable to assault from those we love and trust, and that when an assault actually comes from that quarter, we are left feeling particularly blind-sided, stunned, and shocked.

FIVE

THE LANGUAGE OF ABUSE

THE IMPULSE TO COMPETITIVE OUTDOING IN THE SPHERE OF INSULTS (as in others) is not restricted to black ghettos or rap music. A fine specimen can be found in Edmond Rostand's *Cyrano de Bergerac*. Early in the play, the foppish, insolent, beribboned Viscount de Valvert seeks to insult Cyrano's prominent proboscis with the words, "That thing of yours is big, what? Very big." Cyrano responds by waxing eloquent with a veritable dissertation on insults and their styles:

> Nothing more?
> Just a fatuous smile? Oh come, there are fifty score
> Varieties of comment you could find.
> For instance, there's the frank aggressive kind:
> "If mine achieved that hypertrophic state,
> I'd call a surgeon in to amputate."
> The friendly: "It must dip into your cup.
> You need a nasal crane to hoist it up."
> The pure descriptive: "From its size and shape
> I'd say it was a rock, a bluff, a cape,
> No, a peninsula—how picturesque!"

Cyrano continues inventively through modes, from the curious through the pedantic to the practical, concluding . . .

And finally, with tragic cries and sighs,
The language finely wrought and deeply felt:
"Oh, that this too too solid nose would melt."
That is the sort of thing you could have said
If you, sir moron, were a man of letters
Or had an ounce of spunk inside your head.
But you've no letters, have you, save the three
Required for self-description: S O T.
You have to leave my worsting to your betters,
Or better, who can best you, meaning me.
But be quite sure, you lesser feathered tit,
Even if you possessed the words and wit,
I'd never let you get away with it.
        (Rostand, trans. Anthony Burgess, 28–29)

The Viscount, at a loss for words to respond to Cyrano's onslaught of "freshly laundered" insults, responds instead with a glove blow to the face—thus descending to the rudely physical. There too, Cyrano excels. He dispatches his opponent with a sword thrust at the conclusion of an impromptu poem ("Ballade of a Fencing Bout Between de Bergerac and a Foppish Lout") with which he first verbally skewers him.

I'm one who can versify extempore
Even when rattling ironmongery.
I'll improvise a ballade. . . .
Three eight-lined stanzas and then one quatrain.
The quatrain's called an *envoy*. I propose
To fight and, at the same time, to compose
A ballade of strict classical design,
And then to kill you on the final line.
        (Rostand, 31)

Much of our language for describing interactions over insult is in fact that of dueling, with wounds and parries and thrusts, ripostes and counter-strokes.[1] We talk of repartee (not to mention skewering) and say touché.

1. We have already explored something of the deeper level of sexual significances. The honor defended in dueling and the respect gained in rituals are quite generally regarded as versions of masculinity. In dueling, the loser is regularly feminized. Jennifer Low, for example, tells us there is "an implicit analogy between the feminine body and the conquered body" and that in the fencing manuals, "for a man to be permeable is to be shamed; to attack and to penetrate, on the other hand, is to dominate other men

The poetry of vituperation often involves metaphors of physical assault. "A hit, a very palpable hit" and other metaphors seem to have a long association with fencing and other forms of stylized warfare (*Hamlet* V.2.270). An insult is after all a wound to personality or dignity. Indeed, as noted at the outset, in modern medicine the word "insult" can still be used to describe a physical wound or injury, as in "an insult to the brain." It is fitting that the language of gentlemanly combat should have a dual use.

ROMEO AND JULIET

Looking for a fight is not merely an adolescent or purely a lower-class phenomenon. In Shakespeare's *Romeo and Juliet* we see upper crust affiliates of the feuding families engage in aggressive play not unlike Dollard's and Abrahams' gang boys, but they are clearly not from the underclass. And since the parties are rival families rather than in-group members jockeying for honor, violence is foreseeable. The family feud between the Montagues and the Capulets in *Romeo and Juliet* plays out in the early scenes between still adolescent, or delayed-adolescent, young men of the leading merchant families. In the very first scene, Sampson (a Capulet retainer) announces that he is set on provocation: "I will bite my thumb at them, which is disgrace to them if they bear it" (I.1.40–41). (I believe this contemptuous thumb gesture, including variants such as "thumbing one's nose," persists to our time.)[2] He is like the Brazilians set on *briga*, quick to quarrel, looking for a fight. And the very earliest and other scenes are full of wordplay, swordplay, and wordplay about swordplay. Tybalt and Benvolio cross swords in the very first scene, as Benvolio seeks to separate the quarreling family servants

physically." She continues, "That bleeding wounds could be perceived as effeminization should not surprise us. . . . By association with sexual congress, penetrating and being penetrated were perceived in the early modern period as gendered behaviors: to be conquered was to be emasculated" (2003, 71, 75, 76).

2. There is an 1832 book, *La Mimica degli antichi investigate nel gestire napoletano* (*The Mimicry of Ancient People Interpreted Through the Gestures of Neapolitans*) by Andrea de Jorio, a Neapolitan priest, that provides a remarkably comprehensive lexicon of Italian hand gestures. An English translation appeared in 2000 and was reviewed by Joan Acocella in the *New York Review of Books* of Dec. 21, 2000 (48–55). De Jorio argued that many local gestures were of ancient origin, legible on Greco-Italian vases and preserved in ancient literature.

(including the thumb-biting Sampson). Later, when Tybalt says "thou consortest with Romeo," Mercutio responds, "Consort? What, dost thou make us minstrels? An thou make minstrels of us, look to hear nothing but discords. Here's my fiddlestick; here's that shall make you dance. Zounds, consort!" (III.1.44–48). Real swordplay ensues.

In the instance, it is Mercutio and Benvolio, kinsmen and friends to Romeo, who get embroiled in combat. Mercutio claims that Benvolio is wont to look for a fight, "Thou wilt quarrel with a man for cracking nuts, having no other reason but because thou hast hazel eyes. What eye but such an eye would spy out such a quarrel?" (III.1.18–21). But Mercutio is at least equally prone to combativeness and it is he who dies at the hands of Tybalt, despite Benvolio's urgings to avoid public quarrel:

> *Benvolio.* We talk here in the public haunt of men.
> Either withdraw unto some private place,
> Or reason coldly of your grievances,
> Or else, depart. Here all eyes gaze on us.
> *Mercutio.* Men's eyes were made to look, and let them gaze.
> I will not budge for no man's pleasure, I. (III.1.49–54)

Mercutio steps in when Romeo (already besotted with Juliet) refuses to be provoked by Tybalt, and he denounces Romeo for his apparent cowardice, "O calm, dishonorable, vile submission!" (III.1.72). In the event, when Mercutio is given his fatal wound under Romeo's intervening arm, Romeo, in the traditions of honor and masculinity, repents his peacemaking:

> This gentleman, the Prince's near ally,
> My very friend, hath got this mortal hurt
> In my behalf—my reputation stained
> With Tybalt's slander—Tybalt, that an hour
> Hath been my cousin. O sweet Juliet,
> Thy beauty hath made me effeminate
> And in my temper soft'ned valor's steel! (III.1.107–113)

SHAKESPEARE'S INSULT LANGUAGE

> You taught me language; and my profit on't
> Is, I know how to curse. The red plague rid you
> for learning me your language!
> —(Caliban's reply to Miranda, *Tempest* I.ii.363–67)

There is an independent pleasure in clever and witty or just original and bizarre verbal insults, verbal fireworks; an independent pleasure also present in play like the dozens. Rostand's Cyrano has fun with the possibilities and Shakespeare dazzles us with his virtuosity. Someone has seen the commercial potential and produced a *Shakespeare Insult Calendar* (I have one for 2002 and another for 2007) that offers up apposite daily insult quotes from his corpus. Some are rather elaborate:

- February 15, 2002: A whoreson jackanapes . . . takes me up for swearing, as if I borrowed mine oaths of him, and might not spend them at my pleasure. (*Cymbeline* II.1.3–6)
- March 22, 2002: You scullion! You rampallian! You fustilarian! I'll tickle your catastrophe! (*Henry IV, Part 2* II.1.56–57)

This second example illustrates the point that one need not know the meanings of the words in order for the intention to insult to be successfully conveyed. Indeed, the speaker can transform meanings, provided that the manner of expression and the context make the emotional point clear. We saw that Freud's Rat Man as a three-year-old child managed to get around his lack of the appropriate language of vituperation by hurling abuse in the form of words for common household items, "You lamp! You towel! You plate!" In an instance of some consequence, Senator George Allen of Virginia referred to a rival's Indian-American campaign tracker who was videotaping his 2006 appearances as "macaca, or whatever his name is," adding for good xenophobic measure, "Welcome to America and the real world of Virginia." As the clip (captured and uploaded by the object of the epithet) made its viral rounds over *YouTube* (http://youtube.com/watch?v=9G7gq7GQ71c, accessed April 26, 2007), everyone recognized the word as a racial slur, even though Allen himself claimed not to know what the word he had used meant. (And few are likely to have been aware that the word had a prior history, perhaps derived from the name of the genus comprising macaque monkeys, as a dismissive epithet applied to the native population by Francophone colonials in the Belgian Congo; Wikipedia, s.v. "macaca," http://en.wikipedia.org/wiki/Macaca_%28slur%29.) Allen lost his bid for reelection by a narrow margin and the Democrats swept into control of both houses of Congress. Still, while context and emotional cues can fill gaps, knowing the meanings of the words used can enrich the message and its impact. (In the case of the lines from *Henry IV, Part 2*: scullion = kitchen wench; rampallian = scoundrel; fustilarian = frowsy fat woman; catastrophe = backside.)

Some of Shakespeare's exemplary insults are more direct:

- November 26, 2002: This letter [is] excellently ignorant. (*Twelfth Night* III.4.189)
- November 27, 2002: [You are] a very dishonest paltry boy, and more a coward than a hare. (*Twelfth Night* III.4.395–96)
- December 2, 2002: If you spend word for word with me, I shall make your wit bankrupt. (*The Two Gentlemen of Verona* II.4.37–38)
- December 27, 2002: O thou thing! (*The Winter's Tale* II.1.82)

In addition to being a rich source of exemplary insults, Shakespeare's language is a fertile generator of insults. In our day of the World Wide Web, there has been a proliferation of sites that provide the "Shakespeare Insult Kit," and even automated versions of it that will automatically generate insults from columns of Shakespearean vocabulary. The kit is of unknown origin, but can be found at various Internet sites, including: http://www.pangloss.com/seidel/shake_rule.html (at least it was there when I last checked on 5/10/2007).

SHAKESPEARE INSULT KIT

Combine one word from each of the three columns below, prefaced with "Thou":

Column 1	Column 2	Column 3
artless	base-court	apple-john
bawdy	bat-fowling	baggage
beslubbering	beef-witted	barnacle
bootless	beetle-headed	bladder
churlish	boil-brained	boar-pig
clouted	clapper-clawed	bugbear
cockered	clay-brained	bum-bailey
craven	common-kissing	canker-blossom
currish	crook-pated	clack-dish
dankish	dismal-dreaming	clotpole
dissembling	dizzy-eyed	codpiece
droning	doghearted	coxcomb
errant	dread-bolted	death-token
fawning	earth-vexing	dewberry
fobbing	elf-skinned	flap-dragon
froward	fat-kidneyed	flax-wench
frothy	fen-sucked	flirt-gill
gleeking	flap-mouthed	foot-licker
goatish	fly-bitten	fustilarian
gorbellied	folly-fallen	giglet
impertinent	fool-born	gudgeon

SHAKESPEARE INSULT KIT (*Continued*)

Column 1	Column 2	Column 3
infectious	full-gorged	haggard
jarring	guts-griping	harpy
loggerheaded	half-faced	hedge-pig
lumpish	hasty-witted	horn-beast
mammering	hedge-born	hugger-mugger
mangled	hell-hated	joithead
mewling	idle-headed	lewdster
paunchy	ill-breeding	lout
pribbling	ill-nurtured	maggot-pie
puking	knotty-pated	malt-worm
puny	milk-livered	mammet
qualling	motley-minded	measle
rank	onion-eyed	minnow
reeky	plume-plucked	miscreant
roguish	pottle-deep	moldwarp
ruttish	pox-marked	mumble-news
saucy	reeling-ripe	nut-hook
spleeny	rough-hewn	pigeon-egg
spongy	rude-growing	pignut
surly	rump-fed	puttock
tottering	shard-borne	pumpion
unmuzzled	sheep-biting	ratsbane
vain	spur-galled	scut
venomed	swag-bellied	skainsmate
villainous	tardy-gaited	strumpet
warped	tickle-brained	varlot
wayward	toad-spotted	vassal
weedy	unchin-snouted	whey-face
yeasty	weather-bitten	wagtail

There have been other inventive and exhaustive literary generators of insults. (Not that everyone has appreciated Shakespeare's abundance. Robert Greene, a rival dramatist, wrote in 1592 in his *Groatsworth of Wit*: "there is an upstart Crow, beautified with our feathers, that with his *Tiger's heart wrapped in a Player's hide*, supposes he is as well able to bombast out a blank verse as the best of you: and being an absolute *Johannes Factotum*, is in his own conceit the only Shakescene in a country" [quoted in Greenblatt 2004, 213].) The following translation of a string of invective from Rabelais' *Gargantua and Pantagruel* provides a nice example:

. . . prattling gabblers, licorous gluttons, freckled bittors, mangy ras-
cals, shite-a-bed scoundrels, drunken roysters, sly knaves, drowsy loi-
terers, slapsauce fellows, slubberdegullion druggles, lubbardly louts,
cozening foxes, ruffian rogues, paultry customers, sycophant-varlets,
drawlatch hoydens, flouting milksops, jeering companions, staring
clowns, forlorn snakes, ninny lobcocks, scurvy sneaksbies, fondling
fops, base loons, saucy coxcombs, idle lusks, scoffing braggards, noddy
meacocks, blockish grutnols, doddipol joltheads, jobbernol goosecaps,
foolish loggerheads, flutch calf-lollies, grouthead gnat-snappers, lob-
dotterels, gaping changelings, codshead loobies, woodcock slangams,
ninnie-hammer fly-catchers, noddiepeak simpletons, turdy-gut shitten
shepherds, and other such like defamatory epithets. (trans. Urquhart
and Motteux)

In 1970, then Vice-President Spiro Agnew (in a speech scripted by
William Safire) reached a memorable high note of Shakespearean allit-
eration in his attack on the press as "nattering nabobs of negativism" and
"the hopeless, hysterical hypochondriacs of history" (http://en.wikipedia.
org/wiki/Spiro_Agnew). Still, Camille Paglia is perhaps the modern
master of vituperation. She casts original (which is not to say justified)
aspersions largely indiscriminately and with great gusto at fellow women
intellectuals as well as at men. The florid inventiveness of her invective
can be astonishing. She manages in one sustained passage to describe
various named academic feminists as "that imploding beanbag of poisonous self-pity," "that damp sob sister . . . with her diarrhea prose," "the
pompous lap dog of Parisian café despots doing her grim, sledgeham-
mer elephant walk through small points," "schlockmeisters like . . ., the
Pollyanna of poppycock," "chirpy warblers . . . those unlearned, unread-
able bores, with their garbled, rumbling, hollow, rolling-trashcan style,"
"Mrs. Fifties Tea Table," and concludes "Women's studies is a jumble of
vulgarians, bunglers, whiners, French faddicts, apparatchiks, doughface
party-liners, pie-in-the-sky utopianists, and bullying, sanctimonious ser-
monizers" (1992, 243–44).

Whatever the pleasures of verbal assault, it does have its risks. Lord
Chesterfield wrote in his *Advice to His Son, On Men and Manners* that
"wrongs are often forgiven but contempt never is. . . . nothing is more
insulting, than to take pains to make a man feel a mortifying inferiority"
(1795, 62). Honor can oblige the offended to resent and so to challenge. Prudence teaches that contempt is sometimes best concealed, if
possible.

SHAKESPEAREAN THOUGHTS ON
INSULT

As well as providing brilliant, exuberant wordplay and a continuing source of colorful insults, Shakespeare's works offer thoughtful meditations on the nature of insults and on the proper practice and performance of insulting. Already, we've seen Mercutio, who himself goes on to pick a quarrel over the innocuous word "consort," comment on the proneness of some to pick a quarrel (a man with hazel eyes espying insult in the cracking of nuts). We've seen Sampson invoking the power of gesture (biting his thumb). Some of Shakespeare's characters school us in avoiding the escalation of verbal combat into physical fighting. After discoursing wittily on the chivalrous degrees of cause and retort, Touchstone in *As You Like It* praises the pacifying powers of "If": "All these you may avoid but the Lie Direct, and you may avoid that too, with an If. I knew when seven justices could not take up a quarrel, but when the parties were met themselves, one of them thought but of an If: as, 'If you said so, then I said so'; and they shook hands and swore brothers. Your If is the only peacemaker. Much virtue in If" (*As You Like It*, V.4.91–97). Of course, the disguise of hypothetical framing is a subterfuge often readily seen through. As Freud explained to his patient, the Rat Man, "it was well known, of course, that it was equally punishable to say 'The Emperor is an ass' or to disguise the forbidden words by saying 'If any one says, etc., . . . then he will have me to reckon with.'" (1909d, 179). A hypothetical saying is still a saying. The same is true for other forms of bracketing. The ancient rabbis prohibited the repetition of a blasphemy in testimony on the alleged blasphemy (Levy 1993, 13). And as we shall see in our discussion of insult humor, while many a truth is said in jest, the framing may provide only problematical protection.

Surrounding with quotes, like prefacing by "if," may sometimes be a way to distance oneself from the content of insults still delivered, and other forms of indirection may be used to achieve the same effect. In *Henry IV, Part I*, we see Prince Hal insulting Falstaff under cover of role-playing (Hal pretending to be his father and Falstaff to be Hal):

> *Prince.* There is a devil haunts thee in the likeness of an old fat man; a tun of man is thy companion. Why dost thou converse with that trunk of humors, that bolting hutch of beastliness, that swoll'n parcel of dropsies, that huge bombard of sack, that stuffed

cloakbag of guts, that roasted Manningtree ox with the pudding
in his belly, that reverend vice, that grey iniquity, that father ruffian, that vanity in years? Wherein is he good, but to taste sack
and drink it? wherein neat and cleanly, but to carve a capon and
eat it? wherein cunning, but in craft? wherein crafty, but in vil-
lainy? wherein villainous, but in all things? Wherein worthy, but
in nothing? (II.4.425–436)

Not that the pair needs the cloak of role-playing to license their insults.
Shortly before in the same scene, they have the following exchange:

> *Prince.* I'll be no longer guilty of this sin; this sanguine coward, this
> bed-presser, this horseback-breaker, this huge hill of flesh–
> *Falstaff.* 'Sblood, you starveling, you eel-skin, you dried neat's-tongue,
> you bull's pizzle, you stockfish—O for breath to utter what is like
> thee!—you tailor's yard, you sheath, you bowcase, you vile standing
> tuck! (II.4.229–234)

While one is put in mind of the Rat Boy's pointed use of common
objects—"You lamp! You towel! You plate!"—the exchange also illustrates the protective power of context and relationship. We have seen
the framing effect of ritual insult contests. Even without an audience,
friendly banter can be framed by the good will of friendship (or the teasing of courtship) to prevent insult from being taken too seriously. The
comic alternating of speakers, stichomythia, in the combative courtship scenes in *The Taming of the Shrew* (Kate and Petrucio—starting at
II.1.169) and *Much Ado about Nothing* (Beatrice and Benedick—starting
at I.1.100) provide nice examples of the sort of sometimes heated, sometimes playful insult exchanges that continue (if less inventively) right
down to today's sitcoms and ordinary life.

As in life, not all of Shakespeare's insults are playful or in exalted
language. We have already seen some examples. They sometimes take
the form of maledictions, imprecations, and curses, laying a shadow on
the target's future. The curses can sometimes be quite elaborate, as in
the extended, misanthropic, blighting curse laid on Athens by Timon,
wishing, among other things:

> . . . Matrons, turn incontinent!
> Obedience fail in children! Slaves and fools,
> . . . To general filths

Convert o' th' instant, green virginity!
Do't in your parents' eyes! Bankrupts, hold fast;
Rather than render back, out with your knives
And cut your trusters' throats!
. . . Son of sixteen,
Pluck the lined crutch from thy old limping sire;
With it beat out his brains! . . .
Plagues incident to men,
Your potent and infectious fevers heap
On Athens, ripe for stroke! Thou cold sciatica,
Cripple our senators, that their limbs may halt
As lamely as their manners! . . . (*Timon of Athens* IV.1.1–33)

You get the idea. Forward-looking, as opposed to backward-looking or present-assessing, insults call on the magical powers of words. The faith in the efficacy of words has roots in religion ("In the beginning was the Word"), in infantile fantasy (what Freud describes as our, typically unconscious, belief in "the omnipotence of thought"), and in primitive superstition (including naming and other taboos that may ultimately be traced to the same belief in "the omnipotence of thought" analyzed by Freud). But it is also the case that words in fact have effects, especially when addressed directly to individuals in conventionally prescribed contexts ("I now pronounce you man and wife"). We shall be discussing the force of "performative utterances" in the next chapter. And even where we may no longer believe in the magical efficacy of curses, they may nonetheless provide relief for the issuer and instill fear in the object. The vehemence of expressed hatred, of aggression uncontained, has its own force. The struggle for dominance we have seen behind insults often plays out in words.

THE POWER OF WORDS

The main familiar terms of vituperation may usefully be divided into two categories. (Here I follow and make use of the analytical apparatus in the second volume of Joel Feinberg's monumental study of *The Moral Limits of the Criminal Law*, the volume that focuses on *Offense to Others*, 1985.) Obscene language, that is, conventionally offensive and shocking words, may be divided into *profanities* (including blasphemies, vain swearings, and curses) and *vulgarities* (including scatological and sexual "dirty" words as well as racial and ethnic slurs, animal and political epithets, and other subclasses of invective).

While blasphemies may have started as ways of cursing or reviling God, they came to include emphatic ways of showing irreverence broadly understood, i.e. disrespect toward anything that is regarded as sacred and so as "no laughing matter." As Feinberg puts it, blasphemous insults say in effect, "I mock and deride whatever you think is holy" (1985, 193). Think of the various "mother-sounds" so prevalent in the dozens and similar insult rituals. Blasphemous insults often, however, involve the use of forbidden words and so the breaking of naming-taboos. As Freud has taught us, in *Totem and Taboo* (1912–13), such taboos extend to both the holy and the polluted, both dead enemies and supposedly beloved relatives, and they may reveal unconscious hostility, aggression, and ambivalence. They take seriously the link between word and thing. The relation is not Saussure's arbitrary connection between sign and signified, but rather a magical tie. Invoking the word may bring the thing it denotes into play. It was such word magic that was involved in the "oath asseverative" of early contracts, in which higher sanctioning powers or authorities were invoked to provide a guarantee of earthly pledges. These solemn vows later degenerated into some familiar forms of swearing (e.g., "May God blind me" became "Blimey!"). And given the beliefs, words can be used as real weapons, in curses and the "oath denunciatory," as illustrated by Timon's rant against Athens. The evil eye, spitting, and thumbing one's nose (or biting one's thumb, as with Sampson in *Romeo and Juliet*) may have initially emerged as ways of aiming curses. Indeed, "looking the wrong way" at someone as an insult may be connected with earlier magical assaults via curses—both words and looks becoming magical conveyances. Cockatrices or basilisks were reptiles thought to be able to kill with a glance, just as the mythical petrifying head of Medusa could turn men to stone if looked at. As Feinberg summarizes, "the shock value of profane words in the past has essentially depended on implicit beliefs in word magic—sorcery, verbal manipulations of nature, or the efficacy of words and gestures as weapons" (1985, 204). Even absent the beliefs, profane words remain useful for emphasis, for the shock of taboo-breaking. Still, we should not too quickly assume the historically underlying magical beliefs are inoperative. So far as such beliefs may have unconscious origins, they may persist in the timeless unconscious (as with belief in "the omnipotence of thoughts") despite modern surface sophistication. The breaking of taboos has a conventional force with a conventional history, but may still draw on deeper reinforcements.

Vulgarities also get their shock value and emphatic force from conventional taboos. They are generally forbidden in formal and polite contexts, but one need not appeal to ancient traditions of verbal magic to understand why they shock and offend. The excremental and the sexual in particular are fertile sources for abusive language. The etiquette of conversation makes certain subjects, at least on certain occasions, and in certain terms or certain registers of discourse, inappropriate. Still, finding the right register can sometimes be difficult. As C. S. Lewis pointed out, "As soon as you deal with it [sex] explicitly, you are forced to choose between the language of the nursery, the gutter and the anatomy class" (Hughes 1998, 1). One should not assume that such matters are inherently disgusting. (Such an assumption may be especially tempting when talking of "poop," "shit," and "feces," but the point applies to both the sexual and the excremental.) Attitudes are socially shaped, sometimes perhaps for good reasons, sometimes for no reason at all. Disgust is itself generally culturally variable and often purely conventional. As Freud points out, "a man who will kiss a pretty girl's lips passionately, may perhaps be disgusted at the idea of using her toothbrush, though there are no grounds for supposing that his own oral cavity, for which he feels no disgust, is any cleaner than the girl's" (1905d, 151–52; for more on disgust see Neu 2000, 149–50). Whether anxiety centers on the anal erotism we have found so significant in relation to insult or around sexuality in general, our language for such biological functions is fraught. Society seeks to constrain both the activities and the language used for describing them. We have our boundaries, both personal and conventional, and verbal crossings of those boundaries can carry great emotional force.

Of course vulgarities and other obscenities are used for purposes other than offending and insulting. In particular, they can serve for intensification, for vivid description and colorful speech, as well as to express a straightforward or an irreverent attitude or to exhibit strength of feeling. Feinberg (1985, 210) attributes the impact of tabooed words to the element of surprise, but the impact (call it "shock value") may have less to do with an element of surprise than the role, specifically, of norms. Recall from our earlier discussion that shock links to normative expectations while surprise has to do with predictive expectations. The violation of convention in the use of taboo words would seem a matter of normative expectations. Still, the interplay of expectations in the impact of certain words, like the purposes the use of those words may serve, can be complex. In some settings, such as military barracks and other sites where young men live in artificial isolation, the insertion of "fuck" and "fucking" can become the norm. (Feinberg correctly points out that "'fucking' is the chief intensifier in their language, an adjective that can modify any noun, and even fit in between the syllables of individual words" 207.) The liberal sprinkling of obscenities can become so habitual that on occasion they can be surprising (even shocking) in their absence. It is reported that among British soldiers during World War I, it was understood to be a matter of routine if a sergeant said "Get your fucking rifles!" If however, he said, "Get your rifles!" the situation was understood to be truly urgent (Brophy and Partridge, 1930, 17).

That the absence of usually intensifying obscenities can sometimes be more shocking than their presence, like the fact that blasphemous statements can be made without using any profane words, connects with the fact that polite statements can be more wounding than attacks that depend on vulgar language. (These points will become significant when we come to consider issues of the legal regulation of hate speech. It is not the saying of certain words that constitutes the problem, and so the prohibiting of such words cannot provide an adequate remedy.) Miss Manners points out that polite phrases—such as "I beg your pardon" and "I believe you are gravely mistaken," said in the appropriate tones—can be the most powerful weapons in the arsenal of fighting words (Martin 1990, 73–74). Speech that seeks to lower the other can, when in the wrong register, have the effect of lowering the speaker. The language of insult is heightened when it can assume an impersonal, preferably a moral perspective. Northrop Frye writes:

> attack in literature can never be a pure expression of merely personal or even social hatred, whatever the motivation for it may be, because the words for expressing hatred, as distinct from enmity, have too limited a range. About the only ones we have are derived from the animal world, but calling a man a swine or a skunk or a woman a bitch affords a severely restricted satisfaction, as most of the unpleasant qualities of the animal are human projections. As Shakespeare's Thersites says of Menelaus, "to what form, but that he is, should wit larded with malice, and malice forced with wit, turn him to? To an ass, were nothing; he is both ass and

ox; to an ox, were nothing; he is both ox and ass." For effective attack we must reach some impersonal level, and that commits the attacker, if only by implication, to a moral standard. (Frye 1957, 224–25)

In contrast with the scatological and the sexual, other terms of abuse, such as comparisons of persons with animals or with despised objects, need not violate verbal taboos in order to be offensive.[3] It is the disreputable analogies that make certain similies and metaphors and imputations intolerable. To call someone a "rat" or a "pig" or a "louse" is to attack their character. Convention and context remain important, however, in helping make clear that it is not the admirable features of those creatures that are supposed to be called to mind. Paul Grice (1989) has taught us that understanding meaning is a layered process of interpreting intentions in context. Racial and ethnic terms like "nigger," "kike," and "wop" get their offensive power from the attitudes they, by convention, convey. The words used make clear the intention to insult. But conventions, intentions, and meanings, especially given their historical dimensions, can sometimes be difficult to interpret.

FIGURES OF SPEECH AND ETYMOLOGY

We have already had occasion to note that figures of speech may be taken as insults, even if the speaker has lost all conscious sense of the words' insulting character. From "Jew me down" to "welsh on your debts" and "gyp," ethnic stereotypes and implications may have lost their immediacy for some while still resonating for others. Onetime slurs such as "hunky" and "queer" may, by the passage of time or determined reappropriation and transvaluation, have changed their valence, again, at least for some. And there are cases of ambiguity (e.g., "spooks") and simple error (e.g., "nip in the bud" and "niggardly budget"—these being cases where false

---

3. Sometimes, however, category taboos may come into play. Edmund Leach remarks, "The fact that frogs' legs are a gourmet's delicacy in France but not food at all in England provokes the English to refer to Frenchmen as Frogs with implications of withering contempt" (1964, 31). Leach goes on to invoke elaborate structuralist patterns (in terms of edibility, social distance from humans, and the like) to explain abuse in animal terms, while I think more direct analogical thinking suffices.

associations of sounds have lead to fantasy etymologies and unfounded offense) where phrases are taken by oversensitive hearers to have racial implications not intended by the speakers.

"*Nigger*" is perhaps the most combustible epithet in America today. Sensitivities run high, and with reason. The word comes tied to a disgraceful history of slavery, lynchings, oppression, discrimination, denigration, and abuse. The word itself is derived from the Latin word for the color black, *niger*, and was in its earliest uses nonpejorative (according to the *Random House Historical Dictionary of American Slang*). The dominant use is now, of course, highly derogatory and people resort to circumlocutions such as "the N-word" to avoid even the appearance of using the word. Again, with reason. Randall Kennedy reports in his *Nigger: The Strange Career of a Troublesome Word* (2002) on several cases of over-reaction. In 1993, a Central Michigan University basketball coach was fired for using the word "nigger" in what was meant to be an encouraging pep talk to his team (which consisted of eleven blacks and three whites)—despite his having first asked the players' permission to use the term, a term that they often used with each other. Indeed, the coach explicitly used the term as a term of praise, "to connote a person who is fearless, mentally strong, and tough" (Kennedy, 142). But word spread and the coach ended up being fired. Kennedy writes of "an even more deplorable incident" that

> took place in 1998 at Jefferson Community College in Louisville, Kentucky, where an adjunct professor named Ken Hardy taught a course on interpersonal communications. In a class exploring taboo words, students cited a number of insulting terms such as *faggot* and *bitch*. A member of the class mentioned *nigger*, and in the course of the discussion, Hardy repeated it. One of the nine black students in the twenty-two-person class objected to the airing of *that* word. Classmates disagreed, giving rise to a debate in which most of those present participated. At one point Hardy lent his support to the student who had first objected, suggesting that the class should take seriously the proposition that certain words were simply too volatile to be spoken out loud. (Kennedy, 147)

Despite his cautious view, Hardy, like the basketball coach, was fired. Things have reached a sorry pitch when some words are too explosive to be even mentioned (in quotation marks) in a college-level course where the word is properly part of the subject under discussion. Ordinarily, the philosophical distinction between use and mention should be protection enough, but sensitivities run high. Absence of an intention to insult does not defuse the word. Some insist that, given the word's checkered history, it cannot be defused. Richard Delgado, in the course of using the Supreme Court's "fighting words" doctrine to support an argument for a tort action to protect from racial insults, writes: "Racial insults, and even some of the words that might be used in a racial insult, inflict injury by their very utterance. Words such as 'nigger' and 'spick' are badges of degradation even when used between friends; these words have no other connotation" (Delgado 1993, 107; Abbott 1982, 180–81, takes a similar view). Yet Delgado himself, a few pages later, seems to recognize that context can negate a demeaning intention when he allows that "'Hey, nigger,' spoken affectionately between Black persons and used as a greeting, would not be actionable" under his proposed tort for racial insults (110). The "fighting words" doctrine raises issues we shall return to in due course, but the idea of a fixed character for terms of abuse such as "nigger" seems excessive. For one thing, as we have noted, "nigger" itself has a history, having initially been innocuous enough in connotation. For another, as Judith Butler argues, the word can have other connotations in quotation, even if the injurious connotation is retained, and it can perhaps even be ironically transformed between friends and in jokes, as have other words such as "fag," "queen," and "queer" (1997, 100; see also 14, 160). Nonetheless, Delgado insists, "Most people today know that certain words are offensive and only calculated to wound. No other use remains for such words as 'nigger,' 'wop,' 'spick,' or 'kike'" (Delgado 1993, 94). As a matter of usage, this seems simply false. Delgado (here) neglects that other uses do remain and are created and that quotation (such as his own) may insulate the word from its usually insulting effects. Delgado notes that "racial insults are intentional acts," but seems immediately to forget that the use (and certainly the mention) of particular words need not be insulting: "The intentionality of racial insults is obvious: What other purpose could the insult serve?" (Delgado 1993, 94).

Sometimes the intention is merely to define and the word is not directed in a hostile way toward any individual or group. Kennedy (2002, 133–37) reports a controversy in 1997 over the *Merriam-Webster's Collegiate Dictionary* definition of "nigger" as "a black person—usu. taken to be offensive." A black woman computer technician read the definition and took offense, started petitioning and organizing against the dictionary-makers, and even elicited a boycott threat from Kweisi Mfume of the NAACP. But dictionary descriptions of usage should not be taken as intending to insult, even when what they describe are insults—the campaign was misguided. There was no more racism in the dictionary's definition of "nigger" than in the same dictionary's explication of "honky" as "usu. disparaging: a white person."

The dictionary entry, while noting that the word "now ranks as perhaps the most offensive and inflammatory racial slur in English," also notes "its use by and among blacks is not always intended or taken as offensive." Despite Delgado's insistence (most of the time), it would seem that the nonpejorative use is as much a descriptive fact of usage as the "usu. taken to be offensive." And here Delgado's reference to the role of intention in insult may be of some help (though we should never forget the persistent possibility and reality of unintentional insults). Why is it permissible for some, particularly blacks (including black comics), to use the word "nigger" in certain contexts? Part of the answer, surely, is that since the speaker is a member of the category being denigrated, the usual presumption of implied inferiority is removed. Who is speaking makes a difference. And the context makes a difference. It matters who the audience is, as does the joking or otherwise nonserious nature of the occasion. These are all signs of intention. And the intention may sometimes be to use the otherwise offensive word in order to appropriate the enemy's or the oppressor's speech, as when gay activists took over the word "queer" as a proud and ironical self-description. Still, one cannot always assume such factors successfully and clearly defuse explosive words. When white rappers who identify with blacks use the word "nigger," their identity and the acceptability of the word may remain questionable. (Eminem, the leading white rapper of our time, has insisted "that word is not even in my vocabulary"—*Rolling Stone*, 7/15/2000.) And when one woman calls another a "cunt," that does not, in general, take away the opprobrious sting. The problem is that even a member of a denigrated group may use against a fellow member the very terms of denigration typically used by outsiders. It is relatively rare that a woman is called a "cunt" by anyone (male or female) in anything other than a denigratory fashion. Membership in the denigrated category does not always and in all circumstances render use of the conventional terms of abuse non-offensive, in actuality or in intent.

And one's words can mean more than one consciously intends. Think here of Freud's case of Dora, in which Freud insisted both that Frau K's discussions of sexual matters with young Dora were intensely sexual and that his own discussions with Dora of such matters were not. (Contrast 1905e, 62, 105n, 120n with 9, 48–49.) Despite his insistence on the clinical character of his conversations, one must surely conclude that his discussions with the adolescent girl were at least as sexually charged as those of Frau K. Indeed, Freud's own views about the role of transference in psychoanalysis would seem to compel the conclusion. Context can matter in more than one way, sometimes defusing hateful epithets, sometimes adding unintended significances.

ENFORCING STANDARDS

Perhaps any word can be used in a joking manner or in an understood playful and non-insulting way. But some words may be presumed guilty until the case for the non-offensiveness of their use (or mention) has been made. In such cases, are the offended licensed to strike back? And may the state properly limit the speech of some to prevent the (legitimate?) response it might provoke in others? Are some words "fighting words" not protected by the First Amendment? The answer is yes according to the case of *Chaplinsky v. New Hampshire*, 315 U.S. 568 (1942), and the doctrine of that case has been influential in terms of inspiring speech codes on college campuses. But those speech codes, where challenged, have generally failed to pass constitutional muster. We will consider the "fighting words" doctrine in its constitutional and philosophical context in the next chapter.

The law has also recognized the insulting and forbidden status of certain words through its doctrines on obscenity. These doctrines tend to be given especially stringent enforcement when it comes to radio and television. Comedian George Carlin had a routine that mocked the FCC's prohibition against the use of "seven filthy words" on the air waves. Carlin's deliciously extended disquisition on those seven words ("shit," "piss," "fuck," "cunt," "cocksucker," "motherfucker," and "tits") was played by a radio station as part of a discussion program on "the use of language in our society," preceded by a warning that it contained "sensitive language" that some listeners might find offensive. Nonetheless, the broadcast resulted in a complaint to the FCC, which in turn issued a Declaratory Order that was ultimately upheld by the Supreme Court in *Federal Communications Commission v. Pacifica Foundation*, 438 U.S.

726 (1978). Aside from the fact that individuals can usually defend them-selves from unwanted intrusions on the airwaves (say, by changing the channel), the offending words were, unlike insults (or "fighting words"), not personal, i.e., not directed at any individuals. Indeed, they were actu-ally being discussed rather than used. Further, obscene language can have aesthetic value, as D. H. Lawrence observed: "if the use of a few so-called obscene words will startle man or woman out of a mob-habit into an individual state, well and good. And word prudery is so universal a mob-habit that it is time we were startled out of it" (Lawrence 1929, 64). Given the valuable expressive and other functions of such words, it could be argued that it is important that citizens (including young citizens) be educated in their use.[4] This may be one of those instances where words should be distinguished from sticks and stones. Whatever one's attitude toward visual pornography, obscene speech (especially mere mentions of such speech) should perhaps be subjected to different standards. (Feinberg 1985, 281–87 considers the *Pacifica* case in detail.)

Television standards can be both nuanced and arbitrary. Tad Friend reports of Standards and Practices censors at the networks: "'Dick' and 'pussy' are now sometimes allowed, but only as insults (it may thus be permissible to say 'You're a dick,' but never 'Your dick . . . ')" (2001, 48). The concrete particular seems disturbing to some sensibilities. Political correctness also exacts its toll. Friend continues, "In 1994, the producers of the Fox sitcom 'Monty' were told that a character in the pilot could not get food poisoning from a Chinese restaurant. He also could not get it from an Italian restaurant. He could, however, get it from a restaurant. . . . Many producers believe that a show like 'All in

---

4. There have been ludicrous cases where a misguided concern for what chil-dren might hear has led to criminal sanctions for obscene words uttered in ordinary life, rather than over the airwaves. A century-old Michigan law that prohibits cursing in the presence of women and children continues to be enforced. The Associated Press reported (12/4/2000) on two cases. One involved a man convicted for uttering a stream of profanities in front of children after tumbling out of a canoe. He was fined $75 and ordered to work four days in a child-care program. The other involved accu-sations of using foul language in front of children on a school bus. The accused said he had used a mild obscenity, and only because he believed his daughter was being manhandled and verbally abused by the driver. Conviction in that case could yield ninety days in jail.

the Family,' in which Archie Bunker inveighed against 'spics, spades, Chinks, [and] Hebes' in the first episode, would never make it on the air today" (49). The conventions of ordinary life can be equally arbitrary. As Joni Mitchell points out in one of her songs, "An angry man is just an angry man / But an angry woman . . . / Bitch!" ("Lead Balloon" on *Taming the Tiger*, 1998). Social prejudices can make permissible as well as make taboo. Male hostility toward women and the denigration of women is often in evidence in vulgar vocabulary (Greer 1971; Baker 1975; Hughes 1998, chap. 10). While the *New York Times* ("The Taming of the Slur," 7/13/2006, E1) reports that these days "slut" is following "pimp" in moving away from its status as a slur as positive and affectionate uses emerge, the traditional sexual double-standard is still marked by the fact that promiscuous women continue to be denigrated as "sluts" or "whores" while promiscuous men continue to be lauded as "studs" or "players." As Feinberg points out, the cult of macho "is an extreme exaggeration and distortion of the personal insecurity, the resentment of dependence, and sour-grape denigration of females that lies behind much compulsive use of sexual vulgarities: (1985, 312n35). We have seen that in many cultures, reference to an assault on a female relative is perceived as a way of getting at the man. In a twist, Labov (1972, 337) points out that equating a mother with something absurd is a ritual insult against the (ritual) mother, if it is meant to be true (your mother *was* a swine, you had a different mother) it becomes a charge against the opponent himself—thus a personal insult. That Abrahams (1970, 32) found "motherfucker" to be the most common obscenity among men in his study and that it could be used alternatively to praise or to damn matches the ambivalence about mothers that he also detected, and reflects the same rejection of the feminine. It appears even in an example among white sounds from Labov (1972, 321): "A: You motherfucker. B: Your mother told." It is worth noting that "Motherfucker" is very widespread (it appears on Carlin's canonical list of "seven filthy words"), but "father-fucker" is used nowhere (Hughes 1998, 32). The asymmetry may be due to that form of insult typically being aimed by men at other men, but it remains to ask why women don't avail themselves of an appropriate incestuous variant when berating each other. In Fiji, "sisterfucker" is the salient obscenity (Brenneis 1980, 174). Again, the transgression is against a woman, though the words are aimed at a man.

There are a variety of modes in which the language of abuse can be used to effect an insult. Feinberg (1985, 118–24) usefully distinguishes name-calling, calumny, factually based put-downs, genuine accusations, charges, and vilifications, and disparagements. Where not simply venting hostility or drawing a colorful (and perhaps informative) analogy, name-calling may be connected with the hostile wishes found behind curses. From trying to lay an unpleasant future on someone (e.g., "may you go to the dogs") one can ascribe a repellant present ("you are a dog"), thus (in accord with the omnipotence of thoughts) transforming the wish into the deed. Such vituperation thus conceals the role of compelling magical fantasy by using the form of matter-of-fact imputation. While tabooed words are not essential to name-calling, as Feinberg says, "Tabooed words can lend color and vivacity to vituperation as they can to oaths, curses, exclamations, avowals, and jokes. It is a dull insult, for example, to call a person stupid, but it is an insult with a flair to say that "he has his head up his ass" (Feinberg 1985, 119)."

The imputations in primitive name-calling insults include likening to lower animals or depersonalized organs (as with "asshole" or "prick" or "cunt"), describing appearance and characteristics in unflattering terms (again, with or without obscene language), accusing of shameful (most often sexual) acts, and similarly denigrating parents and ancestors (as with "son of a bitch" and "bastard"). Where imputed characteristics or shameful acts might have a basis in truth, they can move toward the categories of factually based put-downs (which may not require a wider audience or be concerned with actually damaging reputation, as with taunting schoolyard attacks on "cripples" and "retards") and genuine accusations or charges (which are usually directed to a wider audience and aim to produce real reputational damage, and more often than not avoid ritualistic obscene language, as with "coward" and "cheat"). Where they might plausibly pretend to truth while being false, they amount to calumnies. (Where they plainly make no pretense to truth, they remain, like Labov's ritual insults, mere name-calling, mere metaphorical jabs.) The malicious falsehoods in calumnies receive legal attention under the headings of libel and slander. We shall turn to the legal doctrines governing defamation after we have considered some of the constitutional and philosophical issues (such as those surrounding "fighting words") that we have already had occasion to mention.

Name-calling, like ritualistic accusation and disparagement of what is held dear or holy, is a way of expressing disrespect. (Feinberg distinguishes a fourth class of insults as "symbolic dominance claims," 224, but we have seen reason for believing that all insults may be symbolic dominance claims: ways of asserting, assuming, or achieving superiority.) Whatever the independent pleasures of verbal dexterity and fireworks in insults, there is no doubt that words can wound, and the law may intervene to prevent harm and (sometimes even) offense. It may sometimes act to prevent (and/or punish) provocations. These interventions are not limited to control of the airwaves. And whatever the standards, the introduction of the coercive powers of the law can change things in ways that require careful thought and, arguably, restraint.

SIX

∎ ∎ ∎

INSULT IN THE LAW

FIGHTING WORDS, OBSCENITY, AND HATE SPEECH

WORDS CAN ALSO BE DEEDS. SPEECH CAN ALSO BE CONDUCT. SO THE schoolyard wisdom that asserts "sticks and stones may break my bones, but words will never hurt me" has its limits. The chant cannot serve as a magical incantation to ward off harm. The categories are, perhaps inextricably, mixed. It is not just that speech can have later effects in the world (saying "Hello" may be the start of a conversation, even of a life-long friendship), but sometimes the effects are peculiarly direct, the mere saying (under the appropriate conditions) can make something so. "I now pronounce you man and wife," said under the appropriate conditions by the appropriate person, may be all that it takes to make a marriage. "You shall be hung by the neck till dead," said under the appropriate conditions by the appropriate person, is not simply a prediction, but a judicial sentence of death. Such constitutive speech acts, called by J. L. Austin "performative utterances" (and described by him, in his later terminology, as having "illocutionary force"), depend on conventions and are essentially complete on utterance (1970b, 1962). This is in addition to the already mentioned power of words (what Austin refers to as their "perlocutionary force") to produce changes causally, over time. The law recognizes the various powers of speech-acts when it attaches legal liability, whether civil or criminal, to the uttering of certain words. This becomes troubling, however, in the context of our commitment to freedom of thought and freedom of expression. Not that this should be thought of as a simple clash. It is, after all, through the operation of legal mechanisms that certain constitutive powers of speech (including the performative powers to marry and to sentence cited in our examples) are created and conferred in the first place. Here as elsewhere, the law both empowers and limits.

It would be foolish to suppose that freedom of speech, enshrined as it is in the First Amendment of the Constitution of the United States, is an absolute. There are any number of offenses an essential element of which, or indeed *the* essential element of which, is speech, that is, acts of symbolic communication. Speech is at the heart of perjury, fraud, conspiracy, defamation (in both its written and verbal forms: libel and slander), extortion by threat, and any number of other offenses. It would, however, also be a mistake—of a different, yet equally significant sort—to suppose that speech has no distinctive privileges. Freedom in general, and freedom of speech in particular, is arguably of great value. The traditional arguments of John Milton, John Stuart Mill and a long and distinguished retinue of champions of freedom of speech appeal to the value of unconstrained communication as a way of discovering truth and uncovering error, of unbinding thought in the pursuit of religious, moral, and scientific insight. But beyond the "marketplace of ideas" as the path to wisdom and understanding, freedom of expression is itself a value, however distasteful the form and content of some expression might be to some, and however erroneous some of the ideas expressed. For all benefit from the opportunity to discover and fulfill their natures through artistic, religious, social, and other "experiments in living." If life has value, surely much of that value is to be found in living it freely. The arguments are powerful and familiar, and we need not detail them here to recognize that their effect is to put the burden on those who would limit liberty. There are always costs in restrictions on liberty (intrinsic costs, along with the instrumental costs of enforcement, secrecy, and the stunting of human potential), and those who would impose the restrictions must bear the burden of showing that the costs are worth it. There is a presumption in favor of liberty. The presumption here, as in the criminal law (where there is a "presumption of innocence"), is a point about who bears the burden of proof. In the criminal law, the presumption of innocence does not mean that no one thinks the accused guilty: the prosecutor, the grand jury, the police, *must* all believe the accused guilty if they are to behave responsibly in bringing the charges at all. What the presumption means is that the prosecution has the burden, in a criminal case, of proving all the elements of the offense. The accused may stand silent and yet prevail if the prosecution fails to carry its burden. Similarly, the presumption in favor of liberty is a point about the burden of proof. And as I have said, given the great value appropriately attributed to liberty, that burden falls and falls heavily upon those who would restrict liberty.

Which brings us back to speech. While freedom of speech is not absolute—as noted, there are crimes constituted by speech acts, from perjury to the treason of a newspaper publishing "the sailing dates of ships" in time of war (*Near v. Minnesota*, 283 US 697 [1931])—our legal system recognizes the priority of freedom of speech through the presumption that puts the burden of proof on those who would limit it. It also does it by disfavoring prior restraint. Even in the case of crimes, the harm in speech may lead to subsequent punishment but only rarely serves as grounds for censoring or prohibiting the speech in advance. The limited and limiting role of injunctions is itself a rather large topic, and so we shall not pursue it here. Freedom of speech is not an absolute. The crimes perpetrated through speech, however, are criminalized because they involve conflicting rights and grievous harms. But what are we, what is the state, to do when the harm to be prevented amounts to mere offense? For the injury involved in insults is most typically offense. It is true that offense can have measurable and even serious effects. And we will have to talk more about what sorts of wrong and what sorts of injury might be involved in offense. We have already said at the start that the injury in insult is typically mental or moral, the cause an attitude of disrespect, an attitude of insufficient attention and regard. Now we can focus on the various attempts in the law to limit the harms and offense that may be done through insults (especially those done through speech or writing or other forms of symbolic communication) by attaching punishments to offensive offenders. We need to pause a bit longer, however, on the notion of symbolic communication in connection with freedom. It is not just about words.

SPEECH/CONDUCT

The distinction between speech and conduct (words and sticks and stones) is also troubled from the other direction. Just as we can perform actions through speech (words can be deeds), we can speak through our actions. For example, the Supreme Court has recognized various forms of peaceful labor picketing and certain civil rights demonstrations as protected speech. Similarly for flag burning. In the case of *Texas v. Johnson* in 1989 the Supreme Court ruled that flag burning as a form of political protest was protected speech, and it affirmed that judgment the following year in *U.S. v. Eichman* when it overturned the Flag Protection Act that Congress had passed in an effort to prohibit flag desecration nationally. Flag burning was particularly common in the United States during Vietnam era protests and it continues as a popular form of expression abroad today. (Of course, American law concerning the burning of flags, whether permissive as now or restrictive at some point in the future, does not govern abroad.) Periodically, there are movements in Congress to ban flag burning (in 2006, a vote in the US Senate for a constitutional amendment to permit such a ban came within one vote of passage), but it is not the action (as such) of burning the flag that upsets the would-be banners. As the Court noted in *Texas v. Johnson* (491 U.S. 397, 411), "federal law designates burning as the preferred means of disposing of a flag 'when it is in such condition that it is no longer a fitting emblem for display,' 36 U.S.C. 176(k)." The Boy Scouts, Veterans of Foreign Wars, and other organizations employ burning as a way of disposing of worn out flags. In those instances, no disrespect is meant or perceived. The would-be banners only wish to ban the disrespectful burning of flags, that is, the burning of flags as a sign of disrespect, as a form of expression. It would seem then that both the permissive Supreme Court and the banners agree in recognizing that flag burning can be a form of symbolic speech. In wanting to ban certain forms of symbolic speech because of the (disrespectful) message conveyed, it would appear that the banners are violating the content and viewpoint neutrality that can be seen as the very essence of freedom of speech. As the Court stated, "If there is a bedrock principle underlying the First Amendment, it is that the government may not prohibit the expression of an idea simply because society finds the idea itself offensive or disagreeable" (414). There is considerable irony in a movement that demands respect for the flag as the symbol of American freedom precisely by undoing one essential aspect of that freedom. As Justice Brennan wrote for the majority in *Texas v. Johnson*, "We can imagine no more appropriate response to burning a flag than waving one's own, no better way to counter a flag burner's message than by saluting the flag that burns, no surer means of preserving the dignity even of the flag that burned than by—as one witness here did—according its remains a respectful burial. We do not consecrate the flag by punishing its desecration, for in doing so we dilute the freedom that this cherished emblem represents" (491 U.S. 397, 420 [1989]).

Again, it is not the act of burning as such that is protected. It is the communicative message in flag burning that earns it privileged status. Not that every message conveyed by burning (any more than every message conveyed by spoken words) should be privileged. There is a dialectic here. The Supreme Court has sometimes been muddled on this point, as illustrated in its holdings on cross-burning. In the case of *R.A.V. v. St. Paul*, 505 U.S. 377 (1992) a municipal statute prohibiting cross-burning was ruled unconstitutional as criminalizing racially motivated acts, and thus violating standards of neutrality. It may be true that we need to allow the Nazis to march in Jewish Skokie if we are to enable the Martin Luther Kings to march in areas where whites do not wish to hear their message. Even racist views may be entitled to be heard. But burning a cross on a black family's lawn is in significant ways not like marching through a neighborhood, however unwelcome the marchers. Leaving aside issues of trespass when a cross is burned on someone else's property (and leaving aside also the issues of underinclusiveness vs. overbreadth in constitutional statutory evaluation focused on by the majority and the concurring opinions in the instant case), there is a history here that must not be ignored. Ku Klux Klan cross-burnings have typically been preludes to violence, and the burning of a cross on a black family's lawn constitutes a readily read threat. Threats are not a form of protected speech. The Supreme Court revisited the issue in *Virginia v. Black*, 538 US 343 (2003) and there finally acknowledged that the state "may ban cross burning carried out with the intent to intimidate." The earlier decision had expressed concern about a statute paying attention to motive, but while the law typically omits motivation in the specification of offenses, it does sometimes take motive into account, as in "hate crime" legislation and when "murder for hire" is given a greater penalty than murder done from other motives. Why shouldn't it? But the crucial point here is that unlike flag burning, cross-burning in the cases under discussion constituted a threat directed at individuals, just the sort of threat historically followed by directed violence, and so the designated punishment is not simply a matter of motive. Scalia, writing for the majority in the *R.A.V.* case, was mistaken to treat cross-burning as protected speech. Nazi marchers may have to be tolerated as the price for allowing civil rights marchers in white areas. But cross-burning in order to get black people to move, as a threat, need not be tolerated, any more than mafia extortionist threats to burn a business if "protection" money is not paid. Speech may be action.[1]

The distinction between speech and conduct (one supposedly being protected, the other not), like the distinction between words and sticks and stones (one supposedly being harmless, the other not), does not get us very far. Fraud, perjury, and any number of other prosecutable crimes are committed through speech, speech can be action; and some actions may constitute symbolic, protected, speech as in flag burning. Ultimately, the distinction between speech and conduct does not provide an analytical tool that can resolve constitutional difficulties. Laurence Tribe puts the legal situation succinctly:

> The trouble with the distinction between speech and conduct is that it has less determinate content than is sometimes supposed. All communication except perhaps that of the extrasensory variety involves conduct. Moreover, if the expression involves talk, it may be noisy; if written, it may become litter. So too, much conduct is expressive, a fact the Court has had no trouble recognizing in a wide variety of circumstances. Expression and conduct, message and medium, are

---

1. In fairness to Scalia, he tries to be clear in his concluding statement for the majority in the R.A.V. case: "Let there be no mistake about our belief that burning a cross in someone's front yard is reprehensible. But St. Paul has sufficient means at its disposal to prevent such behavior without adding the First Amendment to the fire" (396). While his novel and tortured underinclusiveness analysis muddies the waters, he does have a point: the reprehensible cross-burning could have been prosecuted under a number of Minnesota statutes (covering terrorist threats, arson, and criminal damage to property) and was in fact also prosecuted (and the petitioner did not appeal conviction) under a statute covering racially motivated assaults, but the city of St. Paul chose to prosecute under its Bias-Motivated Crime Ordinance, which provided: "Whoever places on public or private property a symbol, object, appellation, characterization or graffiti, including, but not limited to, a burning cross or Nazi swastika, which one knows or has reasonable grounds to know arouses anger, alarm or resentment in others on the basis of race, color, creed, religion or gender commits disorderly conduct and shall be guilty of a misdemeanor" (380). This statute, as the various concurrences argued, is overbroad. As Justice White states, "The mere fact that expressive activity causes hurt feelings, offense, or resentment does not render the expression unprotected" (414). Construing the "fighting words" doctrine as applying to anything that causes "anger, alarm or resentment" would spread a pall of silence—a problem we shall see directly when we come to arguments for codes regulating "hate speech."

thus inextricably tied together in all communicative behavior . . . the distinction between speech and conduct must be seen at best as announcing a conclusion of the Court, rather than as summarizing in any way the analytic processes which led the Court to that conclusion. (Tribe 1988, 827)

That the legal categories are inextricably mixed should perhaps not be surprising. Austin himself introduces the notion of performative utterances by developing a series of contrasts with constative or fact-stating utterances; he concludes his discussion by "taking back" much of the contrast. He points out that even utterances that merely seek to state facts are in a sense performative, for stating is a kind of action. (There is "the bit where we take it all back"—Austin 1970b, 241.) Looking the other way across the saying-doing divide, it is also the case that many performatives may, like statements of fact, be assessed in terms of correspondence with fact. While warnings, verdicts, estimates, and the like may not be simply true or false, neither are statements, for there are many dimensions of assessment (fair or not fair, adequate or not adequate, exaggerated or not exaggerated, too rough or precise and accurate). The coming together of performative and constative utterance, of doing and saying, does not mean that particular aspects may not predominate in particular cases, nor that explicit performative utterances may not be of special interest, but it does mean that one must exercise great care in approaching that mongrel, speech acts (Austin 1970b, 246–52; 1962, Lecture XI).

FIGHTING WORDS

The Supreme Court has sometimes attempted to single out certain specific kinds of speech ("fighting words" and "obscenity" among them) as constituting unprotected conduct. "Fighting words" and "obscenity" also play a central role in insults, and so we shall be giving them particular attention. The doctrines developed in relation to them have in turn had a large influence on those who have pressed for campus codes to limit "hate speech," and those codes help focus questions about who may insult whom and how. Finally, certain parallels in the analysis of fighting words, pornography, and hate speech will bring us back to a broader understanding of speech acts, including the role of intentions.

The constitutional "fighting words" doctrine was introduced in the 1942 case of *Chaplinsky v. New Hampshire* (315 U.S. 568). Walter Chaplinsky was a Jehovah's Witness who was distributing pamphlets in the midst of an unreceptive and increasingly unruly crowd. He was warned by the City Marshall that the crowd was getting restless and when there was later a disturbance he was asked to come along to the police station. Chaplinsky then called the Marshall "a God damned racketeer" and "a damned Fascist" (though he claimed that the Marshall had cursed him first when he had asked that the Marshall arrest the ones responsible for the disturbance rather than him). This resulted in what became the formal charge at issue, a charge over his intemperate words (even the Marshall had admitted the pamphlet distribution was itself lawful activity). He was charged under a state statute that prohibited addressing "offensive, derisive or annoying" words or names or noises to another person in a public place. The state courts held that neither provocation nor the truth of the utterances could constitute a defense to the charge.

The Supreme Court refused to afford cursing a public officer the protection of freedom of speech, saying "it is well understood that the right of free speech is not absolute at all times and under all circumstances. There are certain well-defined and narrowly limited classes of speech, the prevention and punishment of which has never been thought to raise any Constitutional problem. These include the lewd and obscene, the profane, the libelous, and the insulting or 'fighting' words—those which by their very utterance inflict injury or tend to incite an immediate breach of the peace" (315 U.S. 568, 571–72). The Court quoted approvingly words from an earlier Jehovah's Witnesses case, "Resort to epithets or personal abuse is not in any proper sense communication of information or opinion safeguarded by the Constitution, and its punishment as a criminal act would raise no question under that instrument" (*Cantwell v. Connecticut*, 310 U.S. 296, 309–10 [1940]). The apparent purpose of the Chaplinsky court was to restrict words "plainly tending to excite the addressee to a breach of the peace" (573). It is an odd way to prevent violence. Given the general presumption in favor of liberty, one would have thought the way to control those who might become violent is to punish those who actually become violent. Otherwise, the irascible and lawless get to silence those they do not wish to hear. Such a "heckler's veto," silencing the speaker rather than the person inclined to become violent, is not recognized in other court rulings, and the decision in *Chaplinsky* has fallen into desuetude.[2] But it has been resurrected in support of speech codes on college campuses and by minorities who wish to enlist the power of the state in protecting them from abuse. The doctrine deserves closer scrutiny.

It is open to at least two rather different interpretations, one in terms of provocation, the other in terms of performative utterance. The first is a causal notion. The second depends on the conventional understanding of speech acts. The Chaplinsky court cited the state court's construal of the particular statute in question as applying to "words whose speaking constitute a breach of the peace by the speaker" (573). On such a performative or constitutive analysis, the question is whether "racketeer" and "fascist" are the conventional equivalent of a "first blow," entitling the object of the abuse to physical self-defense. (Note that "fascist" in 1942, in the middle of World War II, was doubtless a more charged word than it might be today.) Which words constitute "first blows" or "breaches of the peace"? When should society expect someone to fight back physically? Should society ever expect individuals to engage in physical "self-defense" against verbal assaults?

Historically, throwing down a gauntlet or other symbolic gesture could initiate a fight. But dueling has been outlawed just about everywhere, and it is not clear why the state should endorse a new *code duello*, encouraging physical altercations among its citizens. Why facilitate the escalation of verbal conflict into what would otherwise amount to actionable physical assault? On the other hand, if one has been clearly threatened and an attack is imminent,

---

2. While never formally overturned, the "fighting words" doctrine has generally been very narrowly construed, e.g.: *Terminello v. Chicago*, 337 U.S. 1 (1949); *Lewis v. City of New Orleans*, 415 U.S. 130 (1974); *Houston v. Hill*, 482 U.S. 451 (1987). (The *Lewis* and *Hill* cases, like *Chaplinsky*, involve exchanges with police, but, unlike *Chaplinsky*, expect greater restraint and self control by police in the face of provocative words.) The "inflict injury" prong has never been used by the Court to uphold the conviction of a person using words that cause emotional harm to the listener; and the narrowed, but sometimes still cited, "breach of the peace" prong would seem to make the legal character of the words (and the degree of protection of the speaker) depend on to whom the words are addressed—so one might insult the weak and passive (i.e., those not inclined to retaliate) with legal impunity. Not an attractive result. While that impact might be muted by the judicious application of "objective standards," subsequent Supreme Court decisions have in fact emphasized provocative personal insults directed at individuals, and have insisted on taking into account actual circumstances (e.g., *Cohen v. California*, 403 U.S. 15, 20, 23 [1971] and *Gooding v. Wilson*, 405 U.S. 518, 524 [1972]). For fuller discussion of the constitutional particulars, see Note, 106 *Harvard Law Review*, 1129, 1137 (1993); and Greenawalt 1995.

it is not clear why one should have passively to sustain a first blow before protecting oneself. The way to deal with whatever tension there is between these principles is, I believe, to maintain the distinction between a threat (with violence imminent) and an insult (which can be answered without physical blows). One of the ways the law does this is by placing constraints on "self-defense" as a justification. To count as "self-defense" an action must meet conditions of necessity (the danger must exist or be reasonably believed to exist), proportion (the response should be no greater than needed to avert the degree of harm threatened), and timing (if too early, the behavior is an impermissible preemptive strike and if it takes place after the danger has passed, it is retaliation rather than self-defense). With appropriate attention to these constraining conditions, individuals' safety and honor can be afforded the justified and justifying defense of self-defense without the state sanctioning turning "fighting words" into an inviting gateway to social disorder. Existing conventions may suggest that one should respond to assaults, including verbal assaults, on things which one holds sacred, but there is little reason to think that the response should be in terms more violent than the mode of assault.

Leaving performative notions of responding to "fighting words" as conventional "first blows" aside, it remains true that words can provoke, that is, can cause one to lose control and strike back physically (can "tend to incite an immediate breach of the peace" 572 or be "likely to provoke the average person to retaliation, and thereby cause a breach of the peace" 574). As Feinberg puts it, words can be used "to taunt another . . . for the purpose of goading him into an unpromising attack or a humiliating withdrawal" (1985, 226). We have seen the pattern in the workings of *briga*. Does provocation amount to justification? Looking back once more to the notion of self-defense, the beliefs involved in the constraining conditions might be thought to require different levels of objective validity. At a minimum, some might think that sincere (however unreasonable and mistaken) belief should be enough. That is, on this standard, if one believes one is in danger, one may strike out with legal impunity. But such a standard would be an invitation to anarchy, licensing (for example) the careless, thoughtless, nervous, and stupid to shoot Halloween trick-or-treaters approaching their home, should the edgy homeowner, however unreasonably, become frightened. At the other end of the subjectivity-objectivity scale, one might require that the relevant beliefs actually be correct. But then, it might be asking too much to require citizens to have beliefs which are not merely reasonable but in fact true before they act.

To secure such accuracy (if it can be secured), individuals might have to delay efforts at self-defense until it is too late. Reasonable belief is the generally accepted standard. The usual norm is to expect people to respond to perceived danger only if they have taken reasonable steps in the circumstances to be sure that the danger is real, that their response is not excessive in view of the harm feared, and that timely action is required. Such reasonableness seems an equally appropriate demand when one is dealing with (backward-looking) provocation.

In the case of (forward-looking) self-defense against feared dangers, to be fully justified, one's beliefs may have actually to be true (to say one is "justified" is to say one has done nothing wrong, one has done the right thing, one has done what society would expect). But even if one is ultimately mistaken, one's reasonable beliefs may still excuse (an "excuse" allows that one has done something wrong, but recognizes that for one reason or another one should not be punished to the full extent of the law or be held fully liable — can society legitimately expect that its citizens do more than be reasonable?). Should provocation be regarded as justification or excuse? And by what standard? According to the Chaplinsky court, citing the state court's construal of the statute, a reasonableness standard applies: "The word 'offensive' is not to be defined in terms of what a particular addressee thinks. . . . The test is what men of common intelligence would understand would be words likely to cause an average addressee to fight" (573).

Supposing an individual is not overly sensitive, and they are provoked, is the fact that someone else "started it" a justification (making the action right), an excuse (making it acceptable), or merely a mitigating circumstance (entailing perhaps lesser punishment)? As recently as the 1960s, there was a statute in the state of Texas that made finding one's spouse in *flagrante* with a rival adequate and full justification for homicide. It was as though the state expected a real man to do no less when confronted with adultery—a rather shocking endorsement of private capital punishment and devaluation of life (Feinberg 1970a, 102–3). While insults may not typically provoke murder, there is no reason why the state should encourage violence rather than restraint in the face of taunts. Verbal provocation may mitigate, but it is unclear when if ever it should do more than that.

Expectations are murky when it comes to fighting words, both reading actual societal expectations and establishing what should be regarded as legitimate expectations. People in our society are not licensed to hit each other, with the notable exception of self-defense (and related forms of defense, as of others and of property). But even that exception is, as we have noted, ringed with restrictions (having to do with reasonable avoidability, proportionality, and timeliness).[3] Does the privilege of self-defense extend to provocation by verbal taunts? I think the answer in the United States is generally no. Here the distinction between words and sticks and stones takes legal hold. There is even a widespread criminal law rule that prevents "mere words" (however insulting, offensive, or abusive) serving as grounds for a provocation excuse reducing a homicide from murder to manslaughter (Kennedy 2002, 69–80; see, e.g., *Allen v. United States*, 164 U.S. 492, 497 [1896] and *Girouard v. State*, 583 A.2d 718 [Md. 1991]). But then, there are occasions where a verbal provocation may license self-defense. Take threats. Where the verbal threat announces imminent danger ("I'm going to shoot you," said by a man holding a gun), one need not await the commencement of a physical assault. But preemptive strikes and retaliation for threats (or even feared or prior assaults) remain prohibited—these are issues of timing, and the legal system is meant to provide alternative means of protection and redress. (The Bush doctrine of preemptive strikes in international affairs is multiply troubling.) Even where a threat may license physical action, where retreat may not be available or safe, it is generally in a context of accompanying circumstances and actions (remember, in the example cited the man was holding a gun) that go beyond the merely verbal. So again, I think verbal taunts do not lift the bar against physical attacks. On the other hand, a physical attack in response to verbal taunts is not unprovoked and certain notions of manliness and honor persist, and so social expectations—if not legal standards—may sometimes allow or even require physical response. (The expectations may not rely solely on ideals of manliness. Women may, in certain circumstances, be expected to slap a man. But then, a slap is generally regarded as a symbolic gesture rather than a serious physical assault.) But note that the man who catches his wife in adultery and attacks the other party is also not unprovoked. He may plead provocation as a mitigating circumstance in relation to sentencing, but provocation is not

---

3. There have traditionally been other constraints, such as a "duty to retreat" where possible, but these demands have become increasingly controversial, and in some jurisdictions they have been legislated away.

a justifying or (here) even an excusing condition. Adultery is not a crime. Taunting is not a crime. Physically assaulting is.

According to at least one account, actor Russell Crowe's notorious assault on a New York hotel desk clerk who failed to assist him when he asked for help in getting a call through to his wife in Australia was triggered by the clerk muttering "*whatever.*" The story continues, "Crowe said, 'What's your name?' The clerk said, 'Josh.' Crowe said, 'Well, Josh, I'm coming down right now to kick your ass.' Crowe proceeded to the lobby, confirmed that the man behind the desk was indeed Josh, hurled a phone and a vase at him, took a bow, then assumed a karate stance, whether in anticipation of retaliation or for Oscar consideration it wasn't clear. Enter the cops" (Paumgarten 2005, 38). The word is doubtless provocative. It is usually a way of saying "stop talking, I'm not interested in what you have to say or in having a discussion." As Paumgarten puts it, "'Whatever' is as incendiary as it is nonchalant; the nonchalance is what makes it incendiary. 'Whatever' turns disengagement into something withering and mean." There is a complete lack of sympathy or respect for one's situation or point of view. So, again, the word is doubtless provocative. But is it the equivalent of a blow, of a first strike? Does it justify physical retaliation? One would think that in a civilized society, such escalation must be regarded as unacceptable. (In Crowe's case, the retaliation was preannounced and required him to leave his room and go to the lobby, so it might seem to involve premeditation. Self-defense, recall, even against physical assaults, requires respect for considerations of proportionality and timing. The threat must be significant, the defensive measures no greater than the harm to be averted, and both preemptive strikes and post-situation retaliation fail to meet the time constraints that call for immediacy of response.) That "whatever" may be provocative should give us further pause about the "fighting words" doctrine. In the right circumstances, *any* word might become effectively provocative.

In the final match of the 2006 World Cup, French soccer star Zinédine Zidane head-butted Italian player Marco Materazzi in the chest. Some (relying on lip readers) alleged that the butt was in response to Materazzi calling Zidane "the son of a terrorist whore" (presumably in Italian). Later accounts focus on disrespectful reference to Zidane's sister. Either way, the provocation might produce sympathy, but still would not make the red card ejecting Zidane from the game (and perhaps costing France the championship) any less appropriate. Zidane himself later explained, "Sometimes words are harder than blows. When he said it for the third time, I reacted" (*New York Times* 7/13/2006, C16). Provocation may mitigate, it may even sometimes excuse, but it does not justify. This is a point important to understand for all those who would respond to words with sticks and stones, whether they be outraged soccer players, offended college students, or affronted nations looking for a *casus belli*.

OBSCENITY AND PORNOGRAPHY

There are some who believe pornography is a way of putting down women (MacKinnon 1993), or more broadly, as D. H. Lawrence put it, an "attempt to insult sex, to do dirt on it" (Lawrence 1961, 67).[4] Insult has a variety of voices and genres, including the scorn of sarcasm and the ridicule of satire. Ought pornography to be classed among the invidious genres of insult? Is pornography by design, or in effect, a way of wounding, an assault on women or on the human spirit? Even if it is, ought it (any more than ugly sarcasm or hurtful satire) be subject to legal restriction?

In addition to "fighting words," obscene speech (and especially pornography, whether verbal or pictorial) has often been deemed to be unprotected by the First Amendment. Leaving aside issues of delimiting the unprotected classes, the immediately interesting question from the perspective of understanding the legal status of insults is the character of the harm or offense that obscenity produces. Is it of a sort that justifies legal restrictions?

As with fighting words, there are at least two interpretations, causal and constitutive, perlocutionary and performative, concerning how obscenity brings about its noxious consequences. Each has its difficulties.

Some believe that the playing out of sexual fantasies in books, magazines, movies, plays, and the like can lead to the actual behavior depicted—so the

---

4. It should perhaps be noted that the attitude that Lawrence (author of the notorious *Lady Chatterley's Lover*) execrates is one that he detects in *Jane Eyre*, and Wagner's *Tristan*, and *Anna Karenina*, and "nearly all nineteenth-century literature"—as well as less literary and more lurid "underworld" productions—for, according to Lawrence, "as soon as there is sex excitement with a desire to spite the sexual feeling, to humiliate it, and degrade it, the element of pornography enters." What he advocates is "a natural fresh openness about sex" (Lawrence 1961, 69–70). The great error is to confuse "sex appeal" (or what the language of constitutional interpretation refers to as "appeal to prurient interest") as in and of itself pornographic (65).

harm in behavior becomes grounds for controlling fantasy, at least published fantasy. Does pornography lead to rape? There is no persuasive evidence that it does. And given that the presumption should, as John Stuart Mill argued in *On Liberty*, always be in favor of liberty, the burden falls on those who would limit free expression whether by censorship or by other means. Much of the social science evidence is surveyed and summarized in the British *Williams Report* on *Obscenity and Film Censorship* (Williams 1979). The report concludes, in relation to one central issue, "there does not appear to be any strong evidence that exposure to sexually explicit material triggers off anti-social sexual behaviour" (66). The anecdotal, statistical, and experimental evidence is mostly inconclusive—and, as I have said, given presumptions in favor of liberty, the burden is on those who would restrict.

The *Williams Report* speaks of one typical sort of experiment and its rather question-begging results. "A common tool in studying imitative violence is the Bobo doll, an inflatable toy with a weighted base which resumes an upright position after being knocked over, and a number of studies have observed the reactions of children toward such a doll after they have seen an adult assaulting it" (67). It turns out that observing fantasy violence does sometimes lead to more fantasy violence in the play of children, but that tells us little about whether it leads to violence in real life. Indeed, sexually explicit and even violent images may be a safety valve, giving a harmless outlet to fantasies that might otherwise insist on manifesting themselves in reality. And it is the underlying desires, not the fantasies, that lead to action. Or must one suppose that individuals could not think up sexual and other forms of aggressive activity without the aid of external images to give them the idea and the impulse? The history of such activities before the wide availability of commercial images goes to the contrary. And even if it were shown that pornography (and fantasies) lead to publicly important harms, drawing lines around preventive measures might prove very difficult. As the *Williams Report* states: "The net would have to be cast very wide to prevent actual events from being influenced undesirably by what people see" (65). Is one to prohibit anti-rape films such as *The Accused* (which contains a fairly graphic depiction of a gang rape) in an effort to prevent rape? What of the story of a young boy who self-asphyxiated while sexually stimulated by the image of a bound woman being tortured? The image was in fact of Joan of Arc at the stake (63). Are all such potentially stimulating religious images to be expunged from the public arena? (Some regard the violence in Mel Gibson's *The Passion of the Christ* as appealing to sadomasochistic and pornographic interests.) How far ought society to go? After all, ads for luxury goods may induce fantasies and desires that increase the number of actual robberies and thefts.

There is a rather different sort of argument, associated especially with Catharine MacKinnon, that the harmful impact of pornography is not so much causal as constitutive. Of course speech can have later effects in the world, but as we have noted, sometimes the effects are peculiarly direct, the mere saying (under the appropriate conditions) can make something so — as spelled out in J. L. Austin's theory of performative utterances. MacKinnon claims that pornographic speech itself constitutes the subordination of women.

> Pornography does not simply express or interpret experience; it substitutes for it . . . Pornography brings its conditions of production to the consumer: sexual dominance . . . Pornography makes the world a pornographic place through its making and use, establishing what women are said to exist as, are seen as, are treated as, constructing the social reality of what a woman is and can be in terms of what can be done to her, and what a man is in terms of doing it . . . In pornography, pictures and words are sex. At the same time, in the world pornography creates, sex is pictures and words. As sex becomes speech, speech becomes sex. (1993, 25–26)[5]

There are at least two problems with this performative, illocutionary, constructive, or constitutive argument against pornography (when it is not simply a confused version of perlocutionary causal claims). First, while the speech act in a performative utterance may be in some sense complete on utterance, it may not always be successful. That is, it may be (in Austin's terminology) "infelicitous." To be effective, a performative must be performed under the appropriate conditions. Things can go

---

5. MacKinnon often writes as though all pornography is of the sort that depicts the explicit subjugation of women by men, as in rape scenes. Aside from the genre that depicts men being whipped and abused by dominant women, this seems to neglect the existence of gay and lesbian pornography, in which members of the opposite sex may not even appear. MacKinnon's response, "the one to whom it is done is the girl regardless of sex" (1989, 211), seems perversely inadequate to the diversity of the phenomena. Worse, in addition to begging the question, it would seem self-defeating for a feminist to insist on an *a priori* equation of being female with submissiveness.

wrong in all sorts of ways (many of which are spelled out by Austin in his *How to Do Things with Words*).

But, more important, pornographic speech and images may not be performative, in the sense of creating the reality they depict, at all. MacKinnon insists that "the message of these materials . . . is 'get her,' pointing at all women" (1993, 21). But what MacKinnon reads as an (inevitably effective) imperative to subordinate women, may simply be a depiction of women "as if" submissive. That is, instead of a constitution or representation of reality, pornographic imagery may function as, in the terminology of Judith Butler's critique of MacKinnon, "a phantasmatic scene of willfulness and submission" as "allegory" depicting "compensatory ideals, hyperbolic gender norms" (Butler 1997, 65–69). Misogynist pornography may function as wishful thinking while recognizing its unrealizability, while recognizing that (in reality) not all women are images of voluptuous and available perfection nor are men always attractive and potent. It may function as, in a word, fantasy.

And once again, all of this leaves open (among many other questions) the question of whether pornography may sometimes function as a safety valve, providing a relatively harmless release for impulses and desires that have a source independent of pornography and that (in the absence of the availability of pornography) might have truly abhorrent outcomes. The notion that fantasies, including fantasies provided commercially in the form of pornography, can serve as a safety valve is complemented by Freud's suggestion (speaking not of pornography but of more austere creative writing) that imaginative literature provides both a kind of bonus pleasure derived from the form of presentation and a liberating possibility of self-acceptance: "In my opinion, all the aesthetic pleasure which a creative writer affords us has the character of a fore-pleasure . . . and our actual enjoyment of an imaginative work proceeds from a liberation of tensions in our minds. It may even be that not a little of this effect is due to the writer's enabling us thenceforward to enjoy our own day-dreams without self-reproach or shame" (1908e, 153; see Neu 2002c).

HATE SPEECH

Words have effects in the world and sometimes their transformative power is peculiarly direct, constructing and constituting the world. And sometimes the effects are disturbingly vile. Hate speech in particular is designed to make individuals feel demeaned, despised, and rejected. And aside from causing emotional injury and other harm to individuals, it can harm interests in community: in civil relations, in equality and non-discrimination, and in peaceful and nonhostile environments for work, education, and the other pursuits that must take place in an interactive setting. Hate speech, it could be fairly argued, does no good. If the arguments for privileging speech depended on the good that it does, it might seem that there is no brief to be made for hate speech, that is, the willful denigration of others based on their race, gender, sexual orientation, ethnic origin, religion, or other group characteristics. But leaving aside the fact that all abusive speech might be construed as hate speech, at least when it is not merely the spewing of generic and unspecified venom, because it may always be seen as picking out a property that might constitute the distinctive and defining property of a group (the stupid, the over-weight, the mean-spirited, the sexually anomalous, and on indefinitely), there are arguments for protecting hate speech—not encouraging it, but also not legally penalizing it. These arguments may not be decisive and absolute, for there may be contexts where such speech has features that make it simply intolerable (e.g., when it is a part of personal and persistent harassment, or direct incitement to or threat of violence, or intimidation of members of historically vulnerable groups). But susceptibility to contextual complication and so prohibition is a feature of all speech, not just abusive or hate speech. The arguments for protecting hate speech have to do with securing the protection of more obviously valuable speech; with the value to individuals of being able to express even their reprehensible views, even in vile terms, and the value to society of being aware of those views (which might persist even if their expression were suppressed) and being better able to confront and perhaps change them; and finally with the difficulties of drawing lines and the costs of enforcing controls.

There is no doubt that hate speech can cause a variety of harms, and where it is directed at members of minorities and other historically victimized groups it can be especially hurtful. In such cases, individual psychological trauma may be exacerbated by wider attitudes of denigration and oppressive social structures; and, reciprocally, the emotional distress caused in individuals may reinforce wider patterns of subordination. A safe and nonthreatening environment for work, for learning, for life, may be the right of all and may be especially necessary to and prized by those to whom it has been too often denied. The problem remains of how to achieve such an environment, and in particular whether underlying invidious attitudes can be overcome through controlling their expression in speech.

Many of the harms are catalogued and documented in a collection of essays by a group of legal scholars entitled, *Words that Wound: Critical Race Theory, Assaultive Speech, and the First Amendment* (Matsuda et al, 1993). Many of the difficulties are thoughtfully and, to my mind, compellingly presented in an essay written in response to that volume by Henry Louis Gates, Jr., "War of Words: Critical Race Theory and the First Amendment" (1994). Again we have the alternatives of the causal or the constitutive, the perlocutionary or performative, workings of words.

Charles R. Lawrence III, in the course of an argument for campus speech codes, insists that racial invective "functions as a preemptive strike . . . a blow, not a proffered idea," subordinating and silencing rather than furthering discussion (Lawrence 1993, 68). But at the same time, as if in refutation of his own claim, he brings out that there is indeed a message in hate speech, a denigrating and discriminatory message, and in the end it is the same message that he finds in the racial segregation condemned in *Brown v. Board of Education* (1954). That a message is despicable does not make it any less a message. That the message of racial invective may reduce to a vulgar version of "I despise you" or "you are worthless" does not denude it of content (Gates 1994, 30, 26). And Gates brings out that suppressing the message, whether it takes a verbal or behavioral form, does not overcome the underlying problem. Racial redlining by bankers is no less racist and discriminatory if people are unaware of it, if the message is not broadcast (Gates 1994, 54). The attitudinal issues take concrete form.

Efforts to control hate speech have been most prominent in recent years in the form of speech codes on college campuses. That might seem strange, if only because in that setting hate speech has a greater tendency to discredit the speaker than to persuade or win approval from others.[6] (Part of the explanation for the prevalence of campus codes may be found in the fact that private universities, unlike public universities, are not generally

---

6. Celebrity bad-mouthers, from Mel Gibson to Michael Richards, also face informal pressures, regularly leading them to retreat behind alcoholism and other excuses. (As formerly successful *Seinfeld* star Michael Richards made his round of apologies for N-wording two black hecklers at a comedy club, he was quick to proclaim, "Let the healing begin.") Others, from trial witnesses such as Mark Fuhrman to politicians such as Trent Lott, also have reason to deny or distance themselves from evidences of racism.

regarded as state agencies and so may not be fully subject to the constraints of the First Amendment, which are constraints on state action. Other aspects of the situation and special pressures on campuses are brought out by Gould 2005.) Whether words function as blows or messages, the problem remains of specifying the words that wound. What speech exactly is to be subject to control? In order to avoid curtailing discussion of controversial issues just because they are controversial (which might be death to the sort of free inquiry universities are designed to foster), campus speech codes are often narrowly drawn. They often limit themselves to abusive language directly addressed to despised individuals. The model of "fighting words" is to the fore. For example, the cautiously drawn Stanford Code requires direct address and is restricted to "personal vilification" that is "intended to insult or stigmatize" and "makes use of insulting or 'fighting' words or non-verbal symbols" (Lawrence 1993, 67). But even the most cautiously crafted code may have trouble with borderline cases. In 1993, a white freshman at the University of Pennsylvania was brought up on charges (ultimately dropped) for calling a group of black sorority girls, whose raucous celebrating had disturbed his tranquility, "water buffalo." (Penn's hate speech policy was abolished two years later—Gould 2005, 20–21.) But politely worded speech that clearly stands outside of and so circumvents the "fighting words" standard may be far more troubling than any borderline cases.

The Stanford Code elaborates its standard to apply only to words "which are commonly understood to convey direct and visceral hatred or contempt for human beings on the basis of their sex, race, color, handicap, religion, sexual orientation, or national and ethnic origin." Gates invites us to consider two statements addressed to a black freshman at Stanford:

(A) LeVon, if you find yourself struggling in your classes here, you should realize it isn't your fault. It's simply that you're the beneficiary of a disruptive policy of affirmative action that places underqualified, underprepared, and often undertalented black students in demanding educational environments like this one. The policy's egalitarian aims may be well intentioned, but given the fact that aptitude tests place African-Americans almost a full standard deviation below the mean, even controlling for socioeconomic disparities, they are also profoundly misguided. The truth is, you probably don't belong here, and your college experience will be a long downhill slide.

(B) Out of my face, jungle bunny. (Gates 1994, 46–47)

The politely worded insult is doubtless more wounding and alienating, and yet it is only the crudely worded insult that is likely to be caught in the Code's net. The restrictions have not gone very far toward creating a comfortable and welcoming environment. Hate speech codes may only restrict vulgar speech, which in any case (as noted) tends itself to discredit the user, especially on university campuses. If one seeks to go further and attempts to extend the net to even politely worded speech that individuals find demeaning and injurious, one risks cutting off the free exchange of views that is essential to truly advancing understanding, and risks foreclosing the preferred remedy of "more speech." That is how things have in fact often played out.

The University of Michigan's 1988 "Policy on Discrimination and Discriminatory Harassment of Students in the University Environment" went beyond "fighting words" to reach ideas that people found obnoxious, however they might be worded. It covered "Any behavior, verbal or physical, that stigmatizes or victimizes an individual on the basis of race, ethnicity, religion, sex, sexual orientation, creed, national origin, ancestry, age, marital status, handicap or Vietnam-era veteran status" (*Doe v. University of Michigan*, 721 F. Supp. 852, 856 [E.D. Mich. 1989]). Notice first of all the creeping extension of protected groups. Who may insult whom? If the fundamental purpose is to protect all from "an intimidating, hostile, or demeaning environment," it is not clear how any limit is to be drawn. And in particular hate speech by minorities against members of socially dominant groups might fall under the net. In practice, it has often been minorities who have been prosecuted under municipal statutes and disciplined under university codes. Second, and in a university context especially disturbing, hateful ideas (even politely expressed) are denied the scrutiny and examination needed to refute them. The campus locations concentrated on by the Michigan code were in fact the central sites for analysis and critique: "educational and academic centers, such as classroom buildings, libraries, research laboratories, recreation and study centers" (856). It may be true that sometimes silent dismissal of Holocaust deniers and their ilk may be all that is required, but where there are arguments that need confronting, keeping them from being stated does not count as refutation and does not change any minds—especially not the prejudiced ones whose mouths might have been silenced. An authoritative interpretive guide issued by the Michigan University Office of Affirmative Action provided examples of sanctionable conduct, including: "A male student makes remarks in class like 'Women just aren't as good in this field as men,' thus creating a hostile learning atmosphere for female classmates" and "You laugh at a joke about someone in your class who stutters" (858). In an actual incident, a black graduate student in the School of Social Work at the University of Michigan had to face a formal disciplinary hearing under the antidiscrimination policy. He did not attack any individual, but he put forward in a research class the position that homosexuality was a disease and indicated he hoped to develop a plan for overcoming it through counseling (861, 865). However benighted his view, one might have thought it just the sort of position that ought to be open to examination, rather than silencing, at a university.

Stanley Fish claims that those who argue academic communities must value freedom more than speech codes are mistaken because communities must have limits in order to define their membership (1994, 108). Even if that were so, one can still argue about the proper limits, and there should always be room to ask: Why protect only some groups from insult? It is also to be remembered that rights in general, and the right to freedom of expression in particular, are antimajoritarian. If you have a right, that others—even a majority of others—would prefer you not exercise it does not cancel that right. If you have a right to speak, that most people might prefer not to hear you does not authorize them to shut you up. Fish insists that what speech is protected is really a matter of politics, not principle—"That is how George Bush can argue *for* flag-burning statutes and *against* campus hate-speech codes" (110). Fish treats the First Amendment as a pious mythology. Which, if taken as absolute or as built on a clear distinction between speech and action, it is. That some people may apply their principles inconsistently and that all of us may sometimes find our principles challenged and difficult to stand by, does not mean that the principles do not exist or that they do not have serious weight. They continue to provide significant protection from the tyranny of the majority. Even Fish admits that questionable First Amendment formulas that are subject to political manipulation "slow down outcomes in an area in which the fear of overhasty outcomes is justified by a long record of abuses of power" (113).

It may be that certain sorts of discomfort are to be expected and even desired in an educational environment, in particular the sort of discomfort that may come from confronting previously unexamined beliefs and attitudes. But the notion of a "hostile environment" brings into play the instructive model of sexual harassment law. It may be that MacKinnon's contributions to understanding sexual harassment in the workplace are more valuable than assaultive models of hate speech, on analogy to MacKinnon's views of pornography or appeals to the troubled doctrine of "fighting words." MacKinnon's arguments in an early book, *Sexual Harassment of Working Women* (1979), helped shape the modern tort of sexual harassment. Sexual harassment law has two branches, one concerning "quid pro quo" arrangements ("you do what I want and I'll give you what you want") and the other concerning a "hostile work environment" (the need for a nonthreatening and nondiscriminatory workplace). Speech and behavior can make a work situation untenable; they can amount to impermissible discrimination. That provides perhaps the strongest argument for hate speech codes on university campuses. A "hostile learning environment" may also be insufferable. But one should recall that sexual harassment in the workplace requires repeated and persistent abuses and is typically directed at particular individuals. Some on campuses may be discomfited and offended by words used on a single occasion, even when those words are themselves polite. One must be careful about what is excluded, what is protected, and at what cost, and whether (on the campus at least) there are alternative, less costly and troubling, remedies. After all, education is supposed to be disruptive, unsettling comfortable convictions.

Tolerating does not amount to endorsing, especially where all views can be openly expressed and contested. Mari J. Matsuda argues that when racist speech goes unpunished in the university, the university is perceived as "taking sides" (1993, 44–45). It shouldn't be. Henry Louis Gates, Jr. pointedly asks, "Why is it 'mere words' when a university condemns racist speech, but not when the student utters the abusive words in the first place? Whose words are 'only words'? Why are racist words deeds, but anti-racist words just lip service?" (1994, 39). Commitment to freedom of speech may sometimes appear to come into tension with promoting equality, but the very point of freedom of speech is to protect unpopular opinions (which may, it must be admitted, be uncivil, may be irrational, may even be wrong and wrong-headed) from suppression by the majority. And one should not be too quick in assuming what view the majority holds or that the view the majority holds is the correct one. Matsuda tells us that racist speech is "universally condemned"

(37). But that is surely false. The racists who use such speech obviously do not condemn it. And if there were no racists, there would be no call for codes to constrain them. Charles R. Lawrence III, who is with Matsuda in arguing for speech codes, sees racist speech as a manifestation of a "ubiquitous and deeply ingrained cultural belief system" (Lawrence 1993, 74). Racists may in some places be the majority. But then, who are the "racists"? This may be a difficult and contested matter in a world divided into Hutus and Tutsis, Palestinians and Israelis, Irish Protestants and Irish Catholics. Part of the point of our risky commitment to the airing of objectionable views is that, under the right conditions, views can shift—both minority views and majority views. In the history of the United States, there was a crucial shift between *Plessy v. Ferguson* (1896) and *Brown v. Board of Education of Topeka* (1954) on the constitutionality of segregation. A shift may take place first at the level of the Supreme Court or it may work its way up from wider political and social arenas, but surely universities ought to be part of the conversation (as they were in contributing to the Supreme Court's shift on "separate but equal"). Is it possible to write a statute that cuts off polite disparagement without also stifling the expression of invidious views that need exposure to discussion and critique? A federal district court overturned the Michigan policy as unconstitutionally overbroad (both on its face and as applied) and impermissibly vague (*Doe v. University of Michigan*, 721 F. Supp. 852, 866, 867 [E.D. Mich. 1989]). If academic institutions seek to protect what all right-thinking people know from criticism, we must be prepared to discover, at some point and whatever our views, that we are not counted among the right thinking by the powers-that-be. Silencing is a dangerous weapon. Once drawn, it can be pointed at anyone. Voltaire understood this perfectly well.

In practice, who gets shut up? Not surprisingly, it is often the very minorities that the First Amendment and the supporters of speech codes aim to protect. Gates offers a telling example of the discriminatory enforcement of "fighting words" statutes: "An apparently not atypical conviction—upheld by the Louisiana state court—was occasioned by the following exchange between a white police officer and the black mother of a young suspect. He: 'Get your black ass in the goddamned car.' She: 'You god damn mother fucking police—I am going to [the Superintendent of Police] about this.' No prize for guessing which one was convicted for uttering 'fighting words'" (1994, 25; see *Lewis v. City of*

New Orleans, 415 U.S. 130 [1974]). It may be recalled that Chaplinsky himself claimed that the "fighting words" for which he was prosecuted were preceded by similar abuse directed at him by the marshall who arrested him.

Gates cites other examples where regimes of hate speech regulation end up getting used as weapons against minorities. In Canada, a version of MacKinnon's statutory definition of pornography was adopted and "the first casualty of the MacKinnonite anti-obscenity ruling was a gay and lesbian bookshop in Toronto, which was raided by the police because of a lesbian magazine it carried. (Homosexual literature is a frequent target of Canada's restrictions on free expression.)" And "copies of a book widely assigned in women's studies courses, *Black Looks: Race and Representation* by the well-known black feminist scholar bell hooks, was confiscated by Canadian authorities as possible 'hate literature'" (Gates 1994, 43; a fuller account of the Canadian experience can be found in Sumner 2004).

Once one has expanded the area where speech can be restricted, the government has a tool that can be used to harass minority groups or minority opinions and to suppress dissident speech. The lesson of recent history is that, too often, that is just what happens (Note, 106 *Harv. L. Rev.* 1129, 1142–45 [1993]). Kathleen M. Sullivan puts the point well, "One argument for presumptive commitment to content neutrality is that gearing the First Amendment for the worst of times requires practice even in the best. A benevolent government promoting messages of racial equality one day may be taken over by rogues the next, and content neutrality is an emergency preparedness device" (1992, 40).

The risks of misdirection and abuse, which should be of concern to all, are not the only costs of silencing. Some of the dangers of banning hate speech may be to the individuals putatively being protected. Sullivan provides a useful summary: "Bans on hate speech may have perverse effects: they may replicate the very marginalization that they are meant to subvert, carrying a subtext that the victims cannot talk back for themselves. They may stifle in the name of civility and reason the most empowering responses, which sometimes consist of shouting back angrily in like kind. They may backfire by turning the haters into martyrs, giving their hate speech magnified publicity and effect. And by punishing a periphery of extreme outbursts, they may perversely reinforce a core of 'politer' racist thoughts" (Sullivan 1992, 40).

MORE SPEECH

As Justice Holmes pointed out (in ringing dissent), freedom of speech is needed to protect the idea that we hate. Inoffensive ideas that we agree with need no such shield. As he famously put it: "if there is any principle of the Constitution that more imperatively calls for attachment than any other it is the principle of free thought—not free thought for those who agree with us but freedom for the thought that we hate" (*United States v. Schwimmer*, 279 U.S. 644, 655 [1929]).

When the Chaplinsky court carved out its "fighting words" exception to freedom of speech, it wrote:

> There are certain well-defined and narrowly limited classes of speech, the prevention and punishment of which has never been thought to raise any Constitutional problem. These include the lewd and obscene, the profane, the libelous, and the insulting or "fighting" words—those which by their very utterance inflict injury or tend to incite an immediate breach of the peace. It has been well observed that such utterances are no essential part of any exposition of ideas, and are of such slight social value as a step to truth that any benefit that may be derived from them is clearly outweighed by the social interest in order and morality. (315 U.S. 568, 571–72)

The last point is meant to refute the "marketplace of ideas" argument for freedom of speech. Being more like a physical blow, having no substantive ideational content, hate speech might be thought to have no value calling for constitutional protection. But that is to neglect that, however repugnant, hate speech may indeed have content, be more than a blow, and by its manner give greater force and clearer expression to the attitudes manifested. It is also to neglect that in addition to the marketplace of ideas, freedom of speech is meant to serve the values of self-expression and self-fulfillment, which may have more to do with the interests of producers than consumers. Even if a pornographic image has no intellectual content (though MacKinnon tries to have this both ways, likening pornographic speech to a physical assault and yet ascribing it constitutive attitude-shaping content), it may give expression to certain interests and allow certain life choices a say in the conversation of society (Dworkin 1996). Finally, speech has an emotive impact in addition to whatever cognitive content it may convey, and that makes for a communicative value that the Supreme Court has recognized in various decisions, notably *Cohen v. California*, 403 U.S. 15 (1971). That case involved a Vietnam War protester entering a courthouse wearing a jacket emblazoned with the phrase "Fuck the Draft." Justice Harlan wrote for the *Cohen* majority, "much linguistic expression serves a dual communicative function: it conveys not only ideas capable of relatively precise, detached explication, but otherwise inexpressible emotions as well. In fact, words are often chosen as much for their emotive as their cognitive force. We cannot sanction the view that the Constitution, while solicitous of the cognitive content of individual speech, has little or no regard for that emotive function which, practically speaking, may often be the more important element of the overall message sought to be communicated" (26). As the Court also noted, since "one man's vulgarity is another's lyric," allowing the regulation of speech to promote general tranquility might create an "inherently boundless" censorship (25).

What is wanted is more speech, not less. When antigay Christian fundamentalists bring their "Fags Will Burn in Hell" signs to San Francisco's gay Castro district, they are met by prancing Sisters of Perpetual Indulgence (a group of drag queens in nuns' habits). Venomous condemnation is answered by flamboyant ridicule. When the Nazis march in Skokie, what is needed is a counter-demonstration. When someone burns a flag, waving and saluting are, as Justice Brennan counseled, the way to honor it. That "more speech" is the most appropriate remedy for objectionable speech is a corollary to the traditional "marketplace of ideas" defense of free speech. Justice Brandeis provided the classic statement:

> Those who won our independence believed that the final end of the State was to make men free to develop their faculties; and that in its government the deliberative forces should prevail over the arbitrary. They valued liberty both as an end and as a means. They believed liberty to be the secret of happiness and courage to be the secret of liberty. They believed that freedom to think as you will and to speak as you think are means indispensable to the discovery and spread of political truth; that without free speech and assembly discussion would be futile; that with them, discussion affords ordinarily adequate protection against the dissemination of noxious doctrine; that the greatest menace to freedom is an inert people; that public discussion is a political duty; and that this should be a fundamental principle of the American government. They recognized the risks to which all human institutions are subject. But they knew that order cannot

be secured merely through fear of punishment for its infraction; that it is hazardous to discourage thought, hope and imagination; that fear breeds repression; that repression breeds hate; that hate menaces stable government; that the path of safety lies in the opportunity to discuss freely supposed grievances and proposed remedies; and that the fitting remedy for evil counsels is good ones. Believing in the power of reason as applied through public discussion, they eschewed silence coerced by law—the argument of force in its worst form. Recognizing the occasional tyrannies of governing majorities, they amended the Constitution so that free speech and assembly should be guaranteed.

Fear of serious injury cannot alone justify suppression of free speech and assembly. Men feared witches and burnt women. It is the function of speech to free men from the bondage of irrational fears. . . . Those who won our independence by revolution were not cowards. They did not fear political change. They did not exalt order at the cost of liberty. To courageous, self-reliant men, with confidence in the power of free and fearless reasoning applied through the processes of popular government, no danger flowing from speech can be deemed clear and present, unless the incidence of the evil apprehended is so imminent that it may befall before there is opportunity for full discussion. If there be time to expose through discussion the falsehood and fallacies, to avert the evil by the processes of education, the remedy to be applied is more speech, not enforced silence. Only an emergency can justify repression. Such must be the rule if authority is to be reconciled with freedom. Such, in my opinion, is the command of the Constitution.

. . . Among free men, the deterrents ordinarily to be applied to prevent crime are education and punishment for violations of the law, not abridgment of the rights of free speech and assembly. (*Whitney v. California*, 274 U.S. 357, 375–78 [1927])

PERFORMATIVE UTTERANCES

Since Austin's performative analysis of language provides much of the inspiration for the understanding of fighting words as first blows, of pornography as sex discrimination, and hate speech as subordination, we should conclude by a closer consideration of aspects of that analysis. We have already noted that it should not be surprising that the constitutional distinction between speech and conduct cannot actually do much work, not only because explicit performative utterances reveal that saying can be doing, and because conduct can convey messages, but also because, in the end, all statements may have a performative aspect and even performative utterances may have, like constative ones, a significant reliance and relationship with facts about how the world is. Explicit performative verbs, however, remain interesting.

Austin points out that there is no distinctive performative verb for insulting (1970b, 245). Unlike "I reprimand you" or "I censure you," we don't have a normal use for "I insult you" (though the Germans in the days of dueling were occasionally known to say things like "consider yourself slapped"—McAleer 1994, 47–48). This leaves room for occasional ambiguity. Having an explicit performative verb can help resolve ambiguity. Saying "I shall be there" might be a promise, or an expression of intention, or a forecast of future behavior, of what is going to happen to me, or any number of other things. Saying "I promise" or (in one of Austin's standard variant forms) "I hereby promise" resolves the ambiguity. "I hereby insult you" does not effect the designated act. But that does not mean that insulting is not a speech act of a performative sort, with a conventionally given significance.

Insulting can in fact often be ambiguous, our words can be misapprehended. Sometimes we ourselves may not be sure of our intentions or we may, without any intention, but in fact and in effect, insult. Nonetheless, despite the absence of an explicit performative verb and with all the attendant possible confusions, we do have all sorts of words and all sorts of means of making our point. This is, as Austin explains, the normal situation for doing things by saying things, even when an explicit performative might also be available. Explicit performative verbs are not essential to performative utterance.

"I will do it, count on it" is as much a promise as "I promise I'll do it." One can make one's point in a variety of ways. "Shut the door" may do duty (perhaps sometimes ambiguous duty) for "I order you to shut the door." And manner can be as crucial as matter. As Austin says, "There are a great many devices that can be used for making clear, even at the primitive level, what act it is we are performing when we say something—the tone of voice, cadence, gesture—and above all we can rely upon the nature of the circumstances, the context in which the utterance is issued" (Austin 1970b, 244). In the realm of insult, we have already discussed aspects of our distinctive language of abuse, and there are even syntactical markers

and canonical formulas. Everyone understands that a statement introduced by "Yo momma" is meant as an insult, usually a playful one. The
quality of imagination exhibited does not much matter (e.g., "Yo momma
is so fat she sweats Ragu"). "Yo momma" syntactically marks the start of
an insult. Such insults may these days be as common among trash-talk-
ing athletes as among dozens-playing adolescents. Contemporary trash
talking, from basketball to soccer, may involve less structured disses than
are typical of the dozens, but it usually maintains the distinction between
clowning and disrespecting as well as the focus on family. (According to
some accounts, the focus was maintained though the distinction failed in
the case of Materazzi's triggering words to head-butting Zidane.)

Austin's suggested reason for the absence of a performative verb for
insulting, namely, our low esteem for the practice ("since apparently we
don't approve of insulting, we have not evolved a simple formula 'I insult
you'"—245), is not particularly persuasive. We may approve more of flattering than insulting, but we still cannot flatter by saying "I hereby flatter
you." Or if flattering is thought to share the low esteem of its opposite, we
can still find any number of generally approved practices—for instance,
praising—that have not evolved simple explicit performative formulas.
More important, as Wilde reminds us, insults do have their place. There
is even a minor subliterature of effective insults.[7] And again, we do have
a wealth of conventionally obscene language, profanities and vulgarities,
that typically breaks verbal taboos and yet plays a distinctively significant
role in our insulting discourse. The vocabulary of abuse can be useful.
And in addition to "Yo momma"–type formulas, we have a range of verbs
(from "I wish to excoriate" to "I hereby denounce" to, the elliptical, "fuck
you") that, in context, make it clear an insult is intended.

To recur for a moment to our earlier discussion, restrictions on hate
speech that confine themselves to profane and vulgar language would
doubtless be underinclusive, omitting politely worded insults, and thus
failing to serve much of the protective purpose envisioned. And if one
sought to prohibit politely worded insults as well, one would risk stifling
all controversial discourse—after all, some might take offense at any

---

7. There are any number of collections (e.g., McPhee 1980). There is even a journal that keeps track of developments worldwide, *Maledicta: The International Journal of
Verbal Aggression*.

questioning of their commitments. Worse, since insults need not be verbal, those who aspire to impose civilization and good will and avoid the wounds of insult will find their work is barely started even should they succeed in limiting words that wound. And that would be the most that could be limited, for the attitudes and desires that lead people to insult others, the underlying causes (the various incentives and drives to put down and belittle and ignore), would not be addressed. And the stifling of discussion of volatile issues might ensure that those underlying causes never can be addressed.

We have seen repeatedly that, despite whatever resources may be available, intentions can be unclear. Must an utterance or action have the actual effect of producing offense in order for it to count as an insult? Is the mere, though perhaps ineffectual, intention to offend enough? (On a Gricean model [1989], in order for an utterance or act to be meant as an insult, the speaker must intend the utterance to be an insult and that intention must be, or be capable of being, recognized as such by the object of the insult or a third party, a reasonable third party who understands the relevant reigning social conventions.) Certainly, as we have noted, some may feel offended when no offense is meant. Some, that is, are oversensitive. Some make mistakes. Though, it is to be remembered, some may in fact be accurate readers of the thoughtless affronts perpetrated by others. There are unintentional insults. But here the question is whether a bare intention to offend is enough to constitute an insult, when no offense is taken. Well, have you "warned" someone if they do not hear your shouts? Certainly you have tried to warn, you have attempted to warn, but whether that is enough to count as warning depends, I want to say, on one's purposes in asking.

Two useful ways of thinking about the issues here can be found in Austin's theory of speech acts and in Ryle's notion of "success verbs" (1949, 149–53). First, speech acts. Austin distinguishes three types of uses of sentences or things we do in saying something: a *locutionary* act is the speaker's act of saying whatever it is he says, "which is roughly equivalent to uttering a certain sentence with a certain sense and reference, which again is roughly equivalent to 'meaning' in the traditional sense"; an *illocutionary* act is one performed *in* saying something, "such as informing, ordering, warning, undertaking, etc., i.e., utterances which have a certain (conventional) force," i.e., performative utterances; and a *perlocutionary* act is "what we bring about or achieve *by* saying something, such as convincing, persuading, deterring, and even, say, surprising or misleading" (Austin 1962, 108). Illocutionary acts (if felicitous) are complete at the time of speaking and rely on convention. Perlocutionary acts have later consequences and rely on causing effects. The difference between illocutionary and perlocutionary is the difference between the constitutive and causal analyses of fighting words, pornography, and hate speech that we have been considering.

But illocutionary acts are not inevitably successful, things can go wrong. One kind of infelicity Austin draws attention to is "securing uptake" of performative utterances. Has one "warned" if one speaks *sotto voce* and is not heard or "protested" if one's words are not taken as a protest (1962, 138)? Has one insulted if the object of one's invective is not offended? Or is that a perlocutionary effect rather than an uptake condition? We may wish to think of insulting as illocutionary (complete on speaking, as "arguing" is) and offending as perlocutionary (a causal effect, as "convincing" is). But, then, when I insult someone without their feeling insulted, that is, perform an illocutionary act without uptake, is that an infelicitous illocutionary act or a failed perlocutionary effect? Certainly unintentional insults would seem best understood as perlocutionary effects (Butler 1997, 17; Austin 1962, 106–7). The tension, or perhaps even collapse, of the illocutionary/perlocutionary divide is really just a special instance of the inherent flexibility of action description. We can (depending on our purposes) build more or fewer consequences into the description of a given act. Was my action "pulling a trigger" with the consequence that someone died, or was my action "killing that person" with the consequences, whatever they were, all being subsequent to his or her death? And this is really part of a yet more general difficulty about the specification of action: actions may be described, understood, and interpreted on many levels, and the level of conscious intention is only one among them, and not necessarily the most important. Moreover, very different bodily movements may make for the same action—a man signing his name, if he is a governor signing a death warrant, may be as much killing someone as a man pulling a trigger. And a further intention may make the same bodily movement into a different action—consider wounding done with an intent to kill, as opposed to wounding, as by a surgeon, with intent to heal. How far our intentions carry us may depend, at least in part, on how we wish to describe and delimit actions and their consequences.

Now, is "warn," is "insult," a success verb? "See" and "remember" are success verbs, as is "know." We can only know what is true, remember what happened, or see what is there. For Ryle, a success verb entails the truth of an embedded clause or the achievement of some result. To say "I saw the dagger" is to imply that there actually was a dagger and that my perception was actually caused by it. To say "It was an hallucination" is to refute the claim that "I saw the dagger." I cannot see a dagger when there is none to be seen, any more than I can remember an event that did not happen. Intentions can always fail in their ambitions, but the particular issue (does insulting in fact depend on insulting in effect?) depends, I want to say, on what is at stake. Have you "warned" someone if they don't hear your shouted words? For some purposes, you may have done your duty, all that could be required. For others, perhaps not. Think of a municipality with a duty to warn visitors that certain cliffs by the ocean are dangerous. Is posting a sign enough? Must it be large and readable? What if people never read such signs? Must the city post guards to keep people off the cliffs, whatever the expense? What is the standard of due care, the limit of negligence? Or consider the duty to give legal notice to someone you are suing or evicting. Can they thwart your attempts at notice and so your suit by refusing to accept certified mail and avoiding process-servers? The law has ways of establishing such standards. In the social world of insult, there are some generally accepted conventional standards, but they may be unclear in particular cases. And then I again want to say one has to look at what is at stake, why one is asking about the conditions for insulting, in order to determine whether it is a success verb (so a person has not insulted someone else, whatever their intent, if the victim does not feel insulted). If one is assessing a speaker's character, that they intended to insult may be enough. If assessing damages, it might not be. (And of course, there can be unintentional insults, perhaps even unintentional insults that fail to offend.)

There is magic in imprecations and curses. In the infantile and the primitive mind, the fantasy of the omnipotence of thoughts turns wishes into accomplished deeds, and that mechanism persists in the modern adult mind. The magic of words has its counterpart in the conventional efficaciousness of performative utterances. But all statements may have a performative aspect, at the least, even less florid speech acts amount to the making of statements, which is itself a kind of act in the world which can have effects (both conventional and nonconventional). Putting down others via insult aims at or reflects their being lower on various scales of valuation. Didier Eribon points out that "The act of naming produces an awareness of oneself as other, transformed by others into an object" (Eribon 2004, 16). He is here picking up on Genet's insight about the effect of being declared a "thief" by a judge early in his life. It was a designation that became an identity, an identity that he went on to fulfill luxuriously, elaborately, fully. (The effect is described in Genet's *The Thief's Journal*, and the process was described even more fully by Sartre in his massive *Saint Genet* and discussed in terms of the concept of "interpellation" by Althusser, who develops the notion that calling can be a calling into being in *Lenin and Philosophy* [1971].) Eribon makes his point in the context of homosexual identity, but it extends to every denigrated category, to every discourse of disparagement.

> Insult is a linguistic act—or a series of repeated linguistic acts—by which a particular place in the world is assigned to the person at whom the acts are directed. . . . insult is a performative utterance. Its function is to produce certain effects—notably, to establish or to renew the barrier between 'normal' people and those Goffman calls 'stigmatized' people and to cause the internalization of that barrier within the individual being insulted. Insult tells me what I am to the extent that it makes me be what I am. (Eribon 2004, 17)

SEVEN

∎ ∎ ∎

INSULT IN THE LAW

LIBEL AND SLANDER

OSCAR WILDE WAS UNDONE BY A QUEST FOR SATISFACTION OF HIS honor. But it wasn't a duel, at least not a duel with swords. The field of honor was a British courtroom, and the rules of engagement were set by the law of libel. He had been accused by the ninth Marquess of Queensbury of being a "posing Sodomite" and Wilde sued for the slur. (Wilde had been sharing "the love that dare not speak its name" with the Marquess's spoiled son, Lord Alfred Douglas, aka Bosie, and the ill-tempered and generally brutal Marquess had left his card at Wilde's club with the offending words inscribed—though misspelled "Somdomite.") Unfortunately for Wilde, the slur was essentially correct and the Marquess (using Wilde's writings and letters and the testimony of blackmailing rentboys) was able to prove his case in court. While one may, as we have noted, certainly be insulted by the truth, it remains the case that truth (or, as in this 1895 English case, "justification") is an absolute defense in libel. There were subsequently criminal charges against Wilde and he was on his way to his descent through Reading Gaol. (The full story is well told in Ellmann 1988.) Our concern, however, is not with Wilde's unwise quest for vindication of his honor, nor with the injustice of attitudes toward homosexuality at the time (though the working of related attitudes in more modern libel suits, such as Tom Cruise's over allegations of homosexuality, will be of interest), our concern now is with the recognition and attempts at mitigation of (or compensation for) the harm in insults in the law.

Truth is an absolute defense in libel—at least in modern times and in most jurisdictions.[1] The harm in libel is the publication of falsity, producing damage to reputation, humiliation, and exposure to public ridicule—all of which are also among the standard harms aimed at by insult. These harms subsequent to the spreading of falsity may, of course, also be the result of the spreading of the truth, and yet the truth is privileged in libel law. Individuals may have to pay the price of their damaged reputations when the besmirching is founded on fact, and so the ignominy and ill repute deserved. Libel law is intended to protect individuals only against unfair damage to their reputations, and the emotional distress and shunning and economic harm it may bring in its train. (There are now laws, "Megan's Laws" among them, that sanction and even require the publication of the identities of convicted sex offenders living in a given area. They are thought to have earned their opprobrium.) Not every false statement, however, is an insult. After all, people receive and often welcome undeserved praise and flattery, and other erroneous statements need not reflect badly on their subjects or offend them. But falsity, combined with a negative effect on reputation, does make for libel or slander. The knowing or reckless spreading of falsehoods damaging to individuals is given no intrinsic value, and so no special protection, in our system of freedom of speech.

But the law recognizes many different types of harm, serves many purposes, and provides many grounds of liability, and may in its various doctrines seek to prevent the injuries of insult among others, even when truth is what produces the harms. While telling the truth may never be libel, it may, for example, be invasion of privacy. Violations of rights to privacy do not depend on the falsity of information spread in those instances where the offense is the making public of information which is nobody's business. Nor

---

1. The New York State Constitution of 1821 was one of the first authoritative pronouncements explicitly making truth a question for the jury. In England, it was "Lord Campbell's Libel Act of 1843 [that] allowed truth to be proved as a defense" (*Beauharnais v. Illinois*, 343 U.S. 250, 295–97). In France, in the Press Law of 1881, "legislators hoped to shield private individuals from embarrassing courtroom revelations by instructing magistrates to assess only the degree of offense contained in the slander, forbidding investigation into the truth of the charges. Their laudable intention was to secure personal privacy and to permit the civil rehabilitation of every poor wretch earnestly trying to right some past failing in his life" (Nye 1993, 176). With modern privacy law, there are ways to meet such concerns without hobbling the defense of truth in libel law.

does concern for privacy depend on the disreputable character of the information. People may wish to keep private information about themselves that does not put them in a bad light, simply because it is nobody's business. (Think of the fact that people pay to keep their phone numbers unlisted. Think of how a married couple might feel were telephoto pictures of them making love in the, presumed, privacy of their bedroom published in the press.) So truth is not, at least not always, a defense where the charge is invasion of privacy. What unites utterances which injure an individual because they falsely damage the individual's reputation with utterances which reveal the individual's intimate secrets, "and separates both from most cases of injury caused by talk, is that 'more talk' is exceedingly unlikely to cure the injury: a lie once loosed is hardly quelled by self-serving denials, and once a secret is out of the bag it cannot be put back in again" (Tribe 1988, 838–39). There are, of course, other ways in which the law seeks to restrict insults and their consequences. These include damages for the intentional (and "outrageous") infliction of emotional distress, the regulation of hate speech on campuses, and radical feminist efforts to control pornography.

In the most important modern libel case, *New York Times Co. v. Sullivan*, concern for free and open discussion and debate, especially of matters of public interest, lead the Court to protect even (some) false statements, at least in the case of public officials (and in later cases, public figures).[2] The ensuring of effective self-government through an informed and vigorous democratic process is at least as central to the value of freedom of speech as the pursuit of truth through an open "marketplace of ideas" and the achievement of self-fulfillment through uninhibited "experiments in living." The Court sought to provide immunity from libel suits for "erroneous statements honestly made" in order to free up criticism of officials. The formula in Justice Brennan's opinion for the Court held:

> The constitutional guarantees require, we think, a Federal rule that prohibits a public official from recovering damages for a defamatory falsehood relating to his official conduct unless he proves that the statement was made with "actual malice"—that is, with knowledge that it was false or with reckless disregard of whether it was false or not. (376 U.S. 254, 279–80 [1964]; see also Lewis 1991)

2. In France in the nineteenth century the law of defamation favored public functionaries over private citizens—the penalties for defaming the former were far more severe (Nye 1993, 175).

Notice that the phrase "actual malice" does *not* refer to ill will or evil intentions. In fact, it has nothing in particular to do with motives. The legal notion of malice, like the legal notion of intention in general, has to do with knowledge rather than attitude. (Intention in the criminal law is typically a matter of knowledge of circumstances and foresight of consequences. The ordinary notion of intention adds a concern for desires as well.)[3] The phrase, "with malice aforethought" in many first degree murder statutes typically refers to premeditation, the calculated

---

3. Lawyers (following Jeremy Bentham) distinguish between direct and oblique intentions. Direct intentions, closest to the ordinary notion, involve knowledge of circumstances, foresight of consequences, as well as a desire that the natural consequences ensue from one's doing of the relevant act. Thus a person who pulls the trigger of a gun fully and directly intending the death of the person aimed at (whether or not the bullet in fact hits its mark) both foresees and desires that outcome. The law against murder aims to inhibit that intention. Oblique intention matches the knowledge and foresight conditions of direct intention, but the outcome need not be desired, indeed, the agent may be indifferent to the foreseeable outcome. Thus someone might blow up a bank, wanting only to destroy the building, but recognizing that a building may be occupied even during hours of closing, they are held to intend the death of anyone who happens to be killed by their bomb—not because they desired that death, but because they were willing for it to happen. Indirect or oblique intentions can, from the point of view of the law, be just as lethal as direct ones and it may be equally important to discourage them. Thus, when a statute requires an act be intentional in order for the agent to be fully culpable, indirect intention is generally held to be as culpable as direct intention. Putting it slightly differently: it is one's intention (what one knowingly does), not one's motive (why one does it, the desires behind it), that counts.

So former President Richard Nixon was misunderstanding the nature of *mens rea* and intention in the law when he claimed (in a May 1977 television interview with David Frost) that he had no "criminal intent" in relation to Watergate. In fact, he both knowingly obstructed justice and, indeed, *desired* that justice be obstructed. His intention was "direct." The requirement of "criminal intent" has nothing in particular to do with motive. It is not as though Nixon did not break the law so long as he did not "desire to break the law" as such (act out of a desire to eat forbidden fruit), or so long as his motives were political rather than economic (unlike the typical bank robber's). He intended to do what the law prohibited. He knew it was prohibited. And he desired that the prohibition (against obstructing justice) be overcome. It was his purpose. And, once more, it is the aim of the law to discourage such purposes, and even intentions (knowing actions) that foreseeably achieve such consequences even if the purpose itself is not what motivates in a particular case.

causing of harm. The law's concern is with knowing and intentional, that is, deliberate, action—not with the desires that might motivate such action. (Nonetheless, motives may sometimes mitigate penalties, especially in the eyes of a sentencer sympathetic to an accused's motives, or aggravate them, as when murder is committed for hire or when a particular criminal act is categorized as a "hate crime.") Notice further that the "maliciousness" referred to in the *Sullivan* opinion does not require knowing ("intentional") falsity. "Reckless disregard" of truth is enough to bring with it liability, and "recklessness" is a matter of a knowing disregard of an unjustifiable risk, or as the Court put it in a subsequent case, reckless disregard for the truth encompasses "only those false statements made with [a] high degree of awareness of their probable falsity" (*Garrison v. Louisiana*, 379 U.S. 64, 74 [1964]). Thus a reporter who in good faith (having taken due care to check sources, etc.) publishes a statement about, say, a senator that puts him in a bad light may still have a defense despite the falsity of the statement. A reporter who entertains serious doubts about the truth of his allegations but does not trouble to check sources or take other standard precautions to assure the truth of his statements, may be held liable for his neglect—even if he had no hatred in his heart toward his victim and even if that victim is a public figure.

The high hurdle that *Sullivan* sets for recovering under defamation law follows from "a profound national commitment to the principle that debate on public issues should be uninhibited, robust, and wide-open, and that it may well include vehement, caustic, and sometimes unpleasantly sharp attacks on government and public officials" (*New York Times Co. v. Sullivan*, 276 U.S. 254, 270). This can leave problematical, however, who exactly counts as a public official or public figure for purposes of the rule. A person may be employed by the government, but at a very low level, so all government employees may not count as government officials in relation to a concern for public debate. And celebrity (which may, after all, sometimes merely be the result of the papers having printed a story about one), may not be enough to make one a public figure. So factors such as whether a person has thrust him or herself into a public controversy or otherwise sought public attention, and whether a person has the sort of prominence and celebrity that provides ready access to the media have been taken into consideration by the courts. It may also be that a person is a public figure within a relatively narrowly circumscribed "public" (say, the community of medical doctors), but not in the wider universe. By what standard should their reputation be protected from false charges within their community? Which is the relevant "public"? Again, the *Sullivan* hurdle is high: it is a heavy burden to have to prove the falsity of an allegation as well as knowledge or recklessness in its making; by contrast, ordinary defamation plaintiffs typically have the advantage of presumptions of falsity and of damages as well as strict liability (which obviates inquiry into states of mind) when smeared or maligned. The presumptions and standards can make the difference between winning and losing. (See Lewis 1991 and Jones 2003 for detailed discussion.)

NOT "FIGHTING WORDS"

Defamation (libel where written, slander where spoken) is essentially concerned with damage to reputation, and because of that, unlike "fighting words," there are requirements that the damaging assertions be published and that the assertions at least purport to be factual. That is, direct denunciations or insult of a person is not enough for damage to reputation; third parties must be made aware of the allegations. And there must be allegations. Derogatory opinions alone or emotional expressions of distaste and loathing are not enough, there must be some express or implied assertion of fact. While there can be difficulties in drawing a line between fact and opinion, opinion need not raise issues of truth or falsity, and the law of defamation insists on factual content. This puts the courts into the sometimes difficult position of having to adjudicate claims of fact, but it protects opinion, even highly insulting opinion.[4]

Unbelievable statements that take the apparent form of statements of fact can no more defame than can opinions. One may ridicule and insult with false depictions, but in order to defame they must be at least potentially believable. After all, how else could they be damaging to reputation? Clear fiction, like opinion, is protected. (In this connection, recall how

---

4. In *Gertz v. Robert Welch, Inc.*, 418 U.S. 323, 339–40 (1974), the Court made clear the protected status of "opinion": "Under the First Amendment there is no such thing as a false idea. However pernicious an opinion may seem, we depend for its correction not on the conscience of judges and juries but on the competition of other ideas."

it is the possibility of truth that can mark the line between a ritual insult and a personal insult—what one might call an "actionable" insult—in the dozens.)

The ridicule of satire, which can be politically potent, is a part of the robust climate of open discussion that the courts have sought to preserve. Jerry Falwell, a public figure for all purposes given his prominence as founder of the Moral Majority, sued *Hustler* magazine for a fictitious advertisement entitled "Jerry Falwell talks about his first time." It was modeled on a series of Campari ads of the period and depicted Falwell as engaging in drunken incest with his mother in an outhouse. It also had him saying, "I always get sloshed before I go out to the pulpit. You don't think I could lay down all that bullshit sober, do you?" In addition to the unlikelihood of the portrayal (a trial jury found it could not "reasonably be understood as describing actual facts . . . or events"), the spoof came with an explicit small-print disclaimer: "Ad parody—not to be taken seriously." Even though the main remaining cause of action was intentional infliction of emotional distress (the libel charges and invasion of privacy claims having been dismissed at the earlier trial), the Court held the parody was nonactionable opinion and that even "outrageous" conduct from bad motives does not override the First Amendment's interest in uninhibited open debate when public figures are involved. The point, the Court insisted, applies to deliberately distorting political cartoons and caricatures, though they may well go beyond the bounds of good taste and violate conventional manners (*Hustler Magazine v. Falwell*, 485 U.S. 46, 53–54 [1988]). (This last is a point that will be worth remembering in connection with our consideration in the next chapter of Muslim outrage over Danish cartoons of the Prophet Muhammad.)

One might think that the law of defamation, of libel and slander, is the central law of insults. But it is actually quite narrow in its concerns, given the vast terrain covered by insults. It might be more accurate to think of the adjudication of libel suits as the modern substitute for duels of honor—they both deal with a kind of truth. Traditional duels did not, of course, settle matters of fact in dispute, but they did purport to settle truths of character and standing—not so much by their outcome as by the willingness to engage, the willingness to risk all for honor. The claims at issue in modern libel suits turn on matters of fact, but the particular matters of fact are generally only of interest in so far as they impinge on and have implications for character and reputation. Whether libel suits are any better than traditional duels or trials by combat for adjudicating matters of fact may be questioned. Anthony Lewis (1991) points out a number of difficulties, including how the huge costs of discovery and litigation in modern libel suits may lead to self-censorship and may in the end obscure rather than uncover truth.

Forum shopping can also distort outcomes. Roman Polanski, while residing in France, won a libel suit in England against *Vanity Fair*, an American publication. This occurred at a time when the filmmaker could not return to the United States because of his having fled before sentencing for having had sex with a minor. He did not attend the trial in England, instead testifying via video link, because of the risk of extradition to the United States (Carter 2005). The magazine had claimed in an article that Polanski had propositioned a model in Elaine's in New York while on the way to the funeral of his murdered wife, Sharon Tate, a victim in the 1969 Manson "Helter Skelter" murders. England has neither the First Amendment nor the *Sullivan* hurdle for public figures in its libel law, indeed the defendant has the burden of proof, making the country a favored venue for the questionably reputable maligned.[5]

Given a global economy, the lowest local standards can end up laying down the law for all, leading to enforcement of standards favored by the plaintiffs who choose their forums. In 2003, an Australian court agreed to hear a lawsuit against Dow Jones and Co., the publisher of *Barron's*, concerning an article that had appeared on *Barron's* US-based Web site (*PC Magazine*, 2/25/2003, 8). The Web site is available in Australia, but does that mean local libel laws should apply? After all, Web sites can be viewed from just about anywhere, and if any government objecting to criticism could use its own courts to enforce its own standards, could anyone still speak freely on the Web? The problem has a number of low-tech counterparts. The "contempo-

---

5. In October 2006, in the case of *Jameel v. Wall Street Journal Europe*, the Law Lords for the first time made a significant move in the direction of America's *Sullivan* standards. Journalists were held to have the right to publish allegations concerning public figures (the case concerned a secret United States and Saudi Arabian government antiterrorism program to monitor the bank accounts of prominent Saudi businesses and individuals), provided the reporting is responsible and in the public interest (*New York Times*, 10/13/2006). It is a change that one can hope will ease the chilling effect of earlier British standards, and contribute to the sort of "robust" discussion the First Amendment was designed to encourage after America's revolutionary break with Britain in the eighteenth century.

rary community standards" criterion commonly used in United States obscenity cases (since *Miller v. California*, 413 U.S. 15 [1973]) subjects pornography produced in Los Angeles to the standards prevailing in Salt Lake City and Biloxi, if it is available in those cities. Given the facts of national distribution of pornography, local standards can become stifling. This is not merely speculative. Harry Reems of "Deep Throat" fame (or infamy), was prosecuted along with others in Memphis in 1976. Should people who live in San Francisco or elsewhere where the local community standards are more liberal (not to say libertine) have what they wish to view or read be subjected to the local community standards of more conservative communities—so that the most restrictive get to set the standards for all? One might have thought that this goes against the very local prerogatives the notion of "contemporary community standards" was meant to preserve and defeat the aims of diversity the legal criterion was meant to support. The problem is perhaps inevitable in a world where pornographic, as well as intellectual, political, and religious material is typically locally produced but nationally or internationally distributed. Looking beyond obscenity, local standards for libel may pose a threat to critical discussion anywhere and everywhere.

REPUTATION AND SOCIETAL ATTITUDES

Many insults, like most hate speech, do not aim at truth. Their message is one of hatred and contempt and dismissal. The law of libel and slander is not designed to protect from such messages, however offensive and hurtful they might be. Its focus is on reputation. Feinberg distinguishes name-calling, which is "a form of pure insult," from "calumny or malicious and usually false statements seriously meant to hurt someone's reputation" (1985, 221). Pure insults, like ritual dozens insults, do not much concern themselves with truth. Calumny, like degenerative dozens personal insults and like libel and slander, at least purports to be true. There are also "factually based put-downs," a distinct category: "Unlike calumny it achieves its whole purpose through face to face confrontation whether or not third parties ever learn of it. But unlike pure insult it does purport to make serious factual imputations, it is not purely a venting of hostile spleen. . . . The mercilessly derisive taunts of the school yard are perhaps the most familiar examples"—attacks on cripples, the retarded, the poor and the unattractive being staples of the genre (1985, 222). Such put-downs may aim at separating and excluding those who are attacked, somehow raising and enhancing the excluders in their own estimation, and defamation may serve the same aims. But again the law of libel and slander is rather narrow in its protection, concern for the economic consequences of damage to reputation being especially prominent. In defamation, the law presumes certain societal values and protects those who are falsely or wantonly devalued by those standards. Viewpoint neutral standards for freedom of speech do not necessarily endorse any given view. Prosecutions for libel and slander, however, would appear to endorse, assume, and support particular valuations.

One cannot sue for being called an upstanding citizen.[6] When Wilde sued for being called a "posing Sodomite," his cause of action assumed the attitudes of his time. Tom Cruise has periodically sued those who have suggested that he has engaged in homosexual activity. Does it matter what Cruise thinks of gays? Does it matter what the public thinks of gays? Have attitudes changed? The crucial issue might be whether it would be damaging to Cruise's reputation—presumably as a macho action hero—if true. (In the most recent instance, in 2001,

---

6. In an interesting case in which a truck stop owner's reputation among his clientele was impaired by the statement that he had reported work hour rule violations by truckers to the Interstate Commerce Commission, he was unable to collect (*Connelly v. McKay*, 28 N.Y.S.2d 327, 329 [Sup. Ct. 1941]). The Court explained:

> At most the language claimed to have been used accuses the plaintiff of giving information of violations of the law to the proper authorities. Are such acts reprehensible? Is such language defamatory? This court thinks not. It is true that informers are not always held in too high esteem, and violators of the law might have good cause to shun one who engaged in such practice, but, nevertheless, such acts cannot constitute a foundation upon which to build an action for slander. "The fact that a communication tends to prejudice another in the eyes of even a substantial group is not enough if the group is one whose standards are so anti-social that it is not proper for the courts to recognize them." (Restatement of the Law of Torts, § 559, p. 142)

As William K. Jones puts it, "the New York court was reluctant to place a judicial seal of approval on plaintiff's claim that it was defamatory to depict him as a law-abiding citizen" (2003, 141). The current "Don't Snitch!" street code does not, and cannot, receive legal sanction.

the porn star involved in the suit ultimately denied he ever gave an interview about Cruise to the French magazine that had published the charges and the magazine itself apologized—*Time*, 5/14/2001.) Whatever Cruise's view, whatever the public attitude, there might be a problem in the state providing a legal remedy for a person accused of being homosexual. Is there such a remedy for a person accused of being heterosexual, or is that like being accused of being an upstanding citizen? Imagine a person accused of being black. Richard Delgado reports that "in at least three older cases, white plaintiffs were permitted to sue for defamation defendants who indicated that the plaintiffs were Black." He argues that "whether or not the conclusion is true, it is not desirable that the law view membership in a racial minority as damaging to a person's reputation, even if some members of society consider it so" (1993, 100).

It is significant that false imputations have not always been treated symmetrically. As Robert C. Post recounts,

> In the South before World War II, for example, defamation law enforced the values of the dominant white culture, making it defamatory to say that a Caucasian was black, but not permitting blacks to sue for defamation upon being labeled white. This result followed from the fact that defamation law understood itself to be reflecting 'the intrinsic difference between whites and blacks,' a difference inhering in the fact that, 'from a social standpoint, the negro race is in mind and morals inferior to the Caucasian.' Wolfe v. Georgia Ry. & Elec. Co., 2 Ga. App. 499, 505–06, 58 S. E. 899, 901–02 (1907). (Post 1988, 300n18)

I have argued that the state failing to prohibit hate speech (or Nazis marching in Skokie) does *not* mean it endorses it, because the state also protects the expression of views that contradict the message of hate speech. The state cannot be taken to endorse all the incompatible views it protects. But punishing as libel charges of blackness or gayness (that is, false claims that a person is black or gay) may indeed endorse a denigratory view of blackness and gayness. It might be responded that the state in its libel laws would merely be reflecting society's views (the dominant, hegemonic, "assimilationist" views—in Post's language) without endorsing them. But the asymmetry involved in not treating false charges that a person is white or heterosexual as libelous would seem to turn the reflected view into an endorsed one. The apparent analogy with state neutrality toward hate speech fails. In thinking about Tom Cruise, the crucial test might be how the state treats people who make their living partly through their homosexual identity (e.g., Harvey Fierstein). Equal treatment might suggest that the real slur is imputation of hypocrisy and false presentation of self, rather than a disfavored sexual identity. If, however, the state allows damages for defamation for suggesting someone is gay, but does not regard as defamation suggesting a gay person is actually straight, then the state is not simply noting a sociological fact, but endorsing and enforcing (and reinforcing) a social attitude.[7]

Justice O'Connor in her concurrence to *Lawrence v. Texas*, the case that overturned *Bowers v. Hardwick* and with it sodomy laws throughout the United States, stated: "Texas law confirms that the sodomy statute is directed toward homosexuals as a class. In Texas, calling a person a homosexual is slander *per se* because the word 'homosexual' 'impute[s] the commission of a crime.' [citations] The State has admitted that because of the sodomy law, *being* homosexual carries the presumption of being a criminal" (539 U.S. 558 [2003]). The Court concluded, on wide liberty as well as narrow equal protection grounds, that the state may not discriminate amongst classes of its citizens on the basis of moralizing animus. In *Palmore v. Sidoti*, the Court reversed a Florida state court ruling that removed a child from the custody of his white mother after she married a black man on the ground that the child would suffer social stigmatization from living in a racially mixed household. The Court stated: "It would ignore reality to suggest that racial and ethnic prejudices do not exist or that all manifestations of those prejudices have been eliminated. . . . The Constitution cannot control such prejudices but neither can it tolerate them. Private biases may be outside the reach of the law, but the law cannot, directly or indirectly, give them effect" (466 U.S. 429, 433 [1984]). As with heckler's vetoes, socially undesirable responses should not dictate legal norms.

---

7. It has been suggested that in a suit under false light privacy, rather than defamation, "it is unnecessary to determine whether white is better than black or straight is better than gay. It is enough that an important aspect of plaintiff's character has been falsified in a manner most plaintiffs would find highly offensive" (Jones 2003, 141). Offensiveness to a reasonable person differs as a standard from damage to reputation—as we have noted, people may well wish to keep aspects of their lives private that are not necessarily disreputable in any way.

GROUP DEFAMATION

In addition to the requirements of publication and factual assertion, there is another constraint in defamation law that makes it difficult for it to serve as a basis for hate speech legislation. Defamation must be "of and concerning" the plaintiff. That was actually an issue in *New York Times Co. v. Sullivan*. L. B. Sullivan was the commissioner in charge of the Montgomery, Alabama, police at the time an ad seeking to raise funds to support the civil-rights movement in the South was published in the *Times*. The ad described some of the behavior of the police and government officials and lawless citizens in response to student protests in Montgomery. Sullivan was never mentioned by name and there was other reason to question whether the ad had in fact defamed him personally, that it was "of and concerning" him. To have standing to sue for defamation, you must be the party defamed. This is quite apart from other reasons for the *Sullivan* court making it harder for public figures to win libel suits, such as the need to encourage and protect criticism of government officials and actions, the need to avoid self-censorship of the press in the face of large libel damages, and the notion that intermediaries should not be held accountable for aspects of publications (such as ads) about which they lack culpable knowledge.

The constraint that a claimed defamation must be "of and concerning" the plaintiff creates great difficulty for those who would use the notion of group defamation to provide a foundation for hate speech codes and legislation, especially given that charges against groups are often vague and may be more matters of opinion than of justiciable fact. William K. Jones argues, "If the plaintiff is not identifiable as the object of the falsehood, her reputation cannot be impaired. Similarly, if the statement is directed at a large and amorphous group—'all politicians are crooks'—no individual member of the group may sue. Nor may the group. The charge is too diffuse to impair the reputation of any individual" (Jones 2003, 20). The notion of group defamation received its strongest constitutional endorsement in the case of *Beauharnais v. Illinois*. Joseph Beauharnais had arranged, as president of the White Circle League, for the distribution of leaflets that sought signatures for a petition that called on Chicago's mayor and city council "to halt the further encroachment,

harassment and invasion of white people, their property, neighborhoods and persons, by the Negro." The leaflets also called for "one
million self respecting white people in Chicago to unite . . ." with the
statement added that "if persuasion and the need to prevent the white
race from becoming mongrelized by the negro will not unite us, then
the aggressions . . . rapes, robberies, knives, guns and marijuana of the
negro, surely will" (343 U.S. 250, 251–52 [1952]). Beauharnais was
convicted and fined $200 under an Illinois statute that prohibited cir-
culation of any publication that "portrays depravity, criminality,
unchastity, or lack of virtue of a class of citizens, of any race, color,
creed or religion which [exposes them] to contempt, derision, or
obloquy or which is productive of breach of the peace or riots."
Beauharnais had not been permitted to proffer proof of the leaflet's
claims, it having been held that, as a matter of criminal libel, truth
alone was not a defense unless the statements were also made "with
good motives and for justifiable ends" (265). The Supreme Court sustained the statute and the conviction.

It might seem that group libel is simply individual libel multiplied. But however outrageous the assumptions and concerns of the
leaflet, its factual assertions are irresolvably vague. Are the various
crimes ascribed to "the negro" being alleged of all "negroes"? Is it
being claimed that most engage in such acts? Some? A higher proportion than of whites? Kent Greenawalt concludes, "If falsity is an
aspect of criminal liability, people should be punishable only for clear
assertions of fact, and much vague scurrilous comment about groups
would remain unpunishable. Trials about truth, with their publicity
for harsh claims about groups, could easily do much more damage
than the original communications. Whatever the constitutional status
of a law precisely limited to false assertions of fact, adopting such a law
would be senseless" (Greenawalt 1995, 63 and 167n79). Does racial
invective even pretend to assert facts? "You cannot libel someone by
saying 'I despise you,' which seems to be the essential message common to most racial epithets" (Gates 1994, 30). The Supreme Court
supported the Illinois courts' denial of truth as a defense, permitting them to focus simply on "good motives" and "justifiable ends,"
and the defendant was not permitted to demonstrate those either (as
emphasized by Justice Jackson in his dissent, 343 U.S. 250, 300). The
truth of matters of opinion and broad, vague claims of fact is difficult

to adjudicate. And where the issue is arguable, perhaps the argument should not be foreclosed by silencing those who hold unattractive and even obviously false views (as with Holocaust denier statutes in Europe, discussed in the next chapter—in the United States, some who wish to regulate hate speech would criminalize "cold" anti-Semitic literature, such as Holocaust denial, along with "hot" name-calling [Matsuda 1993, 42]). Permitting such speech does not count as endorsement by the state, so long as the state protects equally the statement of opposing views—and even less when the state actually acts to create and enforce equality. The proper protection against Beauharnais-type advocacy is not restrictions on speech, but legislation to prevent discrimination in housing, schools, employment and the like—legislation that did not exist at the time of *Beauharnais*, but which has been enacted and enforced subsequently. As Laurence Tribe puts the point about viewpoint neutrality in relation to freedom of speech in his treatise *American Constitutional Law*: "If the Constitution forces government to allow people to march, speak, and write in favor of peace, brotherhood, and justice, then it must also require government to allow them to advocate hatred, racism, and even genocide" (1988, 838n17).

Beauharnais has been weakened and narrowed by subsequent cases. *Sullivan* changed the landscape. Where Justice Frankfurter in *Beauharnais* had thought group libel as a form of defamation was wholly without First Amendment protection, stating "if an utterance directed at an individual may be the object of criminal sanctions, we cannot deny to a State power to punish the same utterance directed at a defined group" (343 U.S. 250, 258 [1952]), *Sullivan* declared that regulation of "libel can claim no talismanic immunity from constitutional limitations. It must be measured by standards that satisfy the First Amendment" (376 U.S. 254, 269 [1964]).

In addition to the especially relevant "of and concerning" requirement emphasized in *Sullivan*, that truth must be accepted as an absolute defense without regard for the motivation with which defamatory statements are made was held in *Garrison v. Louisiana*: "Debate on public issues will not be uninhibited if the speaker must run the risk that it will be proved in court that he spoke out of hatred; even if he did speak out of hatred, utterances honestly believed contribute to the free interchange of ideas and the ascertainment of truth. . . . Moreover, in the case of charges against a popular political figure . . . it may be almost impossible to show freedom from ill-will or selfish motives" (379 U.S. 64, 73–74 [1964]).

Where *Beauharnais* had put the burden of proving truth and motivation on the defendant, *Philadelphia Newspapers, Inc. v. Hepps* followed up on *Sullivan* by holding that the First Amendment requires that a "plaintiff bear the burden of showing that the speech at issue is false" when a defamation involves matters of public concern (475 U.S. 767, 777 [1986]). And *Cohen v. California*, 403 U.S. 15 (1971), offered protection to emotional expression and invalidated breach of the peace and disorderly conduct statutes insufficiently linked to immediate danger of actual violence in the circumstances (an "imminent lawless action" requirement emphasized also in *Brandenburg v. Ohio*, 395 U.S. 444 [1969]).

Group epithets and slurs are presumably entitled to the same protection from content and viewpoint discrimination that permitted the Nazis to march in Skokie and that protected even burning crosses in the *R.A.V.* decision. And however repulsive Beauharnais' views, his leaflets had perhaps a special claim to protection. As Justice Black pointed out in dissent (343 U.S. 250, 268), Beauharnais and his group were seeking to petition their government representatives, and the First Amendment explicitly protects such petitions: "Congress shall make no law . . . abridging the freedom of speech, or of the press; or the right of the people peaceably to assemble, and to petition the Government for a redress of grievances." It is true the Beauharnais petition was addressed to local government officials rather than Congress, and that the petition was in favor of segregation, but the Fourteenth Amendment has been regularly held to extend the restraints of the First Amendment to the states. Black also points out that to treat criminal libel as though it extended to groups has a sorry history (going back to "Seditious Libel," where the government was the group being protected) and sanctions a broad censorship. It might even stifle discussion of any proposed legislation that might have differential impact on defined groups (as much legislation does) should criticism of the affected groups be part of the argument.

Justice Douglas notes the risk of further, unwelcome, regulation. "Today a white man stands convicted for protesting in unseemly language against our decisions invalidating restrictive covenants. Tomorrow a Negro will be haled before a court for denouncing lynch law in heated terms. Farm laborers in the West who compete with field hands drifting up from Mexico; whites who feel the pressure of orientals; a minority which finds employment going to members of the dominant religious group—all of these are caught in the mesh of today's decision" (343 U.S. 250, 286). As Zechariah Chafee put the point, "Once you start group libel laws, every influential body of men will urge that it has an equal claim to be protected by such legislation. And the wider the protection, the narrower becomes the field for unimpeded discussion of public affairs" (quoted in Post 1988, 332; the example of a professional association of offended "rug merchants" is discussed by Post at 332n178). Given the flexibility and variety of group identities, there is no limit to claims of protection. Douglas concludes that the majority view "represents a philosophy at war with the First Amendment—a constitutional interpretation which puts free speech under the legislative thumb. It reflects an influence moving ever deeper into our society. It is notice to the legislatures that they have the power to control unpopular blocs. It is a warning to every minority that when the Constitution guarantees free speech it does not mean what it says" (287). While the group defamation model of *Beauharnais* differs from the assaultive model of *Chaplinsky* (unlike "fighting words," Beauharnais's pamphlet was not addressed to the individuals it attacked), the risk of licensing a dangerous weapon that may then be turned against those who first wanted it is a problem shared by both.

While "fighting words" involve direct confrontation, one should not make the mistake of generalizing that into a requirement on all insults. Robert M. Adams asserts "insult is always a face-to-face affair. You can slander a man in the public prints (and for that his recourse is the law), but you cannot insult him" (1977, 28). The statement is doubly false. First, because defamation in print is called "libel," not "slander." Slander is precisely what is done when a person defames another in speech. One ought to keep one's legal terminology straight when speaking of recourse to the law. Second, the notion that one cannot insult a person in print is absurd. The medium permits all the name-calling, attacks on a person and what he holds dear, and other varieties of insult available via oral/aural media. Certainly a reader can take offense as readily as a hearer can. And certainly a writer can have all the malicious intent that a speaker might—though, we should always remember, in both the case of speakers and writers, insults can be unintentional.[8]

REASONABLE EXPECTATIONS

Feeling insulted is largely a matter of expectations. Whether one has in fact been insulted (whether one "properly" feels insulted) may be a matter of the reasonableness of those expectations. Which expectations are reasonable? Who is the reasonable man or the reasonable woman? We have already seen

---

8. Adams makes a third error in the same paragraph when he continues, "Without personal intent on both sides, there can hardly be insult" (29).

While Adams provides one of the few direct discussions of our topic by a philosopher, one quickly begins to lose count of his false gratuitous generalizations. Just a few sentences on, he opines "you can't disdain a man whom both of you recognize as a social superior." But surely contempt can flow upwards. An ordinary citizen may have the greatest disdain for the President of the United States, though both might recognize the august dignity of the office. Perhaps it would be in some way unseemly for a president or a king to take offense at the attitudes of those below, but surely the attitudes are readily available. Adams tells us, "Being out of the ordinary range, presidents are as hard to insult as priests or pariahs; and kings, it's to be suspected, can be insulted only by other kings" (29). Here Adams treats "insult" as a success verb; but while greatness of office may make one immune from insult in the sense that one might be foolish to take offense, it does not follow that those below cannot point insults and disdain in one's direction. Where the pretensions are successfully punctured, the low may actually succeed in humiliating the high—even if some in high office might be too oblivious to notice. (One could imagine, were the aspersions not so correct, President George W. Bush reading and being offended by Calvin Trillin's *Obliviously On He Sails: The Bush Administration in Rhyme*, 2004.)

No doubt grievances against equals may be felt more bitterly than those against superiors in power. Grievance and felt harm and insult depend on expectations, and where one has equal status one might have greater expectations of respectful treatment (see Miller 1993, 76–77). At any rate, social conventions may make certain statements (whether written or spoken) breaches of etiquette, of expectations of respect, of the norms which constitute the boundaries of insult. And again, from the point of view of outcome, written abuse may be at least as effective as spoken abuse; indeed, the possibility exists for larger audiences, especially over time, as written statements are generally more widely preserved than spoken ones. At least this has been true until the recent coming of cell phone and digital camera videos and the *YouTube* effect. (Ask former Senator George Allen.)

that "fighting words" may require a discrimination that is difficult to make, given that any words may be an incitement to some. The problem of how much to individuate arises regularly in the law when it seeks to guide juries by the standard of the "reasonable man." How much of the individual history and knowledge of the accused ought one to build into the reasonable man to make his expectations relevant to the case in hand? Was Bernhard Goetz, the man who in 1984 shot four black teenagers on a subway when one of them approached him and said "Give me five dollars," acting in self-defense?[9]

9. Recall that a cognizable defense of self-defense depends on claims concerning necessity (the plausibility of the threatened harm and lack of alternatives), proportionality (no excessive force), and timing (no early preemptive strikes or later retaliatory acts are permissible). As we have discussed, one can ask whether these claims must be based on truth, or on reasonable belief, or whether merely sincere belief might suffice. (Note the order of increasing subjectivity in these standards.) The defendant may have a *justification* if true but still an *excuse* if reasonable. Should mere honest belief also provide an excuse? In the Goetz case, the New York courts in the end required a trial using an *objective* standard (a trial which ended in acquittal on all but a single possession charge for the handgun in June 1987). Goetz served eight and one-half months of a one-year term in jail. To follow out the legal trail, in 1990, the paralyzed youth (Cabey) sued Goetz civilly for $50 million. In 1996 Cabey won, though Goetz, being penniless at that point, was "judgment proof."

Whether the issue is one of *standards* or of the *facts* can be unclear—and can matter: it is normally for the judge to instruct on standards and for the jury to be the trier of fact. That the standard for reasonableness must be objective was well argued by Judge Wachtler (then chief judge of the New York State Court of Appeals and subsequently, unfortunately, imprisoned for attempted intimidation of a former girlfriend):

> We cannot lightly impute to the Legislature an intent to fundamentally alter the principles of justification to allow the perpetrator of a serious crime to go free simply because that person believed his actions were reasonable and necessary to prevent some perceived harm. To completely exonerate such an individual, no matter how aberrational or bizarre his thought patterns, would allow citizens to set their own standards for the permissible use of force. (*People v. Goetz*, 68 NY2d 96 [1986])

We should note that the Court's opinion allows including Goetz's background and other particular characteristics under an objective standard as part of "the circumstances" or "situation." Should it? The more one includes in the "situation," the more individualized and so "subjective" the standard. (The real difference between objective and subjective standards is ultimately the degree of individuation.) But one must include *some* knowledge and experience in the description of any situation, or the "reasonable man" will always misread the neutrally described circumstances. Thus

He said he feared they would rob him. Was it reasonable to believe a mugging was in the offing? (A 1991 Federal District Court opinion in California protects panhandling as free speech.) Before the shooting, Goetz had been mugged several times and had been carrying an unlicensed gun for three years because of his fear of being mugged again. (He had actually drawn his concealed weapon and stopped robberies on two occasions without firing a shot.) Is it reasonable for an individual with Goetz's particular history to have these expectations? Does the reasonable man have a history? How much of the defendant's individual history ought one to build in? If we leave out everything, the jury will always get it wrong. (Surely the reasonable man in New York knows about the dangers of the subway, but should one presume he has "victim" written on his forehead and has been mugged three times before?) In the Goetz case, he was in fact correct in believing he was being robbed under an unspoken threat of force (one of the would-be assailants admitted as much to the police at the time). But if we include every detail of an individual's history, then perhaps whatever the individual does is always (subjectively) justified, despite apparently objective standards of "reasonableness." The New York courts ultimately ruled in the Goetz case that the reasonable man standard is objective (the jury must consider what a person of ordinary capacities and experience would know, expect, and do in the circumstances), but also allowed building individual history into the "circumstances" in which the reasonable man is called upon to act. So the problem of how much to individuate, how much individual history to include is left largely in the hands of the

every member of the jury (all being from New York) understood that the words "Give me five dollars" were more than a bare request, more than innocent panhandling, that *in the circumstances* the words carried an implicit threat and a shakedown was in process (though it would be difficult to predict what level of violence would ensue on a crowded subway—on which, it should be noted, the other passengers were grouped at the other end of the car, away from the young toughs, at the time Goetz got on the train). One should be aware that, for example, in 1990, a twenty-two year old visiting New York with his family for a tennis tournament was knifed to death on a subway platform by a gang of youths who first stole his father's wallet and punched his mother. There were two other men in his party. It was 10:30 PM on a crowded platform. There were eight or nine youths in the gang. What constitutes reasonable expectations in such a subterranean setting?

jury. Juries tend to identify the reasonable man with themselves (i.e., the reasonable thing to have done is whatever they would have done). What other standard could a juror be expected to turn to?

One way the courts control what counts, what gets included when determining what beliefs and which expectations are reasonable, is via the rules of evidence. One way to resolve how much of the circumstances in a given case the reasonable man knows is by how much the jury gets to hear. The problem then focuses on what evidence should be presentable to them.[10] We have already noted in passing that when the court, in the person of the judge, decides, reasonable expectations (say of privacy) often turn out, circularly, to be those the court will enforce. Social conventions, when they are clear and clearly knowable, may sometimes provide a way out. But different groups, as well as different individuals, may have different sensitivities and expectations (as we have noted in our discussion of cross-cultural misunderstanding).

In judging whether expectations are reasonable, whether feeling insulted in the circumstances is legitimate or perhaps the result of over-sensitivity, in searching out an Aristotelian mean in determining how sensitive we ought to be, the standard of the reasonable man (as it operates in the law) provides some clues. This is as true for libel law (where one might wish to know, among other things: would the reasonable man believe that such-and-such a statement was damaging to reputation, that it was not reckless to believe it and publish it on the basis of the evidence to hand) as for the law of assault. Of course, the purposes of the law place special demands on legal deliberations (conclusions

10. For example, prior criminal records of the "victims" in the Goetz case were not admissible—in fact, Goetz would not have been aware of their records at the time. One of the youths stated to a detective at the time of the shooting, "We were going to rob him but the white guy shot us first." That might have been excluded as hearsay (in relation to proving the youths intended to rob Goetz), but an exception to the hearsay rule admitted the statement to impeach the speaker's credibility once he took to the stand and told a different story. (This and many other aspects of the case are fruitfully discussed in Fletcher, 1988.)

There are, of course, other questions. Was the use of force excessive? One of the youths is still paralyzed from the waist down. Goetz had successfully drawn without firing in the past and some of Goetz's statements, at the time of the shooting as well as both before and after, suggest he was fed up and out for vigilante justice.

need to be reached, conclusions that may have serious consequences for all the parties concerned), and the procedure and apparatus of the law provide mechanisms that may not be generally available. The crucial importance of rules of admissibility of evidence in connection with establishing standards of "reasonableness" has no ready analogue in judging when someone feels insulted in ordinary life. Nonetheless, our less methodical thinking about what to take into account and how to weigh it can receive some illumination from the more strictly ordered requirements of law. After all, looking to just one aspect of everyday situations, we often in our ordinary determinations have to consider what the parties "should" have known.

EIGHT

INSULT IN THE LAW

BLASPHEMY

WHEN IT COMES TO RELIGION, PEOPLE READILY TAKE OFFENSE AT WHAT others say and do, indeed, even at what they think. Wars have been fought to convert others to a particular group's way of thinking. Modern freedom of thought has been hard won, and it typically goes with a right to freedom of expression—one need not keep one's views, even one's widely disapproved of views, to oneself. But the law recognizes many limits to freedom of expression (libel, slander, obscenity, invasion of privacy, state secrets and national security among them) and many think those limits should include matters of religion as well: blasphemy. And where the law fails to provide protection to religious sensibilities, some will take matters into their own hands; indeed, some religious leaders call for such self-help as itself a religious duty. Of course, when states enforce religious respect, they tend to single out a preferred—sometimes an official, established state—religion for special protection. That too can cause offense. Certainly it raises issues of equity, especially in a context of supposed religious freedom. How can freedom of belief, freedom of expression, and freedom of religion coexist in a world where people readily express disagreement with and refuse to obey the prescriptions and proscriptions of others—especially when those others may view such disagreement and refusal as disrespect and so take offense? Can the law enforce a harmony that centuries of war have failed to impose? Should it try? Is the alternative prospect, in an ever-more interconnected world with intermingling and minority populations, simmering hatreds and more religion-inspired war? Does irreverence have a place? A protected place?

THE MUHAMMAD CARTOONS

In early 2006, much of the Muslim world was inflamed because of a series of cartoons depicting the Prophet Muhammad that had been published in a Danish newspaper some months earlier. The set of twelve cartoons (including one with the Prophet wearing a turban in the shape of a cannonball bomb with a lit fuse) had been solicited by an editor at the *Jyllands-Posten* because of incidents of apparent fearful self-censorship. Among them: the writer of a children's life of Muhammad had had difficulty in finding someone to illustrate the book. It needs to be understood that, for many Muslims, *any* depiction of the Prophet Muhammad risks idolatry and constitutes blasphemy. This is true for sympathetic portrayals as well as critical caricatures.[1] In the event, the fears of the self-censors were not unwarranted. With spreading awareness of the cartoons in the Muslim world, demonstrations turned into riots, people were trampled and shot by police, embassies were assaulted, trashed, and burned, ambassadors were recalled (by Saudi Arabia, Libya, and Syria, among others) and diplomatic missions closed, and Danish products were boycotted and employees of Danish companies beaten in the Middle East. People died in demonstrations from Indonesia to Afghanistan and Gaza. By any measure, the response was excessive.

Clearly, there were other things going on. With America at war in Iraq and continuing tensions between Israel and the Palestinians, with unrest surrounding Muslim immigrant communities in Europe and elsewhere, one does not have to look far. There had been rioting in the impoverished, immigrant *banlieues* of Paris in fall 2005, before word of the cartoons fanned flames worldwide. The marginalization and exploitation of increasingly large Muslim minorities in Europe doubtless gave the perceived insult special force. Conditions in the Middle East, North

---

1. Christians and Christian reformers have disagreed about the place of images in their religion. Iconoclasts since at least Byzantine Emperor Leo III in the eighth century have taken offense (and occasionally arms) against images. In 2001, the Taliban in Afghanistan went so far as to destroy the images of another religion, the monumental statues of the Buddha at Bamiyan.

Africa, and other parts of the Muslim world — including the degradation of massive unemployment — also doubtless contributed to the explosive response, aided perhaps by the fact that oppressive oligarchies, theocracies, and despotisms that rarely tolerate internal dissent sometimes may have welcomed the release provided by demonstrations directed outward. Nor were the Danish cartoons the first triggers to Muslim outrage against the West in recent years.

There was the *fatwa* by the Ayatollah Ruhollah Khomeini, spiritual and political leader of Iran, in 1989 calling for the death of British author Salman Rushdie after the publication of his *The Satanic Verses*. The novel was taken to insult the memory of Muhammad. Rushdie and his publishers were declared *madhur el dam* ("those whose blood must be shed"). Twenty-two people died in violence connected with the publication of the book. Rushdie was compelled to take various self-protective measures; and subsequently, the Japanese translator of the book was killed, its Italian translator was stabbed, and its Norwegian publisher was injured in a gun attack. In 2004, Dutch filmmaker Theo van Gogh was murdered after making a film called "Submission" (2004) about violence against women in Islamic societies. But it is not just a matter of a clash between civilizations.

Even within the Muslim world, responses to perceived blasphemy in modern times have been (to Western eyes) harsh, and not just in theocratic states such as Afghanistan under the Taliban or Iran under the Ayatollahs. In heavily Muslim Pakistan (what became the "Islamic Republic of Pakistan" was established on Muslim principles when it was hived off from dominantly Hindu India in 1949), a man was sentenced to death as recently as 2001 for defaming the Prophet Muhammad. That sentence was particularly problematical because Dr. Younus Shaikh's alleged offense was to claim "the Prophet had not become a Muslim until age 40 and that before then, he had not followed Muslim practices concerning circumcision or removing his underarm hair" (*New York Times* 8/20/2001). To many that might seem not only a truthful claim (based on the practices of the Prophet's tribe), but (with regard to the first part of the claim) even a logically necessary truth, given that Muhammad is not thought to have received the revelations which became the foundation for the new religion of Islam until age 40. And of course, in states like Afghanistan, *Shari'a* law can be harsh and unforgiving for heresy, blasphemy, or apostasy. Abdul Rahman faced the death penalty in spring 2006 for having converted to Christianity, at least until he was spirited away from Afghanistan to asylum in Italy.

Having noted the world-historical context of the events surrounding the Danish publication of the cartoons, the perhaps special sensitivity of less powerful groups to perceived insults from arrogant, dominant societies, and the perhaps special stringency of Muslim law and Muslim cultures, it is time to turn from the specific triggering insult, the Muhammad cartoons, to focus on offense to religion in general, that is to say, the concerns of blasphemy.

THE NATURE OF BLASPHEMY

Who are blasphemy laws concerned to protect? From what? At what cost? Traditionally, blasphemy was concerned with insults to God. Among the ancient Hebrews, for example, even to utter God's name was sometimes considered an affront (who are we to call upon God—as in a curse, "God damn you"—who are we to presume to summon and command? [Feinberg 1985, 201]), though the Talmudic offense typically involved speaking evil of God, or cursing God, or, at the least, speaking disrespectfully of God. As we have had occasion to notice, the ancient Hebrews went so far as to bar the quotation or repetition of the blasphemy in testimony (Levy 1993, 13)— thus neglecting the use/mention distinction we have ourselves had frequent occasion to rely on. This attitude of reverence for the magical efficacy of words persists in the later power attributed to swearing oaths (the invocation of God's authority to ensure the sanctity of contracts and the veracity of testimony), as well as in the special significance attached to certain swear words and curses in general. "Blasphemy" is centrally and most often a matter of speech. While sometimes used as synonyms, "sacrilege" is typically broader and (as we shall spell out in a moment) "heresy" narrower.

The concern in prohibiting blasphemy was to ensure that proper respect be paid to communal objects of veneration. But surely God, especially an all-powerful God, can do his own smiting. Even where communal enforcement was said to be for the sake of God, it would seem that there must have been concern that a vengeful God might extend his wrath beyond particular disrespecters and blasphemers and extend his punishment to those who failed to ensure the appropriate worshipful attitude, that is, to all and any. In the end, the community of believers was doubtless protecting itself from harm when it sought to protect its God or gods from offense. For the crops not to fail, respect must be paid. Indeed, depending on the religion, often sacrifices (whether vegetable, animal, or even human) had to be made. But at the least, the central beliefs of the religion were not to be questioned and its prohibitions and taboos, the presumed commands of the divinity, had to be observed. The details of offensive conduct might vary from group to group and sect to sect, but every religious group had its sense of proprieties to be observed. And where state and religion came together, the machinery of legal enforcement would come to bear along with whatever sanctions the religious community might impose. This has continued into modern times, wherever there has been an established church or a theocratic state, and some have insisted that even secular states must ensure respect to people's religious sensibilities. After all, the state often acts to prevent or punish offense of other kinds (whether by smells, indecent displays, or obscene literature). But still, whose religious sensibilities are to be protected and from what precisely? As we have seen, the penalties have often been severe (including death).

Blasphemy takes insult into the realm of religion. Supposing it is the orthodox believer rather than God who is the object of insult, that may provide a settled victim, but what counts as blasphemy remains inherently open to dispute: what many regard as intolerably abusive and scurrilous attacks on religious feelings, others regard as healthy and courageous protests against dubious and dangerous beliefs. Does this contrast in perspectives turn simply on the differing content of beliefs? Not if attitudes are central, as I have argued, to an understanding of insult.

Heresy is to be distinguished from blasphemy. Heresy involves deviation from doctrine, but it is crucially confined to coreligionists, those within the fold (at least up until the moment of heresy).[2] It is an offense confined to a circle of believers, whose shared beliefs may come under challenge from within—leading sometimes to discord, sometimes to change, sometimes to proliferating sects. Heresy is very much a matter of content. Blasphemy, I wish to suggest, is very much a matter of attitude. What attitude? Dr. Johnson defines a blasphemer as "A wretch that speaks of God in impious and irreverent

---

2. T. S. Eliot, in *After Strange Gods*, argued that blasphemy too should be understood as restricted to believers. He desired that people be shocked at disrespect, and not just at its manner: "blasphemy is not a matter of good form but of right belief; no one can possibly blaspheme in any sense except that in which a parrot may be said to curse, unless he profoundly believes in that which he profanes; and when anyone who is not a believer is shocked by blasphemy he is shocked merely by a breach of good form . . . I am reproaching a world in which blasphemy is impossible" (1934, 52). Eliot's nostalgia for an age of reverent belief, however, goes against both biblical and legal doctrine on the subject.

terms." (The rabbinic tradition takes its start in a biblical passage expressing a similar sentiment, Exodus 22:28, "You shall not revile God, nor curse a ruler of your people.") Content can be an indicator of attitude, but so can the manner of expression. Sometimes who does the speaking may be taken as decisive. The history of selective prosecutions and changing legal standards suggests that class has played as large a role in determining the acceptability of attitudes (and of the language in which they are expressed) as the particular content of beliefs. The contrast between matter and manner, content and form, that pervades the law can be seen particularly sharply in the history of prosecutions for blasphemy in England.

MATTER AND MANNER

In England in 1880, an elected member of Parliament refused to swear the oath of office on the Bible and was denied his seat. That radical politician, Charles Bradlaugh, was the publisher of the *Freethinker*, and along with his colleagues in that magazine, George William Foote and William Ramsey, he was tried in 1883 for blasphemy. Foote, the editor of the penny weekly, had written in its first issue, "The *Freethinker* is an anti-Christian organ, and is therefore chiefly aggressive. It will wage relentless war against superstition in general, and against the superstition of Christianity in particular" (Levy 1993, 479). There had not been a prosecution for blasphemy in England for forty years, but the political situation of the moment and the ill-mannered fierceness of the *Freethinker* (including cartoons lampooning God, one illustrating a biblical passage in which God "shows his backside" to Moses) conspired to bring about the trial.

At least since the Blasphemy Act of 1698, the denial of God's existence or of the truths of Christianity or of the divine authority of the Bible, however politely or civilly stated, had been enough for criminal conviction.[3] Though

---

3. As Robert C. Post explains: "In England, blasphemy was a common law crime. It was one of the four branches of criminal libel, the other three being obscenity, sedition, and defamation. All four branches of libel sought to ensure that speech did not violate established norms of respect and propriety. The particular province of blasphemy was to prevent disrespect toward God, which according to Blackstone could be manifested 'by denying his being or providence; or by contumelious reproaches of our Saviour Christ'" (1988, 305).

prosecutions had grown rare, that standard—combined with a biased charge by the presiding judge, Justice North—proved sufficient for the conviction of Foote and Ramsey in an initial trial based on a special Christmas issue of the *Freethinker*, Foote being sentenced to prison for a year and Ramsey for nine months. By the time of Ramsey's *Freethinker* trial later in 1883, there was a different court with a different judge who introduced a new standard for blasphemy and all three got off. What exactly had changed?

While generally unenforced, and so already arguably dead-letter law, the black-letter law had been spelled out by Blackstone in his *Commentaries on the Laws of England* in 1769 and Justice James Fitzjames Stephen maintained in his *History of Criminal Law of England*, published just before the *Freethinker* trials in 1883, that "the true legal doctrine upon the subject is that blasphemy consists in the character of the matter published and not in the manner in which it is stated" (Levy 1993, 490). So understood, Stephen (in sharp contrast to Blackstone) argued prosecutions for blasphemy are repressive and unjust. Indeed, they are persecutions for they privilege and protect only certain Christian denominations, and they leave the feelings of unbelievers unprotected from Christians' insults. While Stephen offered criticisms, Lord Chief Justice John Duke Coleridge, who presided over Bradlaugh's separate trial and Foote's later trial, effectively changed the law in England for the next century. He insisted that blasphemy concerns not the matter but the manner of expression and ruled: "if the decencies of controversy are observed, even the fundamentals of religion may be attacked without the writer being guilty of blasphemy" (Levy 1993, 487). Nonbelief was not by itself criminal. In a time when a Jew might become Lord Chancellor, Christianity was no longer the law of the land in the way that it had once been. Even if it were, any part of the law of the land, on Coleridge's view, was open to attack, whether it was religion, the monarchy, primogeniture, or the laws of marriage.

But making manner the crux and requiring a malicious intent to insult the Christian majority (typically manifested in the manner of expression) did not remove all difficulties in blasphemy doctrine. There remained the inherent unfairness in the law's being solicitous of the feelings of (some) Christians while failing to protect the feelings of freethinkers or Jews or Muslims. And even where a blasphemy statute might seek to protect all religions and all believers' (and perhaps even nonbelievers') feelings against intentional wounding, we must recognize it can do little to enforce harmony. Macaulay's even-handed Indian Penal Code provision did little to defuse the murderous expression of hatred between Muslims and Hindus in that divided country (Levy 1993, 494, 548)—the divisions coming ultimately to be marked by the troubled border between India and Pakistan. Further, an emphasis on manner risks turning prosecutions for blasphemy into a class weapon of the ruling classes against the poor. The well-educated could state their views, but the penny press and its working class readers could not. Educated writers such as Matthew Arnold and T. H. Huxley might make some of the same arguments as the *Freethinker* with impunity, their elevated discourse providing them cover. As Stephen put the point, "You cannot really distinguish between substance and style. You must either forbid or permit all attacks on Christianity. You cannot in practice send a man to gaol for not writing like a scholar and a gentleman when he is neither one nor the other, and when he is writing on a subject which excites him strongly" (Levy 1993, 491–92). And what exactly is being protected when one focuses on abusive epithets and scurrilous ridicule? The feelings of the attacked? As we saw in our earlier discussion of modern hate speech codes, polite hate speech can be far more wounding than a stream of vulgar epithets. Or, to cite Levy's example, "saying that Jesus was the illegitimate offspring of a passing Roman soldier is not much less offensive than calling him a 'bastard' and his mother a 'whore'—one of the conventional blasphemous statements" (Levy 1993, 488). In general, scholarly arguments may be more subversive than abusive insults.[4]

---

4. And fiction may be more subversive still. The enormously popular turn-of-the-millennium religious mystery-thriller, *The Da Vinci Code*, stirred demonstrations and outrage (though no legal prosecutions) at its novelistic theology of a mortal, married Jesus and an early Christianity centered on the sacred feminine. Is it blasphemy if it presents itself as a suspense novel? Are the orthodox offended entitled to protection by the state?

The *Gay News* case in England was a private prosecution for blasphemy instigated by Mary Whitehouse (an activist censor of public morals) in 1977, based on the publication of a poem ("The Love That Dares to Speak Its Name") by James Kirkup that graphically depicted a homosexual Christ. The prosecution resulted in convictions and penalties for the magazine's editor and publisher. The prosecutor had conceded, "You can say Christ was a fraud or deceiver, or that Christ may have been a homosexual, provided you say it in a reasonable, measured, reflective, decent way." Mrs. Whitehouse herself stated that the prosecution for blasphemy was based on the poem being "so offensive in its manner to Christians and sympathizers with the Christian faith that it would be liable to cause a breach of the peace"

The sources quoted by Coleridge in his definitive opinion (notably *Starkie on Libel*) had emphasized "a malicious and mischievous intention" as essential to blasphemy. "The wilful intention to insult and mislead others by means of licentious and contumelious abuse offered to sacred subjects . . . is the criterion and the test of guilt" (Levy 1993, 546, 486). If the real target of prosecutions for blasphemy are malicious intentions—so that the Muslims who take offense at Danish cartoons but not at unbelievers eating pork are taking offense at the underlying intentions, the insult depending on the intention to insult—the problem remains that intention or motive cannot simply be read from either matter or manner. It may be that, as a matter of class, some express themselves less elegantly than others—that cannot be proof of intent. Nor is vehemence of language proof of malice. As Leonard W. Levy summarizes an argument at the time of the 1883 trials in his valuable history of blasphemy, there is a risk in inferring the existence of malice from the character of the defendant's language: "anyone shocked by that language would discover a malicious intent to offend. Coleridge's decency test, if enforced, would have convicted Luther, Calvin, and Fox, as well as Jesus" (1993, 489). Further, for there to be an intention to insult an individual's feelings, the target must be in the presumed audience. Foote's paper was sold to be purchased by like-minded individuals. The Danish cartoons were not published for distribution in the Middle East, and it took some time and a concerted effort for awareness of them to make its way there. (Indeed, since some of the twelve actually published Danish cartoons might have seemed too tame, some bogus cartoons—including one of the Prophet mounted by a dog—were widely distributed by Muslim clerics seeking to foment offense.)

In the end, an intolerable subjectivity and vagueness is introduced by appeal to "the decencies of controversy" and malicious intentions. As Foote put it, "an overt act of crime is the broad boundary between right and wrong . . . [The] law of blasphemous libel is simply a noose

(Levy 1993, 542, 538 cf. 543). The standard was Coleridge's manner test, the spirit American "fighting words" doctrine.

In the United States in recent years, certain conservative commentators have fantasized a "war on Christmas" because some stores, to their reverent minds, have not mentioned Christ enough in their holiday decorations, ads, and commercials. (It has been alleged that some stores go so far in their crusade as to substitute a slyly secular "Happy Holidays" for "Merry Christmas" in greeting their shoppers.) It seems, amazingly, blasphemy may sometimes be marked by absence of utterance.

round the neck of every man who writes or speaks on the subject of religion; and if he happens to be on the unpopular side, somebody will pull the string" (Levy 1993, 489). It happened that in Foote's own case, in Coleridge's court under Coleridge's "manner" interpretation of the law, the jury was hung and Foote escaped conviction despite the fact that it is difficult to imagine a more blatant transgression of "the decencies of controversy" than by the *Freethinker*. That does not obviate or overcome the problem of vagueness, it simply illustrates that vagueness can occasionally work in a defendant's favor.

The English contrast between matter and manner in blasphemy law has its parallel in American law, in particular in the First Amendment contrast between content-based restrictions on speech (which are prohibited) and restrictions based on time, place, and manner (which are permitted). So, for example, campaigns for a particular candidate cannot be proscribed, but sound trucks (whether trumpeting the virtues of a political candidate or a bargain at the local mall) can be prohibited from circulating during certain hours or broadcasting their messages above a certain volume. The concern is not to protect individuals from offensive beliefs, but to preserve their sleep and the quiet enjoyment of their pleasures. But notice that vulgarity and vehemence are not relevant aspects of "manner" in American doctrine. Whether obscenity and "fighting words" should be, we have already discussed. The predominant strain in American law is to protect the free exercise and even the vilification of religion under the First Amendment. As Stephen had pointed out during the debates surrounding the 1883 prosecutions, "heat, exaggeration, and fierce invective" are inherent in religious as in political controversy (Levy 1993, 492). In its 1940 *Cantwell v. Connecticut* decision, the United States Supreme Court extended the protection of the First Amendment to prevent infringement by the states (incorporating it through the due-process clause of the Fourteenth Amendment), unanimously declaring:

> In the realm of religious faith, and in that of political belief, sharp differences arise. In both fields the tenets of one man may seem the rankest error to his neighbor. To persuade others to his own point of view, the pleader, as we know, at times resorts to exaggeration, to vilification of men who have been, or are, prominent in church or state, and even to false statement. But the people of this nation have ordained in the light of history, that, in spite of the probability of excesses and abuses, these liberties are, in the long view, essential

to enlightened opinion and right conduct on the part of the citizens of a democracy. The essential characteristic of these liberties is, that under their shield many types of life, character, opinion and belief can develop unmolested and unobstructed. Nowhere is this shield more necessary than in our own country for a people composed of many races and of many creeds. (*Cantwell v. Connecticut*, 310 U.S. 296, 310 [1940])

In both England, with its established church, and the United States, with its constitutional prohibition of an establishment of religion and its insistence on the separation of church and state, the last significant prosecutions under the laws of blasphemy were in the 1970s. But we have seen that times have not changed everywhere, and even where believers have no state sanctioned special protections, religious feelings often run high and find extralegal expression. Where the law does provide protection to religious sensibilities, it is at some considerable cost, whether the focus is on matter or manner. One might object to coarse attacks. One might object to refined satire as well. One might wish to protect all equally from all forms of offensive discourse. But in protecting all or any from offense, the victim becomes free thought, inquiry, and argument.

FREEDOM OF SPEECH VERSUS RESPECT

While the *Jyllands-Posten* editor responsible for the publication of the Muhammad cartoons apologized for any offended feelings, he did not retreat on principle.[5] He complained that protesters were not asking merely for his respect, but his "submission" (*New York Times* 2/5/2006, p. 5). What exactly does respect require?

Leviticus 24:16, 22 has the Lord saying to Moses, after a man with an Egyptian father had cursed the name of the Lord, "He who

---

5. To say "I apologize" does not always mean to admit wrongdoing. It can, like "I'm sorry for your loss" and as in "we apologize for the inconvenience," sometimes merely be an expression of sympathy, regret, and compassion for misfortune and suffering. In such empathic uses, "I apologize" does not mean the apologizer would not do the offending act again. The ambiguity is usefully considered by Lazare 2004, 23–27.

blasphemes the name of the Lord shall be put to death; all the congregation shall stone him; the sojourner as well as the native, when he blasphemes the Name, shall be put to death. . . . You shall have one law for the sojourner and for the native; for I am the Lord your God" (Revised Standard Version). Thus the Third Book of Moses inaugurated a standard for blasphemy that applied to believers and nonbelievers, natives and foreigners, alike. But such a universal standard cannot prevail in a world of multiple religions with conflicting prescriptions and proscriptions, with minorities in one area forming majorities elsewhere. Even if a locally dominant group could enforce its requirements where it held sway (e.g., prohibition of liquor in Muslim countries) what counts as blasphemy would vary from jurisdiction to jurisdiction, and so would what counts as "respect." But perhaps what is wanted (in regions where a different majority holds sway) is not an impossible universal conformity in behavior, but simply a biting of would-be blasphemous tongues. Perhaps what respect requires of those who reject particular religious beliefs is silence.

The Vatican weighed into the Muhammad cartoon controversy by deploring violence, but added that "The right to freedom of thought and expression cannot entail the right to offend the religious sentiment of believers" (*New York Times* 2/5/2006, p. 5). The believers in question in this instance were, of course, Muslims. The Catholic Church has not, however, always honored the sentiments of its own dissidents, reformers, and heretics nor the views of those it has sought—in its apostolic, evangelical, missionary, and crusading zeal—to convert to "the one true faith." Worse, the problem is not just a selectively respectful and tolerant Catholic Church. History suggests that just about any set of beliefs can be organized into a religion. If so, assuming all religions merit the same respect, the Vatican view would entail that freedom of thought and expression have no scope at all. If the right to speak is limited by a right not to be offended, the offended could silence the world. (The Catholic Church had troubles of its own with an offended Muslim world a year after the original publication of the Danish cartoons, when Pope Benedict XVI quoted and appeared to endorse a fourteenth-century criticism that everything new Muhammad had brought was "evil and inhuman, such as his command to spread by the sword the faith he preached" [*New York Times* 9/15/2006].) If there is to be discourse and disagreement, freedom of speech must be taken to protect insults, even irreverent blasphemous insults. While that does not make freedom of speech limitless (Mill's "harm to others principle" remains in force), offended feelings must in general be regarded among the costs, the generally acceptable costs, of honoring such freedom. As Justice Oliver Wendell Holmes Jr. pointed out, freedom of speech is needed to protect the idea that we hate. Inoffensive ideas that we agree with need no such shield (*U.S. v. Schwimmer*, 279 U.S. 644, 655 [1929]).

Even unspoken thoughts may need protection. God is typically thought to see into the heart, so deviant thoughts have sometimes been believed as subject to observation as deviant conduct. Blasphemy laws have traditionally insisted on conformity to orthodox belief within, *in foro interno*, as well as in outward expression. And we need to consider conduct further. The line between speech and conduct, here as elsewhere, is problematic. We have seen that conduct may be speech and speech may be conduct. As we have also seen, religions differ in their prescriptions and proscriptions for conduct, and so it might be impossible to "respect" them all where they conflict. But where it is possible, does respect require conformity in conduct? When the religious rules of Islam (or any other religion) clash with the secular ideals of freedom of speech and freedom of action, which should prevail?

What if the Muslims object to my eating pork—not just to depictions of the Prophet Muhammad? John Stuart Mill (1975, 104–5) pointed out that Muslims find scarcely anything as offensive as the eating of pork (a taboo actually shared with Orthodox Jews). No religion that I am aware of *requires* its adherents to eat pork, so abstaining need not involve conflict of religions. Nonetheless, there does not seem to be a call from the mullahs for non-Muslims to observe the taboo. Does respecting Islam require that no one eat pork or only that believers not eat pork? How about making images of the Prophet? How is it that some rules are selective in their application and others universal? Why should those thought to be bound by stringent religious rules be different from rule to rule? Of course, no one should blow up or desecrate a mosque (or a church or a synagogue or any other place of worship), but that has happened repeatedly in Iraq without stirring worldwide protests. The inner divisions of Islam seem better tolerated than Western slights.

The clash of convictions between individuals from different cultural backgrounds may lead to differing expectations and thus feelings of insult. Differences between dominant cultures and subcultures can be similarly problematical. Consider the historical conflict between Mormon polygamy and American law. John Stuart Mill himself, when writing about the Mormons, was torn between his liberal commitment to the toleration of differing religious beliefs and his fierce opposition to the subjugation of women (the subject of one of his many books), of which even apparently consensual polygamy may be an example. As Mill wrote of such polygamy at the end of chapter 4 of *On Liberty* in 1859, "far from being in any way countenanced by the principle of liberty, it is a direct infraction of that principle, being a mere riveting of the chains of one-half of the community, and an emancipation of the other from reciprocity of obligation towards them" (Mill 1975, 113). Mill in the end supported the right of the Mormons as a sovereign people to practice their preferred ways free of coercive interference by others. He was writing, of course, before the region that the Mormons had fled to, what he referred to as "a solitary recess in the midst of a desert," had become the state of Utah (which it did in 1896). The conflict between freedom of religion and secular law was taken up by the Supreme Court while Utah was still a territory of the United States, and the dominant culture's views prevailed (*Reynolds v. U.S.*, 98 U.S. 145 [1878]).[6]

Now eating pork, unlike depictions of Muhammad in cartoons or other media, may not seem "aimed" at believers. It may be easier for the orthodox to accept deviations from doctrine and behavior among outsiders when they do not perceive these as propelled by an intention to disrespect and conspicuously flout the demands of their religion. We see once more that a perceived intention to offend can itself produce or deepen offense. But reading intentions here as elsewhere can be prob-

6. There are other strands in American law. Robert C. Post (1988) interestingly explores them under the headings of *assimilationism* (which is what is illustrated by the rejection of Mormon polygamy by the sustaining of the federal anti-bigamy statute in the *Reynolds* case), *pluralism* (which is illustrated in cases such as *Wisconsin v. Yoder*, 406 U.S. 205 [1972], where group rights and diversity prevailed when the Amish community was given ultimate authority to school their children in their preferred traditions), and *individualism* (illustrated in the case of *West Virginia State Board of Education v. Barnette*, 319 U.S. 624 [1942], where the question of swearing allegiance to the flag was left to individual student conscience, thus overturning the Court's own 1940 *Gobitis* decision). On this analysis, the English law of blasphemy is assimilationist, while the American law of blasphemy, like First Amendment law in general, is predominantly individualist.

lematic. Must an illustrator of a children's life of Muhammad necessarily aim at offending? Religious doctrine may itself distinguish between constraints on believers and on nonbelievers. But that was not the view of the ancient Hebrews as expounded in Leviticus. Let us suppose that the strictures against depictions of Muhammad are meant to apply to Muslims and non-Muslims alike. Suppose further that the non-Muslims are well aware that the stricture is meant to apply to them, and that violation of the prohibition will be perceived as willful, pointed disrespect (and not as due to the compulsions of hunger or other acceptable motivations). Certainly the editor of the *Jyllands-Posten* was aware that publication of the cartoons would be seen as a provocation. But his aim was not a macho confrontation of the sort we have seen in the *briga* of Brazilian street life. He wished to make a point against self-censorship. He knew Muslims did not want to hear or see certain things, but in a free society that some wish not to see or hear certain things, that they might be offended by them, is not grounds to silence those who would speak. So a genuine clash of principles was set up.

Several papers elsewhere in Europe republished the cartoons in solidarity with the principled stand of the Danish editor, among them Italy's *La Stampa* and Barcelona's *El Periodico* and Madrid's *El Mundo*. Germany's *Die Welt* printed one of the cartoons on its front page, arguing that a "right to blasphemy" was anchored in democratic freedoms (*Washington Post* 2/2/2006, p. A17). While the daily *France Soir* initially joined the chorus, the paper subsequently fired its managing editor — its owner, Raymond Lakah, an Egyptian-born French businessman, explaining the firing as "a strong sign of respect for the beliefs and intimate convictions of every individual" (*New York Times* 2/3/2006). But does firing one of the parties in a conflict of convictions show respect for "every individual"? Could it? Can one? Hamid Karzai, President of Afghanistan at the time, issued a statement condemning "in the strongest terms" *France Soir*'s publication of the cartoons, affirming: "Any insult to the holy prophet (peace be upon him) is an insult to more than one billion Muslims" (*New York Times* 2/3/2006). The various reprintings led to further demonstrations and the brief kidnapping of a German (mistaken for a Dane) in the West Bank. While many political leaders in Europe called for condemnation of insults to any religion, French Interior Minister Nicolas Sarkozy (now President of France) said he preferred "an excess of caricature to an excess of censorship" (*Wall Street Journal* 2/25/2006).

CONSISTENCY

Some have accused the Muslim world of inconsistency: expressing outrage when their religious beliefs are not respected or conformed to, while blatantly libeling and blaspheming against Judaism, Christianity, and other religions on a regular basis. Egyptian TV has broadcast a 41-part series based on *The Protocols of the Elders of Zion*, a hundred-year-old anti-Semitic forgery that purported to be a Jewish master plan to control the world. Syrian television has depicted rabbis as cannibals, one series showing rabbis slaughtering a gentile boy in order to ritually drink his blood (*New York Times* and *Washington Post*, 2/3/2006). Not long after the Muhammad cartoon furor, a ten million dollar Turkish film (the costliest every made in that country), *Valley of the Wolves—Iraq*, became that country's biggest hit ever (*New York Times* 2/14/2006). It portrayed American soldiers as killing Muslim children in order to sell their bodies to Jewish doctors who harvest their organs. This caricature of Americans played to packed houses in a country that at about the same time was bringing to trial its most famous author for daring to insult Turkishness by referring to the unmentionable 1915 Turkish massacre of a million Armenians. Not that American films are any kinder to Muslims in their portrayal as conscienceless terrorists prepared to indulge in murder, hijackings, and nuclear annihilation of whole populations. But, under the protection of the First Amendment, American films have greater leeway to be equal-opportunity offenders, not sparing locally dominant religions or powerful political interests from criticism, caricature, and ridicule. The silencing in Turkey may be more troubling than its offensive caricatures.

Under Turkey's law that makes it a crime to "insult Turkish identity," authors who have so much as admitted the World War I Turkish massacre of Armenians have been charged and jailed for defaming the state. The crime is punishable by up to three years in prison. Truth is no defense. Orhan Pamuk, awarded the Nobel Prize for literature in 2006, was charged under the law in 2005 for referring to the Armenian genocide and to later clashes between Turks and minority Kurds in Turkey. He told a Swiss newspaper that "One million Armenians and 30,000 Kurds were killed in these lands, and nobody but me dares to talk about it" (*New York Times* 12/21/2005). With entry into the European Union at stake, however, Turkey went on to temper some of its trials. The charges against Pamuk were dismissed on a technicality. Still, others have been convicted and jailed under the law.

But it is not only Turkey or other Muslim countries that lack a First Amendment or its equivalent. In 2005, Oriana Fallaci was indicted in Italy under provisions of the Italian Penal Code which proscribe the *"vilipendio"* or "vilification" of "any religion acknowledged by the state." She had published a series of books (including *The Rage and the Pride* and *The Force of Reason* and, most recently, *The Apocalypse*) complaining that Europe is on the verge of becoming a dominion of Islam. It must be admitted that the "manner," in particular the language, of the books was intemperate, even scatological; but such language has not always led to indictments in relation to other objects of vilification (*Wall Street Journal* 6/23/2005 and Talbot 2006). And there is other evidence that the ideals of freedom of expression that allowed the publication of the Muhammad cartoons in Denmark and other European countries are not always enforced with an even hand. It is illegal in seven European countries to say that Hitler did not murder millions of Jews. In 2006 in an Austrian Court, right-wing British historian David Irving was sentenced to three years imprisonment after pleading guilty to Holocaust denial. The 1992 Austrian law applies to "whoever denies, grossly plays down, approves or tries to excuse the National Socialist genocide or other National Socialist crimes against humanity in a print publication, in broadcast or other media" (*New York Times* 2/21/2006).

There is a kind of inconsistency here too. A different standard— historically understandable, but ultimately unprincipled—is applied to the Holocaust deniers. The despicable Holocaust denier should be answered by dismissal or ridicule or refutation, not legal sanctions. As Brandeis pointed out, the remedy for objectionable speech is generally more speech, better speech. How else can the most deeply felt convictions of religion and politics be given the airing needed to be persuasive to others or legitimately sustainable for those already convinced? These were the familiar arguments of John Milton and John Stuart Mill in favor of freedom of expression. They must still prevail.

One should go a step further. Freedom of expression is itself a part of human dignity. Whatever the benefits to all of allowing everyone to have their say, and whatever its costs, it is essential to each to be able to express what they think and, so, who they are. In speaking our minds, we give reality, shape and definite content to those minds, as well as potentially influencing others. When one is compelled to shut up, one is stifled and stunted. Which is not to say that it is impossible to speak out of turn. There may be all sorts of reasons to object to the matter or manner, the substance or style, of a person's speech, and the objector may sometimes be—all things considered—right. We thus have reason to note once more that freedom of speech is not (and never has been) an absolute. But the crucial thing is to appreciate how much and what is at stake when some are silenced, so that we are extremely alert to the possibility of error, and so that in our wariness we put the burden of proof on those who would silence. It should be an extremely heavy burden.

RESPECTING RELIGION

There used to be "Blue Laws" in certain states in the United States (beginning in New England) that required all places of business to close on Sundays. That might seem to be enforcing a simple respect for religion. But surely Jews might prefer to close on their day of rest, Saturday, and Muslims on their holy day, Friday. Whose religion gets respected? And if the concern of the Blue Laws was to prevent unfair competition (rather than to show respect for religion), why was it unfair for Christians to have to compete with businesses that stayed open on Sundays but not unfair for Muslims or Jews to have to compete with businesses that stayed open on Fridays or Saturdays? Blasphemy laws in general tend to protect only the majority or dominant religion in a society. Not that an even-handed respect could be easily enforced. If all religions were to be protected equally, all businesses might have to be closed every day. This is but one of many conflicts that the diverse demands of differing religions might lead to. There are advantages to the state permitting what might appear to some as disrespect.

The tradition of tolerating even blasphemy is very strong in the United States. Many Christian (and non-Christian) sensibilities were inflamed by Andres Serrano's "Piss Christ," a crucified Christ immersed (baptized?) in a tank of Serrano's urine. The National Endowment for the Arts had supported the project—one of a series of tableaux by Serrano dealing with fluids: blood, urine, milk, and semen—with a grant. Senator Alphonse D'Amato launched the image into prominence by tearing up a picture of it in the chambers of the U.S. Senate in 1989—a kind of ritual counter-desecration.[7] The subsidized mingling of the sacred and the profane did stir outrage among conservatives and a backlash against the NEA. But toleration and government subsidization are separable issues. While there were political repercussions (calls to cut funding to the NEA and subsequent legislation requiring the agency to take "into consideration general standards of decency" in awarding grants—*New York Times* 6/26/1998), there were no prosecutions or persecutions . . . no one died, no buildings were burned, there was no rioting in the streets. Toleration survived even as subsidization got restricted.

Some might suppose religion and art, like obscenity, do not matter so much in the United States—that the price of toleration is trivialization. But the First Amendment is serious on any accounting. Even the most deeply held political convictions are open to challenge. Not just Holocaust deniers, but Nazis get to express their views in the United States. We have had occasion to refer earlier to the *Skokie* case. In 1977, a group of neo-Nazis wished to parade their repugnant creed, complete with offensive symbols and uniforms, in the Chicago suburb of Skokie. Skokie was a heavily Jewish town, with 7000 Holocaust survivors residing there at the time—an audience hardly likely to welcome the message of the swastika emblazoned marchers. In the case of *Village of Skokie v. National Socialist Party of America* (373 N.E. 2d 21 [Ill. 1978]), with the Nazis represented by the ACLU, the Supreme Court of Illinois lifted an injunction against the march and the Nazis were eventually awarded a permit. When they did march (in the end in Chicago's Marquette Park rather than Skokie) the small band of Nazis were met by thousands of counter-demonstrators. The remedy for offensive speech is, once more, more speech.

---

7. In 1992, singer Sinead O'Connor practically ended her career when she tore up a picture of Pope John Paul II on *Saturday Night Live*. Other singers have had to pay a heavy price for their public insults. The Dixie Chicks were banned for years from many country music radio stations after telling a London audience, in 2003 on the eve of the Iraq war, "Just so you know, we're ashamed the President of the United States is from Texas."

There have been other controversies stirred by tax-funded minglings of the sacred and the profane, notably a 1999 Brooklyn Museum show that included Chris Ofili's "The Holy Virgin Mary," with the sacred image in that case shown clotted with elephant dung and surrounded by pornographic cut-outs.

The principle behind giving a hearing to such unsympathetic speakers may be clearer if one considers the many marches led by Martin Luther King through the Jim Crow South. When he and others marched to Selma and elsewhere, there were many (in the South, likely a majority) who found the demands of the civil rights movement offensive. But sometimes people need to march where they are not wanted in order to be heard. The televised brutal response of southern sheriffs with their police dogs and fire hoses made clear to all what the marchers were contending with and protesting against. The movement's right to speak was protected by federal law and the movement demands prevailed in the end. The rights protected by the American Bill of Rights are precisely rights *against* the majority. In particular, people have a right to speak even if the majority does not wish to hear. And it is salutary to remember (as we saw when we discussed hate speech codes on university campuses), that the right-thinking individuals and groups that would cut off hateful and discriminatory speech may themselves be a minority. It may be a political error to invite the majority to shut anyone up, however distasteful what they have to say, if only because one can never be sure whether one's own views will come to be seen as distasteful. (Recall the record of Canadian efforts to keep out hateful literature. The first victims of the effort were the writings of the very lesbian, gay, and black authors the legislation had been meant to protect.)

We have seen majority sensibilities have received special protections in the history of blasphemy law in England and elsewhere. Some have argued that fairness requires that the protections be spread more widely, that all religions should be protected from offense. I have tried to argue that offense is less of a danger than the stifling of free speech. There might in the end be no limit to religious sensitivities and ultimately no scope for freedom of expression. The demands of democratic open discussion, including room for satire and ridicule, go against it. Mill's call for self-development and self-expression through experiments in living goes against it. This is a lesson not just for Muslims that seek accommodation with the West, but also for Western nations that seek to limit freedom of expression (as of the Holocaust deniers in Austria). As Voltaire and others have repeatedly warned, to give some the power to shut up others is to endanger all. The move should not be to extend the range of blasphemy law, but to curtail it completely. While Justice Brandeis' call for "more speech" may not always provide the remedy desired, in the realm of religion like the realm of politics, our risky commitment to the airing of objectionable views requires that debate be "uninhibited, robust, and wide-open."

To conclude, what exactly does respect require? There is a striking moment in the 1981 Joan Crawford biopic *Mommie Dearest* when the mother viciously slaps her daughter, saying, "Why can't you just give me the *respect* that I deserve?" To demand obedience to one's every desire, whim, and command (which is what the abusive Mommie Dearest expects) is to ask too much. To demand an admiration which one's conduct and character do not warrant is to ask too much. To demand never to be offended is also to ask too much. The thing that all persons are entitled to, according to Kantian moral philosophy, is not obedience, or admiration, or even liking or esteem. It is an acknowledgment of each individual's distinctive and unique rationality and agency. Such an acknowledgment precludes treating persons as mere means to one's own ends, ignoring their personhood or humanity. Kant himself acknowledges respect is a feeling, but insists it must be distinguished from the ordinary run of feelings that can be reduced to inclination or fear, are linked to self-love, and are not purely rational (1785, 401n). Whatever may be the truth about love, grief, and other emotions, we can show respect even if we do not feel it. True virtue, however, may require more. And in our personal relations we expect (or at least hope for) more. At a minimum, however, in our less personal encounters and engagements, we look for the outward form, and that is all that the coercive powers of society can enforce. Still, the outer manner may be easier to maintain if it is generated from an inner attitude. The respect due persons, their dignity, is, within Kantian morality, derivative from or equivalent to the respect due to the moral law. It is supposed to be the effect on us of recognition of the majesty of the moral law. That compelling majesty leaves room for us to mock, ridicule, and laugh at our fellow ends-in-themselves—at least most of the time.

NINE

■ ■ ■

INSULT HUMOR

ONE HARDLY KNOWS WHERE TO BEGIN. THERE IS OF COURSE A DISTINCTIVE genre of insult humor, where the jokes are meant directly to insult the audience and the insult is meant to be the joke. The likes of Don Rickles and Andrew Dice Clay are comics who spew their venom directly at the audience (or at least certain individuals or selected groups within it) and the audience, in the spirit of everything being all-in-good-fun and everyone being a good sport, is cajoled or expected to pretend the venom is not poisonous and that the would-be comics are not mean-spirited, small-minded, and vicious—that is, not funny at all.

Don Rickles, sometimes referred to as "the Merchant of Venom," has made a career out of calling strangers in his audience "hockey pucks." The emptiness of such wit leaves only the groundlessness and pointlessness of the apparent aggressiveness to fuel the relief that is supposed to be felt when Rickles reveals, at the end of his act, that the verbal hostility and facial grimaces were not meant seriously. He typically does this by assuring the audience—with equal emptiness—that he loves them all, leaving them thinking he is really a "nice guy" and that they must be nice too for having tolerated his unjustified abusiveness like good sports. Since the sport is obviously not hockey, it may perhaps be deception and collusive self-deception. We shall see that humor, as Freud teaches, may often involve collusion of various sorts.

Rickles and his ilk are sometimes defended as serving a higher purpose. Zoe Heller explains, "The aggression that is generally understood to

be the subtext of all standup acts is rendered entirely explicit in his performance: aggression is, in a sense, the subject of his performance. He isn't trying
to charm a hostile world. He is coming at it with a baseball bat" (Heller
2004, 33). He rains derision on the audience. His act is basically a stream of
racial and sexual stereotypes (some rather dated, e.g., "but really, we like the
Italians. We do. We gotta kiss their asses, so's the Jews can have ice"—Don
Rickles was 78 in 2004, with more than 50 years in show business) and individual invective (some rather fanciful, like calling people "hockey pucks,"
which may be more a matter of sound effects than incisive characterization). If he is playing with aggression, rather than simply manifesting it, to
what end? Heller continues, "The stated intention of this genial racism is a
liberal one. Rickles is an equal-opportunity offender, the idea goes—a kind
of workingman's Lenny Bruce—deploying stereotype to demonstrate that
we are all different and all equal" (Heller, 33). But even Heller concedes
such ennobling purposes cannot be detected in his progeny, "the ultra-
aggressive shock comedy of Andrew Dice Clay and Sam Kinison" (Heller,
35). Andrew Dice Clay occasionally defends himself by insisting he is only
pretending to be a jerk—but that can be complicated when one actually is a
jerk.[1] One suspects that the line between mocking bigotry and insensitivity
and exhibiting them is not clear and firm even in Rickles' case. He admits to
insulting-to-order in some of his gigs (Heller, 38). Certainly he has exploited
the attitudes of some in his audience for his comedic purposes. Whether
he actually has higher purposes and whether he achieves them are further
questions. That individuals can be co-opted (forced to be good sports in tolerating Rickles' apparent intolerance and open abuse), fits with the general
structure of collusion in tendentious humor detected by Freud.

   Of course, insults *can* be done with good humor. Witness Dame
Edna. As a *Time Magazine* critic says of the "saucy, violet-haired, spangle-

---

1. Actors should presumably be allowed to play any role (despite Plato's view that
demeaning roles demean both actor and audience). Should an actor refuse certain roles
because he or she would not want actually to be that person? Presumably not, but perhaps
a comedian should, because his jokes legitimize underlying attitudes. Still, a particularly
agile comedian might be able to do a somersault and use the apparent legitimization to
flush out the bigots, as Sacha Baron Cohen attempts in his 2006 movie, *Borat: Cultural
Learnings of America for Make Benefit Glorious Nation of Kazakhstan.* And Carroll
O'Connor for years managed to bring out the ludicrousness of bigotry through his masterful portrayal of Archie Bunker in the TV series, *All in the Family* (1971–1979), regularly
making Archie and his bigoted view of the world the object of the audience's laughter.

spectacled matron" played by Barry Humphries in his second Broadway production, *Dame Edna: Back with a Vengeance!*, "Humphries has built an entire show out of that old comedy-club staple of bantering with the audience. But the earnestly solicitous singsong with which Dame Edna delivers her well-practiced sucker punches ('I love the outfit you've chosen.' Beat. 'Is it reversible?') robs them of any meanness or condescension" (Zoglin 2004, 156). Any eviscerating insult would be in the missing meanness and condescension. The redemption is in the comic framing. (In case anyone is tempted to think that the tempering results from Dame Edna being a woman, as though truly vicious insults were a masculine prerogative, remember Dame Edna is played by a cross-dressing Barry Humphries. For good measure, there is Lisa Lampanelli, self-described as the world's only female insult comic, and also as "Comedy's Lovable Queen of Mean," or "The Cunt of Comedy"—i.e., a Don Rickles wannabe.)

Direct insult humor—direct in the sense of being aimed at members of the audience (as by Don Rickles and, more subtly and more genially, by Dame Edna) or at the nominal "honoree" of the occasion (as in roasts)—allows for playing with aggression. As with the insult rituals discussed earlier, the context defangs the insults, which might otherwise be regarded as grievous assaults. The aggression gets both expressed and blunted. The mechanism seems similar to that operating in "carnivale" and other social practices which allow for the (momentary, circumscribed) breaking of taboos and their simultaneous maintenance, affirmation, and preservation. While the crudity of much direct insult humor may be occasion for dismay (think of the "poop"-centered humor of Triumph the Insult Comic Dog)—one misses the envelope of wit in which more clever and thoughtful humor gets delivered—it is when the butt of the joke is not present that unbridled viciousness tends to emerge. And the butt is often a group (racial, religious, ethnic, social) rather than an individual. The humor of denigratory stereotype and group hatred makes pressing the question (in Ronald de Sousa's pointed formulation) "when is it wrong to laugh?"

WHEN IS IT WRONG TO LAUGH?

De Sousa answers his question by insisting that racist and sexist humor presupposes certain attitudes and that to find witless racist and sexist jokes funny, one cannot hold those attitudes merely hypothetically. He offers the example of a witless rape joke: "M. visits the hockey team. When she emerges she complains that she has been gang-raped. Wishful thinking" (de Sousa 1987, 290). There is no shortage of equally witless racist jokes. Randall Kennedy offers the following example taken from a KKK Web site: "Q. What do you call a nigger boy riding a bike? A. Thief!" (Kennedy 2002, 7). The problem, once more, is in the underlying attitudes assumed and revealed.

There are, of course, some circumstances where the normally presumed attitudes might not prevail. For example, in joking between friends, where the slurs against the other's group are part of a mutual exchange and clearly not meant seriously, or where the friends are perhaps both members of the same ridiculed group. (This last is perhaps why Richard Pryor can make "nigger" jokes and non-blacks cannot. The usual denigratory attitudes are typically cancelled out when self-ascribed. But self-denigrating humor and the relation of the joke-maker to the audience will need further examination.) The usually presumed attitudes may also fall away where the joke is clever rather than witless, because that opens the possibility that the object of laughter is the envelope of the joke rather than its content, the manner rather than the matter. But outside of such special circumstances, it is not so easy to laugh and yet dissociate from the racist or sexist or otherwise objectionable attitudes that a joke presumes and requires. One might well understand why someone else might be moved to laughter if they held certain beliefs and attitudes one does not oneself share, but such theoretical understanding would not be enough to provoke one's own laughter (except perhaps in a meta-form, where the joker's benighted and self-satisfied attitudes themselves become the object of laughter, what de Sousa calls the "Monty Python principle"—1987, 291).

A joking context may sometimes belie what would otherwise be taken as a hostile intention—but we should recall that framing is fragile. As Bateson has taught us, frames can shift and they can be misunderstood. Ritual insults fairly readily cross over into personal insults and develop into fights. Saying "I didn't mean it" or "only kidding" may sometimes not be enough. (In the case of children, the familiar "I didn't mean to" defense usually gets offered on occasions in which it is only too obvious that they did mean to. They just didn't mean for the harm that ensued to ensue, or to get caught.) Being a member of the denigrated category may be a more readily read and stable defense. (Again, why blacks can make "nigger" jokes.) That is also why self-deprecating humor is particularly appealing. The object of attack is a group with a membership of one. But then, some minorities are genuinely self-loathing, as are some individuals. And while in this book I have frequently relied on the use/ mention distinction to license my quotation and discussion of invective I would never personally use, even quotation can be equivocal. As we noted when discussing Shakespeare on hypothetical framing, Freud explained the difficulty to the Rat Man when that unfortunate patient tried to repudiate as merely a passing "train of thought" what had in fact been a *wish* that his father might die: "I remarked that he was treating the phrase as though it were one that involved *lèse-majesté*; it was well known, of course, that it was equally punishable to say 'The Emperor is an ass' or to disguise the forbidden words by saying 'If any one says, etc., . . . then he will have me to reckon with.'" (1909d, 179). Bracketed quotations may still carry their original meaning. (A problem pointed to by the ancient rabbis who prohibited the repetition of a blasphemy in testimony on the alleged blasphemy and by those who insist that there is no context that can make the word "nigger" acceptable.) Passing trains of thought may be freighted with significance.

And one can go too far—even in a roast. Ted Danson was met with public excoriation for appearing in blackface at a Friars Club roast in 1993 honoring his then-girlfriend Whoopi Goldberg. She, the ostensible honoree of the occasion, was not offended (indeed, it turned out she had written the bit and thought it hilarious); it was others outside who took offense. Still, even the honoree may sometimes be offended, though the conventions of the genre would generally require him or her to refrain from any public expression of genuine offense. Being able to "take it" can be as highly valued a trait in dignified modern honorees as in ghetto players of the dozens and as among the duelists who were supposed to defend their honor with *sangfroid*. Self-mastery is a way of maintaining superiority to one's tormentors.

Roasts may be a relatively modern institution, but court jesters, licensed fools, are hardly modern innovations. Who may insult whom? Once one accepts Freud's insight that most humor is tendentious, serves purposes and has victims, it becomes interesting to consider the types of insult humor in relation to the position of the victim. There are three possibilities: the teller is himself the victim, as in self-deprecating humor (usually individual, but sometimes also implicating a wider group); the audience is the victim, as in Don Rickles's insult humor (where the audience are "hockey pucks"); or a third party not present is the victim (as in typical racist, ethnic, and sexist humor). Self-deprecating humor is especially appealing because no one is victimized but the agent him or herself. It becomes more interesting when a person is compelled to make fun of him or herself (as the American president must, annually, before the White House Correspondents' Association and the Foreign Press Corps). Insult humor directed at the audience is particularly fascinating, because the audience is needed to collaborate (to license the joker to laugh at his own jokes) while being victimized. Third party victims raise other, more typically moral, issues. As we have seen, so far as the underlying attitudes are reprehensible, so is the laughter that expresses those attitudes while attempting to give them cover.

COLLUSION

In *Jokes and their Relation to the Unconscious*, Freud points out that, very often, "strictly speaking, we do not know what we are laughing at" (1905c, 102). We may think that it is the joke technique that amuses us when it is the joke's hidden purpose that actually has force. This is typical for obscene jokes, hostile jokes, and other tendentious jokes that undo the renunciation of repression. As in cases of blasphemy, it can be difficult to distinguish manner and matter, a joke's witty envelope and its malicious content. One test that sometimes helps is to attempt to substitute a different group with a different stereotype (say Jews or Asians for women or blacks). Many dumbness jokes ("How many x does it take to screw in a lightbulb?," etc.) are relatively independent of the particular group picked out as preternaturally dumb, the effect often depends crucially only on the cleverness of the illustration of dumbness. De Sousa suggests the following thought experiment in connection with the rape joke he cited as involving endorsement of sexist attitudes:

> Just imagine either of two variants. In the first, some nonsexual form of assault is substituted for rape. Apart from some tenuous connection with masochism by which one might try to restore the original point, it will undoubtedly cease to be funny to anyone. In the second variant, substitute some man who (1) is not assumed to be homosexual

and (2) is not the object of any particularly hostile attitude. Again, the joke loses its point. And this cannot be remedied by my saying, "For the purposes of the joke, just ignore the sexist double standard, and pretend that you think that there is something evil or contemptible about a man who fucks a lot." (de Sousa 1987, 291)

The attitudes are clearly endorsed rather than simply entertained or understood. The situation is similar to the endorsement the state reveals when it engages in selective enforcement in libel cases. In cases of selective enforcement, as when the state denies liability for libel where a black is described as white, the state is not simply reflecting but endorsing the underlying societal views. This is different from the situation of the state when it declines to prosecute hate speech. In such cases the state may indeed remain neutral by defending freedom for both of two incompatible views.

We should note that not all humor entails commitment to underlying attitudes, offensive or otherwise. Jokes should be distinguished from the comic. Jokes are made up, constructions, but the comic is presented by life. Consider an MTV television series from 2003, *Newlyweds: Nick and Jessica*. One of its eponymous stars, Jessica Simpson, is a pert and pretty, blonde pop singer with a knockout body. Unfortunately, she is spoiled (her new hubby, Nick Lachey, himself a boy-band graduate, at one point speculates that she has never picked up a towel in her life), whining, talentless (rendering all lyrics in the same undifferentiating scream), and unrelievedly dumb. Jessica Simpson does not tell dumb blonde jokes, she *is* such a joke. There are episodes where she wonders whether the "Chicken of the Sea" (she actually says, "Chicken *by* the Sea") brand tuna she is eating might be chicken, where she declines to eat proffered "buffalo wings" (the Buffalo, New York barbequed chicken delicacy) because, as she puts it, "I don't eat buffalo," and where she says "I'm twenty-three years old, it's almost twenty-five, which is *almost* mid-twenties." To be accurate, she is not so much a "joke" (jokes after all are things made up and told with the intention of provoking laughter) as "comic" (the comic simply presents itself for our perception, it is an aspect of life). Jessica is what she is and seems unembarrassed about it. Indeed, she seems wholly unselfconscious and self-satisfied in her dumbness. (Still, it must be acknowledged that she has managed to capitalize on her apparent ignorance—making buffalo wing commercials and the like—so perhaps she possesses a deeper, a commercial and marketable, wisdom.) The late Anna Nicole Smith (who, in these degraded times, also had a TV show, *The Anna Nicole Show* [2002–2004]) went beyond the comic to the grotesque. Her drunken, slovenly boorishness went far beyond simple ignorance and rudeness. But neither self-satisfied Jessica nor complacent Anna Nicole is or was self-mocking.

There is, as we have seen, great appeal in self-deprecating humor. Aside from the unpretentious attitude toward oneself, and the undeceived self-understanding, it allows for the statement of truths that might be insulting from the mouths of others. The insightful self-criticism that Freud finds in many Jewish jokes about Jews ("stories created by Jews and directed against Jewish characteristics") typically becomes "brutal derision" in the crude and unsympathetic jokes told by outsiders (Freud 1905c, 111, 142). Sometimes what makes it wrong to laugh is not the joke, but who tells it.[2]

2. We have seen that people can go too far in insult rituals, turning ritual insults into personal insults and sometimes verbal sparring into physical confrontation. While self-deprecating humor has its appeals, self-depreciation can go too far. Erving Goffman writes about how our rituals of deference and demeanor, our rules for acceptable interaction, our etiquette, allow for "face-to-face ritual profanation" (1967, 88). In some psychiatric wards "Patients may profane a staff member or a fellow-patient by spitting at him, slapping his face, throwing feces at him, tearing off his clothes, pushing him off the chair, taking food from his grasp, screaming into his face, sexually molesting him, etc." (88). While the early members of this series are part of our common currency of insult, the escalating infractions go beyond our norms. It is important that they do not, however, go beyond our understanding, they still speak the language of insult—but they shout. As Goffman explains, "Whatever is in the patient's mind, the throwing of feces at an attendant is a use of our ceremonial idiom that is as exquisite in its way as is a bow from the waist done with grace and a flourish. Whether he knows it or not, the patient speaks the same ritual language as his captors; he merely says what they do not wish to hear, for patient behavior which does not carry ritual meaning in terms of the daily ceremonial discourse of the staff will not be perceived by the staff at all" (89). The language of insult cannot be a private language, not if it is to be effective. It must be a common currency. We must remember that clowns often achieve their effects via exaggeration. The point to see next is that self-profanation also has its norms. Moral self-castigation is familiar enough, and ordinary self-deprecation (serious or humorous) is familiar enough. But on psychiatric wards, and sometimes outside of them, "female patients can be found who have systematically pulled out all the hair from their head, presenting themselves thereafter with a countenance that is guaranteed to be grotesque. Perhaps the extreme for our society is found in patients who smear themselves with and eat their own feces" (90). But even verbal self-profanation, self-deprecation, can go too far (just as can ritual insult contests,

Thus Richard Pryor can effectively, and (usually) without causing offense, tell "nigger" jokes.[3] Hearers must presume that Pryor himself does not share the racist assumptions of the jokes and think himself inferior because of the color of his skin. Indeed, while an outsider cannot engage in self-ridicule of a group to which he does not belong, an insider can sometimes play with stereotypes, as with blacks making "nigger" jokes and gays making "queen" and "fag" and "queer" jokes— assured that they are not actually self-loathing, they safely play with the opprobrious terms of others and sometimes reappropriate them to more benign purposes.[4] But can one be so assured? One must be ever wary of self-deceptive self-understandings. As we saw in our discussion of "nigger" in relation to the regulation of hate speech, some believe such terms can never be stripped of their hateful connotations. This connects with the general difficulty of determining whether one is buying into hateful stereotypical assumptions when one laughs, or whether there is something about the cleverness of the envelope that does not presuppose commitment to views about the particular butt of the joke (for which substitution of other groups may provide one test). But then, more than group membership and reflexive attitudes toward the self may

just as can roasts). "On Ward B, Betty was wont to comment on how ugly she was, how fat, and how no one would want to have someone like her for a girl-friend. . . . these self-derogations, carried past the limits of polite self-depreciation, were considered a tax upon the others: they were willing to exert protective referential avoidance regarding the individual's shortcomings and felt it was unfair to be forced into contaminating intimacy with the individual's problems" (90).

3. There is a George Carlin bit that goes something like: "Why do Richard Pryor and Eddie Murphy get to say 'nigger' and I don't? [Pause.] Because they're niggers! [Explosive laughter.]" Here we have Carlin's familiar mixture of shocking the audience while making fun of them for being shocked. It is an interesting question whether there is some kernel of actual racism nestled within this self-aware joke that makes it funnier to racists than nonracists, even though one can certainly be amused by Carlin's cleverness (the joke's reflexive and self-mocking envelope) without being a racist. (Point due to Lucas McGranahan.)

4. Transforming formerly pejorative terms may necessarily be the work of former victims. There may be something unseemly (and ineffective) in members of the formerly opprobrious class (say whites) announcing that they henceforth intend some slur (say "nigger") in a nonpejorative sense. We see the point illustrated in the character Randal's hopeless attempt to reclaim "porch monkey" in Kevin Smith's 2006 film, *Clerks II.*

be involved. For Richard Pryor was equally well able to get away with "white" jokes before mixed or even predominantly white audiences, for example mimicking the way white folks walk and talk (which, if you have ever seen one of his shows, can be just hilarious when achieved and displayed through the resisting medium of his person). One presumes that what is in play here is not group-identification but rather the disparity in power in the mocked party. This is insulting up.

Who is listening also matters. Does the audience include the "butt" of the joke, its victim? Sometimes the joke-maker is speaking to an audience's shared prejudices, so that speaker and audience form a cohesive community and reinforce each other's views (a form of preaching to the choir—though, as in the "bicycle-thief" joke quoted earlier, the choir may be a Ku Klux Klan coven).

The roles of speaker and audience may be crucial even where the audience is just one person, for we generally do not (perhaps cannot) laugh at our own jokes. Freud helpfully suggests why. Tendentious jokes, unlike innocent jokes, have a purpose. According to Freud, a tendentious joke "is either a *hostile* joke (serving the purpose of aggressiveness, satire, or defence) or an *obscene* joke (serving the purpose of exposure)" (1905c, 97). As in the competitive insult rituals that we have considered—where there is aggressive play for status and sexual themes may predominate—an audience is crucial. Freud asks why one is supposed not to laugh at one's own jokes and in answering illuminates the multiple roles of the audience. He summarizes his account in terms of psychic economy: "telling my joke to another person would seem to serve several purposes: first, to give me objective certainty that the joke-work has been successful; secondly, to complete my own pleasure by a reaction from the other person upon myself; and thirdly—where it is a question of repeating a joke that one has not produced oneself—to make up for the loss of pleasure owing to the joke's lack of novelty" (144, 156). But the crucial insight involves the collusive nature of tendentious jokes, the fact—clearest perhaps in sexual jokes—that there are *three* parties involved. "A tendentious joke calls for three people: in addition to the one who makes the joke, there must be a second who is taken as the object of the hostile or sexual aggressiveness, and a third in whom the joke's aim of producing pleasure is fulfilled" (100). There is the joker, the butt of the joke, and the audience. The joker uses the audience to enhance and legitimate his own laughter—a kind of ricochet effect.

Let's look a bit more closely at Freud's account of obscene jokes (which, interestingly, resonates with MacKinnon's later view of pornography as victimizing women).[5] Smut begins as sexually exciting speech, with the Gricean reflexive speaker's intention of arousing the addressee through awareness of the speaker's excitement: it is "originally directed towards women and may be equated with attempts at seduction. . . . A person who laughs at smut that he hears is laughing as though he were the spectator of an act of sexual aggression" (97). In such a situation, the audience is in collusion with the joker, and has in effect been "bribed" by the yield of pleasure that the joke provides (103).

Behind the scenes, there is attempted seduction of the butt and a quest for permission from the audience. The various joke techniques (parallel to the displacement, condensation, etc. of the dreamwork) "bribe" the audience (103). It is the reaction of the third party that then allows the joker's own discharge/satisfaction. That we need others before we may laugh at our own jokes is a matter of seduction and permission.

There is a special problem about insults being funny. When are they funny? Why are they funny? Is humiliation funny? Is embarrassment? Is shame? Freud's three-party view of jokes and the complex forms of cooperation and collusion that can take place begins to clarify what is going on. The aggression (personal, group, sexual, and on and on) that gets unleashed in tendentious humor depends on and reinforces invidious and hostile attitudes. The appreciative audience in effect gangs up on the victim, the butt, with the joker. (Though it may be that some audience members do not simply share the joker's attitudes, but rather experience nervous relief that—on this occasion at least—they are not the butt.) Verbal invective and joking insults stand in for more naked aggression. "By making our enemy small, inferior, despicable or comic,

5. D. H. Lawrence suggests the real victim of "the dirty stories one hears commercial travellers telling each other in a smoke-room" may be sexuality itself: "Occasionally there is a really funny one, that redeems a great deal. But usually they are just ugly and repellent, and the so-called 'humour' is just a trick of doing dirt on sex" (1961, 67). But in the end, the attitude to sex emerges as an attitude toward women. Lawrence continues, "Experience teaches that common individuals . . . have a disgusting attitude towards sex, a disgusting contempt of it, a disgusting desire to insult it. If such fellows have intercourse with a woman, they triumphantly feel that they have done her dirt, and now she is lower, cheaper, more contemptible than she was before" (68).

we achieve in a roundabout way the enjoyment of overcoming him — to which the third person, who has made no efforts, bears witness by his laughter" (103). As society becomes more aware of the victimization involved in racist, sexist, and various ethnic jokes, the range of acceptable objects for humor narrows. At this point, it may be only politicians and celebrities, "public officials" and "public figures," who remain clearly fair game.

That attitudes have been changing, and that audiences may not be willing to collude in the same old ways, cost Don Imus his job in April 2007. Imus, a long-time radio talk show host and shock jock, was fired over his reference to members of the Rutgers women's basketball team as "nappy-headed ho's" after their striking rise and then defeat in the NCAA finals. The racist and sexist slur was witless and ill-aimed, very unfunny, but that he got fired for it after a career of wide-ranging and often equally witless insults suggests that standards are shifting. A wave of offense and advertiser withdrawals after the publicity surrounding Imus' crack about the women basketball players made it financially no longer worth while for his employers to support him. Still, the media widely repeated the actual "nappy headed ho's" insult verbatim. (The ancient rabbis would have disapproved.) By contrast, the media generally resorted to "the N-word" rather than repeat Michael Richards' (formerly *Seinfeld*'s Kramer) verbal assault on some hecklers. Which insults are repeatable in quotation? Which words, used by whom, are really unacceptable? Whether black rappers can continue with impunity to denigrate black women in their lyrics remains to be seen.

Of course much humor, not just the sort that reveals repugnant attitudes and assumptions that may make it wrong to laugh, relies on conventions (the very conventions that are attacked in much satire). Just as conventions are the heart of etiquette, they establish the background for humor, at least the humor of stereotypes. As Northrop Frye puts it, "Humor, like attack, is founded on convention. The world of humor is a rigidly stylized world in which generous Scotchmen, obedient wives, beloved mothers-in-law, and professors with presence of mind are not permitted to exist. All humor demands agreement that certain things, such as a picture of a wife beating her husband in a comic strip, are conventionally funny. To introduce a comic strip in which a husband beats his wife would distress the reader, because it would mean learning a new convention" (Frye 1957, 225).

SATIRE

The tendentious character of many jokes may sometimes be hidden and require interpretation to bring it out. In satire, the pointed nature of the employment of wit is writ large and on the surface. Indeed, extended satire may become tiresome precisely because once one has gotten the point, there may not be much beyond that point to engage the intellect or the imagination. In effective satire, aggression and anger are given purposeful expression using the tools of wit. Northrop Frye provides a succinct characterization of the distinctive features of satire:

> The chief distinction between irony and satire is that satire is militant irony: its moral norms are relatively clear, and it assumes standards against which the grotesque and absurd are measured. Sheer invective or name-calling ("flyting") is satire in which there is relatively little irony: o n the other hand, whenever a reader is not sure what the author's attitude is or what his own is supposed to be, we have irony with relatively little satire. (Frye 1957, 223)

By its nature, irony does not require victims. Indeed, it may create a sense of community with the author, who after all grants the reader the courtesy of assuming a capacity for dealing with his or her playful use of language. And even where there are real or imagined naïve victims, divisive irony may mainly serve to build amiable communities—those who share the author's views and appreciate his or her indirect way of stating them (Booth 1974, 28). Aggression is indispensable in satire, though it has its limits. As Frye writes,

> Two things, then, are essential to satire; one is wit or humor founded on fantasy or a sense of the grotesque or absurd, the other is an object of attack. Attack without humor, or pure denunciation, forms one of the boundaries of satire. It is a very hazy boundary, because invective is one of the most readable forms of literary art, just as panegyric is one of the dullest. It is an established datum of literature that we like hearing people cursed and are bored with hearing them praised, and almost any denunciation, if vigorous enough, is followed by a reader with the kind of pleasure that soon breaks into a smile. To attack anything, writer and audience must agree on its undesirability, which means that the content of a great deal of satire founded on national hatreds, snobbery, prejudice, and personal pique goes out of date very quickly. (1957, 224)

Satire is generally not self-deprecating, it is typically directed at others, but there is something not merely untimely but unseemly when it is aimed at despised and denigrated minorities who had no choice about their identities. The ridicule of satire ought arguably to be aimed at the powerful and the successful, including politicians and celebrities, people who have put themselves forward for prominence and have some sort of dominance over others. That is, the very people that American libel law, at least since *NY Times v. Sullivan*, affords less protection from defamation than others. Insult, as the assertion or assumption of dominance, may seem less troublesome when it is an assault on conventional structures of dominance, when it is insult up. Of course, the pretentious are also among the objects of satire, and they are not necessarily powerful. But the pretentious have put themselves forward, have set themselves up, in ways that may make them attractive targets for ridicule. While precisely not self-deprecating, they are indeed self-selecting. Jonathan Swift, the master of satire, made it clear that his weapons were directed only at the pretentious, whose corrigible and intentional vanity made their humiliation appropriate. In Swift's "Verses on the Death of Dr. Swift," he wrote of himself:

> His Satyr points at no Defect,
> But what all Mortals may correct;
> For he abhorr'd that senseless Tribe,
> Who call it Humour when they jibe:
> He spared a Hump or crooked Nose,
> Whose Owners set not up for Beaux.
> True genuine Dulness mov'd his Pity,
> Unless it offer'd to be witty.
> Those, who to their Ignorance confess'd,
> He ne'er offended with a jest;
> But laugh'd to hear an Idiot quote,
> A Verse from Horace learn'd by Rote.
> ("Verses on the Death of Dr. Swift," vv. 467–78)

When dealing with Swift, of course, the possibility of irony—especially in a passage that might be taken as self-praise—cannot be dismissed. In the same poem he writes, "Yet, Malice never was his Aim; He lash'd the Vice but spar'd the Name" (459–60)—this despite the fact that he had just finished attacking thirteen people by name in the very same poem

(Booth 1974, 120–23). And, independent of Swift's intentions, the boundaries between corrigible faults and fated conditions (as between virtues and natural endowment) are open to question. And, while there may be danger, there may still be point in attacking apparently given and unalterable conditions, in mocking the (apparent) fates. Just as some virtues may turn out to be gifts of nature, we sometimes learn that what might appear iron natural laws are in reality malleable social constructions. That surely is one of the lessons of the generally unironical Marx.

We have already seen that stating the truth can be insulting. Calling someone fat can be insulting, even if they are in fact fat, perhaps especially if they are fat. Satire, especially in the hands of its masters, such as Molière, Swift, and Twain, teaches the important related lesson that insults can be true. That the awful truth is told with wit and humor, that one can laugh at what in the end are serious criticisms, marks the special virtue of satire. The laughter may serve to give one license to criticize ever more deeply. Exaggeration, caricature, distortion, displacement, condensation, and the usual tools of comedy all help to make the satirical point and also to give it permission to be made. In discussing blasphemy, we saw how crucial the distinction between matter and manner, substance and style can be. In drawing legal lines, certain forms will protect otherwise objectionable content from prosecution. This is so not just in the world of worship, of God and blasphemy, but in the wider world of defamation, in the courts that hear charges of slander and libel. In the case of *Hustler v Falwell*, and in other cases, the Supreme Court has explicitly allowed that political satire can serve as a defense against the charge of unlawful defamation. Truth is a defense against the charge of libel, but so also is the claim that one is not engaging in an attempt to purvey (literal) truth. Newspapers are generally careful to separate their opinion pages from their straight reportage. Of course, not all newspapers or other media really maintain the separation (think of Fox News' claims to be "Fair and Balanced" and the counterclaims in the 2004 documentary, *Outfoxed: Rupert Murdoch's War on Journalism*) and no paper does it successfully all the time. The line between fact and opinion can be as wavering and unsure as the line between speech and action. But aside from those (very serious) complications, there is a certain irony in the fact that the distortion of satire receives protection from prosecution precisely because it does not pretend to truth (in the *Hustler*

case, the court held that the grotesque character of the sexual parody—
depicting the Reverend Jerry Falwell's "first time" as having been with
his mother—ensured that no one could mistake it for the truth), while at
the same time the aim of satire is most often to convey a rather pointed
version of the truth. Just as the court jester or Shakespearean Fool may
be licensed to tell in his jolly way unwelcome truths under the cloak of
nonsense, so the more sober satirist, in allowing us to laugh as he makes
his point, is in turn permitted to tell us how things really are—so long
as he presents his home truths in the guise of telling us no such thing.
Insofar as insults are a part of the production, they perform invaluable
service.

So far as satire takes the form of provocative critique, it may serve
the truth (even when the side it takes may happen to be mistaken),
and so it should fall under the protection of the traditional defenses of
freedom of speech. Jokes can serve the truth. Warren Buffett, on the
occasion of turning over the bulk of his fortune (about thirty-one billion
dollars) to the Bill and Melinda Gates Foundation for charitable disper-
sal, was asked why he didn't simply pass the money on to his children.
In response, he was scathing on the Bush administration's attempts to
abolish estate taxes (what conservatives call "The Death Tax"), insisting
that the preservation of "dynastic wealth" is offensive to the American
tradition of meritocracy. Buffett explained that he gets particularly upset
at members of his country club who complain about welfare mothers
getting food stamps "while they are trying to leave their children a more-
than-lifetime-supply of food stamps and are substituting a trust officer
for a welfare officer." After being applauded for this remark at his press
conference, he cheerily asked, "Is there anyone I forgot to insult?" (New
York Times 6/27/2006, C4). Once more we see that insults can be valuable, even when their claims to express truth are undisguised.

Parody—a form of satire "in which the victim's style is imitated and
distorted" (Booth, 123)—unlike other forms of satire, need not have a
point beyond simply making fun. Satire, as we have noted, normally
assumes the moral high ground. But making fun serves its purposes, and
as we have seen in the case of *Hustler v Falwell*, so long as a parody makes
its nature plain and does not pretend to be purveying truth, it may have
the protection of the law. Truth is always a defense against libel. Further,
one is not libeled if an untruth is told without seeking to persuade anyone that it is a truth.

Ridicule is the business of satire. It is also an important species of insult. It can be an important business. It can also be simple (or complex) viciousness. The 1996 French film, *Ridicule*, directed by Patrice Leconte, portrays the role of wit, especially malicious wit, in the prerevolutionary French court. Aristocratic ridicule was the maker and breaker of reputations, the determinant of one's placing in the world of courtiers (which was also the world of honor and duels). The movie illustrates Freud's notion of tendentious wit, as well as portraying a kind of social corruption that differs from simple monetary forms. Kierkegaard's suffering under the ridicule of his fellow citizens provides a different sort of illustration. The aggression is more naked, not cloaked in wit. Kierkegaard was rather peculiar in appearance, in particular, his trousers were of unequal length. As John Updike (2005) recounts the story:

> It was this last oddity that the populace of Copenhagen fastened upon as the subject of gibes and taunts, making Kierkegaard's cherished daily perambulations in the streets a torment; he spoke of "that slow death, being trampled to death by a flock of geese." The characterization was witty, but the experience was painful, remembered in his journals long after it had subsided as analogous "to the gladiatorial animal combat of pagan times." If Christ were to return to the world, he wrote, "he would perhaps not be put to death, but would be ridiculed. This is martyrdom in the age of reason." . . . He had imagined himself a friend of the people, an aristocratic dandy engaging even the lowliest Copenhagener in conversation during his strolls. Now every schoolboy and ruffian called insults after him.

The ridicule of satire makes fun with a point—typically a political point. The politics can be either progressive or conservative. At the most general level, there is an important contrast between mockingly self-critical and too comfortably reactionary humor. Seeing how humor can reveal contingency and undermine social complacencies, while also sometimes allowing persons to wallow in a sense of self-satisfied superiority at the expense of others, may help explain how humor can be both comfortingly human and disruptively liberating, even revolutionary (see Critchley 2002). The aggressive edge of satire, that master genre of insult, can sharpen the revolutionary point.

But we have seen that insult can be a playful as well as a political enterprise. In teasing, the ambiguities of aggression reveal yet another form. Play and attack combine to both express and control aggression.

TEASING

The central feature of teasing is the simultaneous deliberate provocation and frustration of desire. At one end, it is seduction. At another, it amounts to goading, annoying, and tormenting. The tension of some level of mutual consent is what is distinctive of the teasing involved in ritual insults and jocular insults of a variety of sorts (from joking relationships to roasts). Still, there is inequality, for typically one party is more venting aggression and the other is more being a good sport—though the roles in certain ritual contexts may shift back and forth.

Of course, teasing itself, with its inherent tension between aggressive destructiveness and controlled and consensual interaction, ranges from getting a rise out of someone, pulling someone's leg, joshing and kidding to bullying and tormenting—without some level of consensual interaction, teasing becomes tormenting, with the absence of aggression, it may just amount to pleasant competitive bantering (Sperling 1953, 458 and 476). While teasing might be regarded as in the same genus as the sort of play between friends we discussed earlier, it seems in general less structured than those rituals. Teasers so often claim to be "only joking," "only kidding," "only playing around" that it seems appropriate to consider the phenomenon in connection with the insult humor that includes the sort of roasts where people are supposed to be similarly "only joking," "only kidding," and "only playing around." Still, the conventional requirements of good-humored tolerance in the roasted do not seem, in general, to carry over to the teased. And the line between good-natured teasing and insulting teasing, or even vicious teasing, seems more tenuous even than the line between ritual insults and personal insults.

The anthropology and psychoanalysis of teasing allow us to see the forces in play more clearly. Joking relationships and the dozens are forms of socially sanctioned teasing. One understanding of the dozens, as we have seen, regards it as a way of turning aggression in an oppressed group inwards, as a way of preventing its dangerous venting outside the group. Among the Balinese, the Sioux Indians, Inuit Eskimos and other groups, systematic teasing is used in childrearing in order to shape character in relation to the expression of anger and aggression (among the Balinese and the Eskimos discouraging such expression and among the Sioux encouraging fierceness). The Arapesh and the Japanese also use teasing to shape character in desired ways. Aggression against the child (including withdrawal during nursing and other threats of rejection) is used to elicit a response from the child that is then reacted to in ways that encourage or discourage certain traits. Aggression is used to shape aggression, under the cover of play. As psychoanalyst Samuel Sperling puts it, "In all teasing, aggression is masked by the pretense of 'just playing.' . . . The playful nature of teasing enables children to test their control of expressing and tolerating aggression. Thus, they learn how to avoid unpleasant consequences, how to meet the disagreeable, how to accept unpleasantries with good grace or humor, and how to hold their own in competitive rivalry" (1953, 470–71).

Among the Inuit Eskimos—a society of isolated and heavily armed hunters, where aggression could be devastating in its consequences— adults play with their aggression by teasing the children, who are taught that anger is itself childish. Jean L. Briggs (1982, see also 1970) explains how the conflict over aggression is dealt with through dramatization of the conflict in interpersonal games or rituals. "Sometimes the older person teases the child in some standardized way: 'Where's your [absent] daddy?' 'Whose child are you?' 'Do you wrongly imagine you're lovable?' 'Shall I adopt you?' 'Shall I hit your nasty old mother?' At other times the game consists in tempting the child to engage in some disvalued behaviour: 'Don't tell your sister you have that candy; it's the last one; eat it all yourself.'" She says the persistence and presence of the games in widely separated Inuit groups "indicates clearly their importance in creating and maintaining an Inuit style of interpersonal relations: smooth, light in tone, controlled, and, at the same time, covertly conflictful. . . . By making conflicts salient to children, they help to create a sense of danger and, ultimately, commitment to the values" (Briggs 1982, 118–19).

Children in our society, in school, in gangs, in groups large and small, learn group standards and gain acceptance through various teasing rites of initiation: "in the form of horseplay, name calling, mock imitation, needling, razzing, heckling, hazing, and practical joking. In these, the weapons of ridicule, disapproval, or playful physical molestations are teasingly utilized to enforce conformity to the group standards of conduct, expression and dress" (Sperling 1953, 472). The trick is to avoid being made permanently a fool of. We become good or bad sports, become known for being able to "dish it out" or "take it."

In an essay "On Joking Relationships" that focuses on Africa but deals with a phenomenon widespread throughout the world, A. R. Radcliffe-Browne describes a "joking relationship" as a form of teasing which takes place in the context of

> a relation between two persons in which one is by custom permitted, and in some instances required, to tease or make fun of the other, who in turn is required to take no offence. It is important to distinguish two main varieties. In one the relation is symmetrical; each of the two persons teases or makes fun of the other. In the other variety the relation is asymmetrical . . . There are many varieties in the form of this relationship in different societies. In some instances the joking or teasing is only verbal, in others it includes horse-play; in some the joking includes elements of obscenity, in others not. (Radcliffe-Brown 1952, 90)

All such relationships of course have their bounds; so, for example, the obligation to take no offense lapses when the other party goes too far. As we have noted, even in a public roast, the target/honoree may properly sometimes take offense. And we have seen how going beyond the limits in the verbal sparring of the dozens can lead to physical fighting. Such bounds are typically defined by custom, though as always in matters of respect, they are subject to the vagaries of individual sensitivities and sensibilities.

Radcliffe-Brown perceptively notes, "The joking relationship is a peculiar combination of friendliness and antagonism. The behaviour is such that in any other social context it would express and arouse hostility; but it is not meant seriously and must not be taken seriously. There is a pretence of hostility and a real friendliness" (91). We have seen some features of this sort of relationship played out in our discussion of the dozens and related rituals. And as we noted there, one should perhaps be more on the lookout than Radcliffe-Brown suggests for subterranean real hostilities that might be given vent and safe release through the conventions governing joking relationships. Psychoanalysts such as Sperling (focusing on individualistic interactions rather than socially structured roles—structured in virtue of kinship and the other factors Radcliffe-Brown emphasizes) tend to speak of a pretense of friendliness and real hostility in teasing, a pretense of playfulness and real sado-masochism. The crucial point is that both are present. (Though they may be less prominent or less readily discernible in that form of teasing which plays with and on the fear of humiliation for being caught out as being more serious about something than is thought appropriate.) The crucial feature of the relation is, as Radcliffe-Brown states, that "the relationship is one of permitted disrespect." Insult at its broadest level involves failures (whether intentional or unintentional, conventional or idiosyncratic) of respect. And "the whole maintenance of a social order depends upon the appropriate kind and degree of respect being shown towards certain persons, things and ideas or symbols" (Radcliffe-Brown 1952, 91). The structures of respect are the structures of our social lives. Joking relationships and their related rituals enable us to play with these structures, test their boundaries while still preserving them, and express disapproved feelings without having them rupture valued relationships. They provide a freer and freeing alternative to more formal relations (such as those between a son-in-law and his wife's father and mother in many African societies), in which direct personal contact is limited and extreme mutual respect is required when contact does occur. Particular people or people in certain social positions (as well, of course, as whole clans or tribes or self-selecting groups such as sports fans) may have genuine divergences as well as conjunctions of interest. When this is so, ways must be found to avoid strife despite the genuine possibility of conflict and hostility. Formal structures of respect are one way to do that. Playful joking relationships are another. Distinctness, self-respect, and pride may be preserved in both ways.

Playfulness in a relationship may be socially prescribed as a part of certain social roles, it may also arise quite naturally between friends. As William Ian Miller (1993, 157–58, 187, 194) notes, teasing, done in a friendly spirit, can be about true flaws. Despite Labov's claims about the need for blatant falsity and ridiculousness in the dozens in order to avoid personal insult and offense, even he notes instances where true weaknesses are touched upon without consequences. Typically, in friendly teasing, the flaws are minor or regarded as charming quirks. The crucial feature in keeping insults from being taken personally (as in ritual insults) may not be that they are not true (as Labov asserts) but that they are not intended to hurt. One sign of innocent intentions might still be blatant falsity and ridiculousness in the taunts. Another might be the context (as in roasts). A joking insult need not lead to offense, because there is no hostile intent evident behind it. Because there is an overriding spirit of friendship. But there is also hostile teasing. Which may be why some see real friendliness and pretend aggression in teasing while others see real aggression and pretend friendliness. Both exist.

Radcliffe-Brown states that "teasing is always a compound of friendliness and antagonism" (104). He develops his special notion of "friends" in his "A Further Note on Joking Relationships." Avoidance relationships and joking relationships are both ways of avoiding open conflict between friends, where "friends" are people who—in virtue of kinship or other social roles—are not supposed to enter into open quarrel or conflict with one another. Thus avoidance relations often also include an obligation to regularly exchange gifts, "because they [e.g., parents-in-law] are great friends." And children who regularly exchange insults or jokes with their grandparents say things like, "we can joke because we are great friends." Both the avoidance and the joking approaches serve the same ends. As Radcliffe-Brown says, speaking of joking relationships, "a relationship in which insults are exchanged and there is an obligation not to take them seriously, is one which, by means of sham conflicts, avoids real ones" (107). But teasing and joking do not just occur between people who stand in special societal relationships. It is, as we have seen, a common pattern between individuals in many societies, though wider groups may join in, as the actively goading crowd commonly does in the dozens. Which should not surprise us, because the needs, conflicts, and constraints of shared interests found in conjunction with mutual antagonisms is a common tension that must be dealt with between individuals, as well as within and between kin groups, clans, and tribes.

The tensions may sometimes call for society-wide release, hence the unleashing of the normally restrained in carnivale and related festivals and rituals. Robert Elliot writes of an Ashanti *Apo* ceremony in which there is license to "freely sing of all the Faults, Villanies and Frauds of their Superiours as well as Inferiours" (William Bosman, 1705, quoted in Elliott 1960, 78). It is a feast of eight days before the Devil is annually banished from their towns. "*Apo*, the name of the ceremony, is a word that seems to be linguistically related to terms meaning 'to speak roughly or harshly to,' 'to abuse, to insult,' but also 'to wash, to cleanse.' In this happy period, this time ritually set apart from the rest of the year, ridicule and abuse are lucky and cleansing and enjoyable for all who participate" (78). The Ashanti themselves see the licensed ridicule as relieving or freeing hatred. They think the king may be better off too for "he will not be sickened by bad thoughts people have of him" (80) — and the same logic applies to the Saturnalia of the ancients, the annual Feast of Fools or Mass of Fools of medieval France, and on and on. Given the dangers of repression and the therapeutic value of *controlled* release of aggressive impulses, the institutionalization of ridicule is a widespread health measure, continuing in modern form in the licensed ridicule of high public figures in the Gridiron Club in Washington, DC, and in other public "roasts." The primary function of ridicule thus gets turned inside out, and what elsewhere may be an insidiously destructive impulse comes to serve societal health.

As always, of course, native peoples may have their own explanations for their cultural practices. For example, in his "A Further Note on Joking Relationships," Radcliffe-Brown draws on the work of M. Griaule to report that the Dogon interpret their regular exchange of insults with the Bozo tribe as "'cathartic' because it rids the livers of both parties of impurities" (1952, 113). Whatever the special significance of such explanations within local cosmologies (in this case, in terms of purification), they may not be incompatible with more general explanations (in regard to joking relationships, interpretation in terms of sustaining a needed balance between cooperation and antagonism — itself commonly associated with liver bile in many Western traditions), and sometimes we may have ample justification for going beyond and behind native self-understandings. (See Neu 2000, chap. 14, "Getting Behind the Demons.")

BULLYING

At one extreme, teasing can become bullying. Lauren Collins (2005), in a piece entitled "Don't Laugh" in *The New Yorker*, reports that there is a movement in education circles, including the Department of Education in New York City, to attempt to counter the painful effects of bullying. While bullying amongst schoolchildren can be a matter of physical assault and extortion under threat (there goes the lunch money), it often importantly involves insult. The New York program, "Operation Respect: Don't Laugh at Me," takes part of its name and much of its inspiration from a country ballad popularized by Peter Yarrow of Peter, Paul & Mary. The song speaks of the effects of ridicule, "I'm a little boy with glasses, the one they call a geek / A little girl who never smiles 'cause I've got braces on my teeth" (Collins 2005, 31). We have seen that it can be wrong to laugh because of the disgraceful attitudes presupposed and revealed by laughing at certain jokes. The butt of the joke need not be present. Laughter at people who are in fact present can be especially objectionable because of the pain it directly causes in them. And the laughter may be a part of broader campaigns of teasing and coercion, bullying and disrespect. Ridicule need not take the form of jokes. It may be a matter of taunts, name-calling, and gesture. (Remember Feinberg's category of "factually based put-downs"—1985, 222.) Disrespect comes in many forms. We all want and need to be valued. There is a modicum of respect due to all human beings, as such, though levels of individual esteem may properly vary with relevant measures of worth of diverse kinds. The lack of respect may cause great pain to its victims, and, on the rebound, in places like Columbine where the denigrated and taunted return to school armed, it may cause great harm to the perpetrators and bystanders. The problem needs confrontation on two fronts. One is in the cultivation of disarming and non-escalating attitudes, sometimes doubtless including forgiveness, in the victims. But not all are capable of Abraham Lincoln's masterful magnanimity to his enemies or of reconciliation with those who have no wish to reconcile. The second front is in the changing of attitudes and behaviors in the bullies. This may be more difficult. Perhaps programs like "Operation Respect: Don't Laugh at Me" can help, perhaps repercussions (including punishment) can too.

GENERAL THEORY

The central need for respect and esteem that makes us vulnerable to insult also plays a role in the general functioning of humor (and not just insult humor), at least according to some prominent theories. Going back at least to Plato and Aristotle, "superiority theory" suggests that dominance and domination, the enjoyment of others' misfortune and the insult of ridicule, is crucial to the production of laughter. Making fun of others is a way of elevating the self. Hobbes fleshed out the theory in *Leviathan*, in accordance with his view of the unique motivating power of the desire for pleasure and the fear of pain and death and their

associated "perpetuall and restlesse desire of Power after power, that cea-
seth onely in Death" (1968 [1651], 161). As for laughter: "Sudden Glory
is the passion which maketh those Grimaces called LAUGHTER; and
is caused either by some sudden act of their own, that pleaseth them; or
by the apprehension of some deformed thing in another, by comparison
whereof they suddenly applaud themselves" (125). According to superiority theory, all humor is insult humor. But that is surely too broad a
claim. Even Freud recognizes a category of nontendentious, innocent,
humor involving wordplay, incongruity, and the like. And in the face
of gross inequalities, what sometimes emerges is an indignant call for
justice rather than an amused sense of superiority. That some, some
of the time, take pleasure in the degradation of others, in making fun
of and mocking others remains true. And the open delight of children
in mimicking the speech, facial expressions, and characteristic movements of others continues throughout life, in forms both open and more
concealed.

The hostility and aggression in humor are often right on the surface. "Other people's physical pain and embarrassment are funny. Mel
Brooks illuminated this problem when he defined tragedy and comedy:
'Tragedy is if I cut my finger. Comedy is if you walk into an open sewer
and die.' With similarly blithe hostility, standup comedians talk about
'cracking up' or 'breaking up' the audience with 'punch' lines, and
equate success onstage with 'killing'" (Friend 2002, 84). The discomfort
and ridicule of others raises us. (F. H. Buckley, 2003, presses the point
with an economic analysis of the costs and benefits in ridicule.)

Group identity may matter as much as individual identity in the
comparative stakes. Christie Davies, in an historical and comparative
study of *The Mirth of Nations* (2002), considers jokes told by or about
particular peoples, analyzing in particular the self-mocking humor of
Scots and Jews as well as humor in which others serve as the butts of stupidity jokes, as in Canadian jokes about Newfoundlanders and American
jokes about Polish people. Stupidity humor is clearly a branch of "superiority humor"—and that the objects of such humor are described as
"butts" fits neatly with the significance I have been attaching to anality
and aggressive sodomy in insult.

Davies himself accepts only a weak, merely descriptive, version of
the superiority theory of humor. He says, "Conflict and hostility are neither a necessary nor a sufficient condition for the generation of jokes

about stupidity. Syrian stupidity jokes are about the familiar unresented Homsiots, the citizens of Homs (and adjoining Hama), on their own periphery" (11). As I have suggested, sometimes the manner rather than the matter, the envelope rather than the content, is what is essential to making us laugh (though, as Freud reminds us, sometimes even we don't know or can't be sure what we are laughing at). Whether superiority and disparagement are linked to, and perhaps cover, genuine hostility may depend on how we interpret "the narcissism of minor differences" that peoples everywhere use to differentiate and distinguish themselves from neighbors and rivals. (See above chap. 4 and Neu 2000, chap. 7, "Pride and Identity.") Such humor can certainly be enormously serious in its consequences. "We ascribe ignoble and ludicrous characteristics to them [minority groups], so that we can legitimize the 'need' for control. In magic art we do not hate and then ridicule, we ridicule so that we can hate. If such laughter is not checked by reason operating through imagination, as in great art, the butt of ridicule soon becomes the scape-goat, whom we torture and kill for our edification" (Hugh Dalziel Duncan, quoted in Elliott 1960, 85).

Of course, superiority theory is only one theory of humor among many, and it fits readily only some jokes. Nonetheless, like Freud's theory, it sheds light on the importance of the audience and the role of collusion. The audience according to superiority theory identifies with the swaggering aggressor who tells a joke or, alternatively, can regard the joke-teller as beneath contempt. Tad Friend writes, "Audiences have felt superior to the people who make them laugh since at least the Middle Ages, when dwarves and hunchbacks were used as court jesters. A 1976 study found that when subjects were asked to characterize American comedians, people often said 'skinny,' 'fat,' 'ugly,' 'clumsy,' 'stupid,' 'weird,' or 'deformed,'" (Friend 2002, 80). The Scottish comedian Billy "Connolly has always believed that comedy is linked to vulnerability. 'When your knickers are down, you're funny,' he frequently says" (Lahr 2003, 107). It is doubtless part of the appeal of self-deprecating humor. Rape is not funny, self-abuse is. Given the importance of the audience, the butt of the joke need not even get it, indeed, their not getting it may be part of the point of the performance. Groucho Marx often (both in his movies and in his television game show) aimed his barbs at people too dim or too self-satisfied to get the insult. (Margaret Dumont often played the role of oblivious straight-man dowager for Groucho, e.g., in

Animal Crackers 1930 and *Duck Soup* 1932.) The assault was for the entertainment and amusement of the audience.

As we have noted, the aggression in insults can be found funny. Straight insults can be amusing, at least if one is not the target (though maybe even then, if one does not take offense). The play of language, the breaking of taboos, and creative forms of critique all have the power to delight. George S. Kaufman, member of the Algonquin Round Table and Broadway hit-maker, was known for his put-downs. For example, "When an inept bridge partner got up to go to the men's room, Kaufman snapped, 'Fine. This is the first time this afternoon I'll know what you have in your hand.'" (Gottlieb 2004, 149). After the *New York Daily News* awarded cash prizes to thousands of lotto-game players by mistake, its rival tabloid, the *New York Post* reviled its reporters and columnists as "scamsters," "goobers," and "pinheads," and bestowed derogatory nicknames on rival executives: "the Cookie Monster, for the *News'* editor-in-chief, Michael Cooke; the Dunce, for its editorial director, Martin Dunn" (McGrath 2005, 23). We have already seen examples from Camille Paglia as the modern master of vituperation, and examples could be multiplied endlessly—there are, as we have noted, whole books collecting insults as well as a journal, *Maledicta*, which documents the language of abuse from around the world. Sometimes it is the clever envelope that amuses, but the aggressive content is not without its pleasures and its significance.

In addition to direct and directly offensive insults, there are, as we have seen, occasions where insults are issued with permission (as in roasts, insult rituals, and joking relationships). And some insults are licensed, or at least open to justification, by social purposes, as with the political and social criticism provided by satire. But whether the aggression comes naked or cloaked, with consent or against resistance, the root significance of insult in assault remains in its modern practice. Laughter may soften the impact of insult, or deepen it, or help us manage it, but the tension between the drive for superiority or dominance and the need for respect (both within and between individuals) compel us to seek to understand the sources and nature of insult. And such understanding may help us forgive—perhaps.

TEN

∎ ∎ ∎

TO UNDERSTAND ALL IS TO
FORGIVE ALL—OR IS IT?

"TO UNDERSTAND ALL IS TO FORGIVE ALL," OR SO THE FAMOUS SAYING GOES. Madame de Staël was actually more measured when she spoke of the relation of understanding and forgiveness in *Corinne:* "Tout comprendre rend très indulgent" (which *Bartlett's* translates as "To understand everything makes one tolerant" [1968, 502b]). She is also credited with the more sweeping and more familiar statement that provides my chapter title and my theme: "Tout comprendre c'est tout pardonner" (which the familiar wisdom "To understand all is to forgive all" captures—near enough). My theme is actually two-fold. First, why is it that the saying does in fact seem wise? My second theme, however, is to question its wisdom, to wonder whether the relation of understanding and forgiveness is perhaps more complex. J. L. Austin is reported to have responded to the notion that to understand all is to forgive all: "That's quite wrong. Understanding might just add contempt to hatred" (Dennett 1984, 32n15). Surely Austin has a point. Suppose that what one learns is that someone did something out of mean and small-minded motives. Such widened understanding need not, as Austin points out, create sympathy. Indeed, all too often, understanding may produce a perception of the insult behind an injury. The mere fact that a person's behavior had causes (and here it is important to note that causes can include reasons) does not lift responsibility. It all turns on the character of the particular injuries, and the particular causes, and on what it is to forgive (or to tolerate). Some sorting out is needed.

On the first theme I can be, at least initially, brief. To say "To understand all is to forgive all" is not only to render a descriptive judgment, but also to offer a prescriptive piece of advice. If someone is not inclined to forgive, the suggestion is that they do not know the whole story, and that if they did this would (properly) soften their attitude. I think that is often good advice. It is often good for the aggrieved to recognize the limits of their understanding, to seek fuller understanding, and to be (at least somewhat) mollified when they achieve that fuller understanding. That I say "often" here rather than "always" connects with my second theme, and I will return to the point. Here we should note that there is also insight in the descriptive aspect of the folk wisdom. To understand all is often to discover that the person who behaved badly "could not help it." Once one knows all the factors that went into bringing about an action, it will often emerge that the crucial determining factors were outside of the person's control. Indeed, if one pushes the investigation far enough, perhaps it will *always* emerge that the factors are outside of the person's control (whether the crucial factors be upbringing, social pressure, genetic inheritance, the force of circumstances . . . or the influence of cosmic rays). It is a deeply Kantian part of our understanding of ourselves and others that where a person is not free to act otherwise, "could not help it," that person is not regarded as responsible or properly blamable for the action done due to the factors outside their control.

But this brings us to some of the limits on the folk wisdom that are also limits on our Kantian intuitions. For if we are determinists about human action, and believe that causal chains can always be traced outside the person, it might appear that we never have ultimate control and so responsibility (if responsibility requires such control as a condition) and so everything must always be forgiven. To refuse to forgive is simply to cling to present ignorance. If we wish to maintain belief in responsibility and to insist that some actions are unforgivable, we may be driven to Kantian belief in a noumenal realm of a pure will where freedom can reign in the face of the ever-expanding explanatory power of science. But I do not think we have to make such a mysterious, such a nonempirical, move to preserve our more retributive, our less forgiving, intuitions. We need not claim that there is some realm beyond the explanatory power of science. We can grant, at least for the sake of argument, that all human actions, like all events in nature, are open to the law-like explanations of science, even if we have not yet uncovered them. (Kant insisted that the fact that we have not yet found a cause does not prove it does not exist [1785, 419]. And even Hume could agree with that, indeed, he insisted that unexpected, uncharacteristic, and unpredictable human actions count no more against the reach of causal explanation than unexpected and unpredictable events in nature such as earthquakes and the weather count against there being causes that we simply have not yet uncovered [1748, §8]. Hume's skepticism about causation was of a different kind.) Rather than retreat to the noumenal, I think we should recognize that there is *always* a story to explain how things have come to be as they are and why a person did whatever it is they have done. But not all stories excuse. The difficult thing is determining which stories excuse, whether our concern is the abstract problem of mapping out a domain of freedom or the more concrete problems of assigning responsibility or, via forgiveness, relieving of some of the consequences of responsibility. This is so whether the particular problem involves determining when a person should be regarded as legally insane in a way that excuses from criminal liability or determining whether a person could not help what they did in a way that entitles them to sympathy and perhaps even forgiveness (if one can be entitled to forgiveness—it is arguable that forgiveness, genuine forgiveness, must always be a free gift, never an entitlement, just as love must be).[1] The sorting out may begin with a closer look at determinism, excuses, and forgiveness.

DETERMINISM AND FORGIVENESS

Determinism as such is not the issue. When we excuse or forgive someone, it is not because of some general belief in causal order in the universe, it is not because we believe that every event has a cause. Resentment is forestalled or inhibited in particular cases for particular reasons, broadly classifiable in terms of the voluntariness of the particular (otherwise) offensive or injurious act (where certain cognitive conditions, such as nonculpable ignorance, or certain control conditions,

---

1. As Murphy (1982, 116) elaborates: "Christians often like to speak of forgiveness as a free gift or act of grace. Insofar as they are making the point that no one has a right to be forgiven, they are making a sound point. But if they are attempting to argue that no reasons can be given in favor of forgiveness, they are mistaken."

such as being pushed or the absence of viable alternatives, prevail) or in terms of the competence or capacities of the agent (where at the time of action or always there are special pressures or the agent is psychologically abnormal, or is simply a child) or in terms of the character of the relation between the injurer and the injured (as when we forgive someone "for old time's sake"). As P. F. Strawson puts it in his discussion of these matters in "Freedom and Resentment": "it has never been claimed . . . that it would follow from the truth of determinism that anyone who caused an injury *either* was quite simply ignorant of causing it *or* had acceptably overriding reasons for acquiescing reluctantly in causing it *or* . . ., etc. The prevalence of this happy state of affairs would not be a consequence of the reign of universal determinism, but of the reign of universal goodwill" (1962, 10–11). Our commitment to ordinary participant reactive attitudes toward each other (attitudes which include resentment, and gratitude, and love) does not depend on a denial of determinism, and an acceptance of determinism need not undermine those attitudes. We can add that an acceptance of determinism would not underwrite universal forgiveness—however desirable or problematic such a universal response. (While Christianity and some forms of therapy might encourage unbridled forgiveness for the sake of communion, community, and calm, an appropriate resentment may conduce to valuable restraint in others as well as be necessary to self-respect and justice.)

If it is not a general thesis of determinism that leads us to excuse or forgive, but rather particular conditions, the relevant conditions call for examination. A good start on that is made by J. L. Austin in "A Plea for Excuses" (1956), and some of the legal ramifications are explored in H. L. A. Hart's *Punishment and Responsibility* (1968). But here we must pause to ask whether the differences between excusing and forgiving matter, whether an excuse can provide a reason for forgiveness or is instead incompatible with it. Despite some possible complications (Richards 1988), it seems to me fruitful to follow Bishop Butler (1726) and Jeffrie Murphy (1982) in taking forgiveness as foreswearing resentment. Thus understood, as Murphy points out, forgiveness is only properly in place where resentment is initially properly in place (otherwise, there is nothing that really needs forgiving), and justified resentment is restricted to responsible wrongdoing (1982, 506). (More on the nature of resentment in a bit. More also on the suggestion that foreswearing, and so forgiving, must be intentional.) Excuses generally undermine charges of responsibility, and so may put both initial resentment and subsequent forgiveness out of place.

But this need not always be so. While occasionally excuses may leave nothing to forgive ("it was simply, purely, unavoidably, an accident"), more typically they merely mitigate or make the offense less serious ("I didn't mean to," if believed, may reduce an intentional fault to mere negligence, but negligence remains a fault). The depth of resentment, as well as the ease of forgiveness, is normally tied to the seriousness of the fault (as well as to the time since the offense—a rankling resentment that may have initially been appropriate may itself become a fault when it persists too long over too minor a matter). A lesser offense may still leave room for resentment (and so forgiveness). And even where an excuse removes all responsibility, and so makes resentment inappropriate, there may be a sense to forgiveness. The therapeutic concerns served by forgiveness may require the overcoming of anger as well as resentment. The kind of responsibility essential to resentment (and so forgiveness as the foreswearing of resentment) may not be essential to anger, and so an excuse that attenuates responsibility may not undermine the anger provoked by an injury. Anger at harm may persist in the absence of resentment at wrong. So far as therapy aims to lessen both anger and resentment, the difference between forgiving and excusing as bars to resentment may not much matter. Our concern is with how understanding might lessen responsibility, and so provide an excuse, or otherwise lead to forgiveness. These (excusing and forgiving) are two different paths to disarming resentment (one by showing it misplaced and the other by renouncing it despite its warrant).

The issues raised by excuses may be seen in perhaps more acute form in relation to justifications. J. L. Austin provides a useful distinction between these two. In a case of excuse, you have done wrong, but there are mitigating factors and your "doing" may not be straightforward. In a case of justification, what you have done is not, all things considered, wrong—no excuse is needed (1956, 176–77, 181n1). It might seem even more obvious in the case of justification than in the case of excuse that talk of forgiveness is, strictly speaking, out of place. Still, I am a bit uneasy at too quickly surrendering some of our looser usages. Even where someone's action is ultimately justified, so they did the right thing, there may still remain something (even perhaps a moral something, a moral remainder) to forgive. Think of the innocent victims of Allied bombing in

Europe in World War II. Their suffering may be seen as the price of defeat of the Nazis (or more accurately as part of the price—the bombers too ran risks and made sacrifices). They (the victims who survived) might well say, "I forgive you my injuries, I would have done it too" or "it was necessary." Even in these cases, it must be admitted, it would make as much sense to say "there is nothing to forgive" as "I forgive you," but it seems to me that the second can be a way of acknowledging a shift in attitude based on a full understanding or appreciation of the situation. It acknowledges justification for a harm. (Forgiveness, in this and certain other cases, may be more a matter of reassurance to another that there is no resentment than a foreswearing of resentment.) To say simply, "there is nothing to forgive, you did the right thing" might fail to recognize and properly note the existence of tragedy. And there are unfortunately many situations—tragic situations—in which the best that one can do is still wrong, has a moral cost that remains to be regretted by the agent and (perhaps) forgiven by the victim (Williams 1973 [1965]). Or, to put it slightly differently, the lesser of two evils may still leave the chosen evil a wrong (an undeserved harm) even while ultimately the right thing to do. Therapy can sometimes be an effort to get someone to see that not every injury is an affront, that harm may be done (even intentionally) without disrespect.

Some contemporary therapeutic movements urge forgiveness (of self and others) as a step toward self-healing. The acceptance (and self acceptance) of limitations may be derived from a variety of sources. Some among these movements worry less about whether an apparent wrong is (from the point of view of objective judgment) excusable, justifiable, or forgivable, than whether it is good for the individual to give up their anger and resentment (whatever the characteristics of the object). But perhaps judgment of the object and judgment about what is good for the subject who experiences anger and resentment are not so simply separable.

MISPLACED ANGER

Let's consider a simple case of understanding leading to forgiveness. Sometimes wider context, more information, changes the perceived character of an action, excusing or perhaps even justifying it. You learn someone has smashed your car window. Anger turns to acceptance when you learn that the parking brake on your car had failed and smashing the window was the only way for a bystander to rescue an imperiled baby. Or you are stood up for a third time. Anger turns to acceptance when you learn that your apparently inconsiderate date was the bystander in the failed-brake case and so detained by the need to smash a window to rescue a baby. But these are the easiest cases. It is hardly surprising that knowledge should lead to forgiveness when the initial anger is based on ignorance or incomplete information. But could it be that anger is always based on ignorance or incomplete information? Is it never right to be angry? (This question might remind one of the notion that some derive from belief in determinism that people may never have ultimate control over, and so responsibility for, their actions. It would be salutary to consider what "control" and "self-control" might mean in this context. That task is nicely started on by Dennett in *Elbow Room* [1984, chap. 3].)

Aristotle certainly thought anger has its proper place. He speaks of those who fail to be angry enough:

> The deficiency, whether it is a sort of inirascibility or whatever it is, is blamed. For those who are not angry at the things they should be are thought to be fools, and so are those who are not angry in the right way, at the right time, or with the right persons; for such a man is thought not to feel things nor to be pained by them, and, since he does not get angry, he is thought unlikely to defend himself; and to endure being insulted and to put up with insults to one's friends is slavish. (*Nicomachean Ethics*, trans. Ross and Urmson, 1126a)

Feeling anger (and variants such as indignation) when appropriate may be a condition of self-respect, and so failure to feel appropriate anger may be a sign of insufficient concern for one's rights and dignity, insufficient self-respect. (See Hill 1973, Murphy 1982, and Spelman 1989.) It does not follow that one should never let the anger go. To think about the proper place and conditions of forgiveness, one must think of the proper place and conditions of anger, and of its more restrained cousin, resentment. I call resentment more restrained because it presumes a certain sort of justification not required by anger (at least by anger caused by frustration of desire). Of course resentment may, like anger, on occasion be unjustified (the beliefs involved may not be true). But resentment, unlike anger, typically asserts a moral claim. "A person without a sense of justice may be enraged at someone who fails to act fairly. But anger and annoyance are distinct from indignation and resentment; they are not, as the latter are, moral emotions" (Rawls 1971, 488). Rawls distinguishes the moral emotions, including resentment and indignation, on the basis of the type of explanation required for a feeling to count as a particular emotion. Rawls writes, "In general, it is a necessary feature of moral feelings, and part of what distinguishes them from the natural attitudes, that the person's explanation of his experience invokes a moral concept and its associated principles. His account of his feeling makes reference to an acknowledged right or wrong" (481).

One of the abuses of resentment that Bishop Butler emphasizes emerges when there is no wrong (which Butler refers to as "injury"), "when we fall into that extravagant and monstrous kind of resentment, toward one who has innocently been the occasion of evil to us; that is, resentment upon account of pain or inconvenience, without injury; which is the same absurdity, as settled anger at a thing that is inanimate" (77). There is something infantile about resentment at what could not be helped.

If something is genuinely outside of a person's control, we ought to forgive them the harm they may have caused. But then (to return to an earlier point), if something is outside of a person's control, is forgiveness needed at all? Where's the wrong? If anger and resentment are out of place, is forgiveness equally out of place? (Is a child forgiving the table it bumps into as absurd as it being angry at the table in the first place?) Not every excuse, however, amounts to a justification. There are, after all, degrees of control. There are different kinds of wrongs. To see this, let us consider accidents.

It might seem that if something was an accident, no forgiveness is needed. An accident is not an intentional wrong (indeed, it is the absence of intention that makes something an "accident"). As Justice Holmes put it, "even a dog distinguishes between being stumbled over and being kicked" (1881, 3). But then, intentional wrongs are not the only kind of wrong, and not all accidents are blameless. Not every accident could not be helped. People are often guilty of negligence, of failure to take due care.[2] (Even stumbling may sometimes show a failure to take due care.)

---

2. Aristotle writes, "Forgetfulness, too, causes anger, as when our own names are forgotten, trifling as this may be; since forgetfulness is felt to be another sign that we are being slighted; it is due to negligence, and to neglect us is to slight us" (*Rhetoric*, trans. Roberts, 1379b). Similarly, Bishop Butler notes, "Men do indeed resent what is occasioned through carelessness: but then they expect observance as their due, and so that carelessness is considered as faulty" (75).

We say the outcome should be in their control, perhaps it would have been in their control had they behaved responsibly earlier. Surely that is what we think in the case of the drunk driver who, we admit, could not avoid hitting the pedestrian, given the driver's impaired reflexes. And we have seen that there are a variety of unintentional insults. That a person is not aware that they might be or are causing offense does not entail it is "out of their control." (Though it does entail that it is "unintentional." Awareness or knowledge is the central condition on intentional action. If you are not aware that you are standing on the garden hose, you cannot be standing on it intentionally.) Unintentional action may still be negligent and, in a sense, in one's control. It might have been the person's duty to be aware (as in the case of the railroad switchman who falls asleep at the switch), or it might simply have been the case that they should have been more careful of what they were doing and more attentive to other people's feelings. It is important to realize that the mere fact that something is caused is not enough to put it beyond one's control. How much care is due may depend, among other things, on the amount and kind of harm risked, and its likelihood in the circumstances. Is clumsiness always an excuse? Is thoughtlessness? Are these not themselves sometimes the central offense? Can't they sometimes be helped?

Bishop Butler notes that proper resentment can have social value: "resentment against vice and wickedness . . . is one of the common bonds, by which society is held together" (75). Since Butler, like Rawls, emphasizes that the object of resentment is wrongful injury rather than mere pain or loss, he insists that its point is to prevent and remedy such injury. Resentment "is to be considered as a weapon, put into our hands by nature, against injury, injustice, and cruelty" (76). As we noted at the outset, Aristotle connects anger with the notion of insult, a kind of wrong. "Anger may be defined as a desire accompanied by pain, for a conspicuous revenge for a conspicuous slight at the hands of men who have no call to slight oneself or one's friends" (*Rhetoric*, trans. Roberts, 1378a). The thing to notice is that the resentment is directed as much at an attitude as at a harm. As Murphy says:

> One reason we so deeply resent moral injuries done to us is not simply that they hurt us in some tangible or sensible way; it is because such injuries are also messages, i.e., symbolic communications. They are ways a wrongdoer has of saying to us "I count and you do not," "I can use you for my purposes," or "I am here up high and you are there down below." Intentional wrongdoing degrades us—or at least represents an

attempt to degrade us—and thus it involves a kind of injury that is not merely tangible and sensible. It is moral injury. (1982, 508)[3]

I would only add that negligence and thoughtlessness can also send a message, indicate lack of due care and regard. Unintentional insults may not directly assert or attempt to achieve dominance, but they may nonetheless assume it. In our interrelations, what needs forgiveness is underlying attitudes. In the case of the child angry at the table, what makes the anger and forgiveness out of place, in addition to the table being faultless, is that the table has and conveys no attitude.

If we understand forgiveness as the foreswearing of resentment, we should recognize that what is involved is an interplay of attitudes. What is resented is an attitude (whether intentional or a lack of due regard that produces an injury or is itself taken as an injury) and what changes when one forgives is one's attitude toward the person whose attitude originally caused resentment. We shall have to ask: are attitudes themselves in our control?

THE INTERPLAY OF ATTITUDES

Following Bishop Butler and Jeffrie Murphy in taking forgiveness as the foreswearing of resentment, more specifically as overcoming resentment for a limited range of moral reasons (including repentance on the part of the wrongdoer but not including for psychological ease on the part of the aggrieved), enables one to see the centrality of an interplay of attitudes in forgiveness. Resentment focuses on the intention or lack of due care and respect that an injury may convey and forgiveness involves a change of heart toward the wrongdoer. So one can begin to see systematic connections among the sorts of reasons that may serve as appropriate grounds for forgiveness. For example, both "repentance" and "old time's sake" enable one to distinguish the attitude manifested in an agent's act and the current fundamental attitude of the agent, and so make sense of St. Augustine's somewhat mysterious counsel to "hate the sin, but love

---

3. There is another kind of moral injury that will need to be attended to. In addition to material harm and insult, there is the kind of injury that can make its victim in turn capable of committing injustice. It was this kind of injury that Socrates regarded as the only true kind.

the sinner." (The mystery arises because people are usually taken to be identified, to some degree, by and with their acts.) As Murphy puts it, "When you are repentant, I forgive you for what you *now are*. When I forgive you for old time's sake, I forgive you for what you *once were*. Much of our forgiveness of old friends and parents, for example, is of this sort" (1982, 510). There is a disparity in messages communicated. The divorce between act and agent, or between the attitude manifested in an act and the attitude of the agent, helps us see what shifts when understanding leads us to move from resentment to forgiveness.

Attitudes, however, are complex. If our resentments are not simple matters of choice, can forgiveness be? And even if we can, somehow, shift our inner attitude, is such a shift by itself enough to constitute forgiveness? In all circumstances? Pardoning or showing mercy certainly require a shift in outward behavior, might forgiveness (at least sometimes) require as much in order for the supposed shift in inner attitude to be taken seriously?

Just as it may be difficult to separate offending wrongdoers from their acts, it may be difficult to separate would-be forgivers from theirs: a change of heart in the would-be forgiver without a change in behavior and treatment may not be enough to constitute genuine forgiveness. While attitudes certainly matter, it is not always clear that an attitude can be taken to have changed if one nonetheless demands one's pound of flesh, insists first (or after) on extracting the full punishment. The poet Heine makes the point in striking ironical fashion:

> Mine is a most peaceable disposition. My wishes are: a humble cottage with a thatched roof, but a good bed, good food, the freshest milk and butter, flowers before my window, and a few fine trees before my door; and if God wants to make my happiness complete, he will grant me the joy of seeing some six or seven of my enemies hanging from those trees. Before their death I shall, moved in my heart, forgive them all the wrong they did me in their lifetime. One must, it is true, forgive one's enemies—but not before they have been hanged. (*Gedanken und Einfälle*, Section I, quoted in Freud 1930a, 110n)

ATTITUDES

Attitudes are not typically under the direct control of our will. Here we may compare deciding to forgive and deciding to care. As Harry

Frankfurt writes of caring, "The fact that someone cares about a certain thing is constituted by a complex set of cognitive, affective, and volitional dispositions and states . . . It certainly cannot be assumed that what a person cares about is generally under his immediate voluntary control" (1982, 85).

So, even if one were persuaded one would be better off if one forgave someone who had trespassed against them, one might find oneself unable to forgive. That is not necessarily something (a further something) to blame oneself for: "I am an unforgiving person." Perhaps the forgiveness is undeserved. Perhaps the offense is in a sense unforgivable (due to its seriousness, its egregiousness, or the depth of betrayal involved). Perhaps the incapacity to forgive is specific to this offense and this offender—not a perpetual unyielding and self-righteous disposition. For example, in the case of the psychopath, insensitive to moral rights and obligations, one may not forgive him (where that involves restoring him to full human relations) because it seems more appropriate to dismiss him (regard him as not a moral agent at all). Perhaps there is no ground for separating the agent from the act. (Understanding is not by itself sufficient for forgiveness. Why forgive the unrepentant wrongdoer?) And perhaps the wound itself is of a kind that renders the victim incapable of forgiveness. The interplay of attitudes needs to recognize a third kind of injury, apart from whatever grievous harm might have been done and whatever morally offensive message might have been sent along with and through it, there is always a risk of moral injury, that the person who is the victim of injustice may become capable of injustice in turn (and withal incapable of forgiveness). It is that sort of moral damage that deeply concerned Socrates, and it is the fear of it that sometimes makes abusers and oppressors relentless: they may fear the justified resentment and revenge of their victims. And all may fear other consequences of such moral damage. Think of the molested child who becomes a child molester. Think of the victims of genocide whose fear of genocide leads them to commit the same crime.

Forgiveness is one path to reconciliation. There are others. Think of the work of "Truth and Reconciliation" commissions after the defeat of evil regimes. The truth, sometimes amounting to confession, insisted on by such commissions is not quite the same as the understanding referred to in our proverb. Nor is it the same as punishment or, for that matter, revenge.

So far as we think of forgiveness as a moral virtue, it must be given for moral reasons. Hence if someone seeks to forgive simply to ease their own mind, for the sake of self-therapy, whatever kind of closure is achieved might not amount to forgiveness (Murphy, 507). Indeed, in such a case, one might suspect that the relevant attitude does not really get shifted, it is just the expression of anger that gets suppressed. Since the attitude of the wrongdoer still presumably stands (the therapeutic interests of the aggrieved give no ground to separate agent from act), a response to the affront is always liable to be provoked anew. It is not clear that forgiveness to make ourselves feel better, to free us to move on, is "forgiveness," that is, a genuine change in attitude toward the offender or the offense. More broadly, the notion that forgiveness is the only way to achieve closure, so one can move on, is of course mistaken. The notion that one must achieve closure before one can move on may also be mistaken. And the notion that understanding inevitably leads to forgiveness and so closure is perhaps least plausible of all. The notion of "closure" is itself problematic when we are dealing with an interplay of attitudes, which by their nature, especially in ongoing relationships, are always in flux.

One may understand the sources of an offense, but to forgive might seem to lessen the offense, to fail to take it and oneself sufficiently seriously. And clinging to grievance may seem to offer other rewards (the rewards of self-righteousness, of dignity, of not having to deal further with the other, etc.). Understanding itself may sometimes be threatening. Even admitting the offense is intelligible (say in the case of genocide or of incest) may seem a risk: understanding might seem to make the offense thinkable and so possible again. Part of the point of taboo is to make certain things unthinkable precisely so as to make them undoable. Still, one might forgive an offense one fails to understand. One might do it because the wrongdoer repents. The wrong may remain unintelligible, yet be forgiven. (Understanding is not necessary to forgiveness.)

Even where one fails or refuses to forgive, one need not be left seething in resentment. (The concern that one might be is one of the therapeutic arguments for urging forgiveness—letting go so one can move on.) It is not just that there are alternative methods of letting go (I shall speak of forgetting in a moment). Nor just that there are alternatives to resentment as a reaction to wrongdoing and neglect directed at oneself in the first place (I shall speak in a bit of an alternative discussed by

Gandhi). It might just be that there are good reasons to let the past rest as past—say, in a political context, the evil is past and so there is no need to struggle further against it, indeed, reason to fear continuing the struggle against the admitted evil might run the risk of reviving it. The mere fact that an evil is past does not mean there is nothing to forgive (despite Aurel Kolnai's concern over an apparent paradox, 1973–74), the harm may persist, as may the attitude it expressed. What other accommodation is needed to maintain moral integrity could be highly variable.

It can, of course, also be the case that precisely because one does understand the forces and the pressures that led to, say, a betrayal, one refuses or is incapable of believing it won't happen again. So despite apologies and apparently sincere promises that it won't happen again, one may refuse to forgive. People often reach such a point in dealing with alcoholics who say they are sorry (and perhaps even mean it, and will go on meaning it each time they lapse and relapse). And even where one understands the circumstances and pressures that led someone to betray, there may remain the feeling that they could have tried harder (Feinberg 1970b, 282–83). The blanket excuse of determinism is faced by our blanket faith in the ability to try.

Even in cases where there may be no alternative, if the outcome reflects the agent's desires, the agent may still be responsible. It is arguable that the mere fact that a person could not have done otherwise need not lift moral responsibility. As Harry Frankfurt puts the point, "The fact that a person lacks alternatives does preclude his being morally responsible when it alone accounts for his behavior. But a lack of alternatives is not inconsistent with moral responsibility when someone acts as he does for reasons of his own, rather than simply because no other alternative is open to him" (Frankfurt 1969, 95). In such cases, the action can still be taken to express the agent's attitude. Moreover, some excuses can themselves be insulting, as in the case of a couple who arrived in the last moments of a party, explaining they had to finish vacuuming first.

Sometimes it is not our understanding but our ignorance that leads to forgiveness. There are cases of too much and too little motive. Sometimes these two may come together in simple difference from the norm. There is the kleptomaniac who is willing to risk much for things that appear valueless to us (and seem, on a conscious level, equally valueless to him). The person who keeps getting in trouble for stealing the apparently valueless may become an object of pity because of unintelligibility. The behavior is not necessarily "compulsive." How, after all, does one distinguish an irresistible desire from one which is simply not resisted? Again, one can always try, and whether one would succeed may depend on which of a host of conditions are held constant and which are allowed to vary. The conditions for determining capacities are too complex to go into here, but J. L. Austin sheds useful light on the notions of "irresistible impulse" and "loss of control" when he tells a story about a sophisticated academic taking more than his share of ice cream at a dinner and dryly concludes, "We often succumb to temptation with calm and even with finesse" (Austin 1956, 198n).

Joel Feinberg (1970b) includes the kleptomaniac in a small set of examples of cases of apparently voluntary actions with bewildering motivation where blame might seem out of place. In addition to the kleptomaniac, Feinberg describes a nonviolent child molester, a repetitive exhibitionist, and a well-to-do man who shoplifts, burgles, and assaults to obtain women's brassieres. All four understand the illegal character of their acts and avoid unnecessary risks of detection. What they don't understand is their own desires. And when we classify them as "mentally ill," we are generally marking the fact that we don't understand them either. What is particularly interesting, however, is that bizarre desires, precisely the sort that puzzle the person who has them and that seem incoherent to us, may lead us to forgive precisely because we do *not* understand. As Feinberg puts it, "Where crimes resist explanation in terms of ordinary motives, we hardly know what to resent. Here the old maxim 'to understand all is to forgive all' seems to be turned on its ear. It is closer to the truth to say of mentally ill wrongdoers that to forgive is to despair of understanding." What seems crucial "is the actor's lack of insight into his own motives" (1970b, 284, 288). Of course, understanding desires may sometimes simply be a matter of their being fairly widespread. Most adults have sexual desires for other adults. Having sexual desires for children seems (fortunately) rare, does not seem to fit in with other patterns of adult desire, and may seem inexplicable. But we should not be too quick to contrast this with a "normal" individual's insight into "normal" motives. People in general would have great trouble in specifying the sources of their "normal" sexual desires. Certainly they have an explanation, but so doubtless do the statistically aberrant or bizarre desires. (It does not follow that all desires are equally desirable. There may be all sorts of good reasons for individuals and societies to seek to restrain acting on certain desires, whether or not we understand their source.) The point here is that the path from lack of understanding to forgiveness is no less strewn with problems than the path from understanding to forgiveness.

In seeking to follow St. Augustine's advice to foreswear resentment by hating the sin while still loving the sinner, the separation is sometimes effectuated not by understanding, but precisely by lack of understanding. The attitude is not so much detached from the wrongdoer as the message that an injury might normally send is not received because the desires and attitude behind the action seem so obscure and unintelligible. So far as the sinner does not understand the appeal of the sin, the usual insulting message may be detached. But, again, do we understand our own desires? Is it a matter of associating with them versus renouncing them? May acting on them sometimes itself be enough to count as associating with them?

POINT OF VIEW

If we cannot simply and directly will our anger and resentment away, steps can be taken, and perhaps sometimes ought to be taken. Therapy depends upon the hope that attitudes can be changed—if not by a direct act of will, by a variety of techniques (which give varying place to reason, thought, and argument). Spinoza's therapy for anger, and for passive emotions generally, involves seeking wider understanding, ultimately *sub specie aeternitatis* (under the aspect of eternity). So the prescriptive advice mentioned at the start of this chapter is not new, and modern therapeutic movements are picking up on a philosophical, as well as a Christian, theme.

Spinoza counsels that we avoid as far as possible passive and painful emotions, such as hatred and anger, and points out, among other things, that if we appreciate "that men, like other things, act from the necessity of nature, then the wrong, or the Hate usually arising from it will occupy a very small part of the imagination, and will easily be overcome" (*Ethics* Part V, Prop. 10 Scol.). In effect, he is suggesting a revision of belief about the operation of causes, so that the object of anger will be seen as just an element of a necessary structure—a change which would inevitably alter the character of the emotion. And the intellectual activity, the search for and consideration of broader causes, is itself a pleasure and hence alleviating. Along similar lines, he points out that if we become aware of the multiplicity and complexity of causes, an emotion will have many objects and we will be less affected toward each than if we had regarded one alone as the cause (*Ethics*, Part V, Prop. 9).

Spinoza's advice, especially the urging to seek wider understanding, contains good sense. Nonetheless, there is a risk, emphasized by Isaiah Berlin in "Historical Inevitability," of mistaking the sort of necessity Spinoza speaks of as some sort of justifying inevitability. It is what leads Berlin to condemn the notion that to understand all is to forgive all as a "ringing fallacy" (1969 [1954], 41). However, I do not think we need to reject determinism outright in order to leave room for judgment. As previously noted, belief in determinism need not provide excuses or, we may now add, be a comfort. Of course, when we manage to take a wider perspective on the travails of our life, even if we don't come to regard them as inevitable, we may come to regard them as trivial. Certainly from a God's-eye-view, our concerns may seem absurd.[4] But it is not obvious that we always can assume such a perspective, or even that we should. Sometimes we are able to direct our attention (though there are limits even on this), and choosing a perspective and so perhaps shifting attitude may sometimes be like that. But why should we take God's point of view or think that the perspective of eternity and the universe is somehow more correct than a more limited perspective? The mere possibility of such an alternative is not enough to make our concerns unjustified—once we recognize that justification must always come to an end. Recognition of alternative views need not leave us with an ironical view of the seriousness with which we take ourselves, when we properly, by our own standards, do take ourselves seriously. After all, what we are looking out onto is our individual human concerns. Such concerns might disappear within some vastly larger picture, but why should a point of view that makes them invisible be thought to make their position (in relation to us) clearer? The concerns remain real for us and the issue is: what is the correct perspective *for us*? (The notion of a "correct perspective" itself determined from no point of view seems

---

4. For Thomas Nagel, absurdity arises from the contrast between the seriousness with which we, unavoidably, live our lives and the arbitrariness of what we care about when we step back, inevitably, to a transcendent standpoint. While Spinoza sees necessity when we view things *sub specie aeternitatis*, for Nagel what emerges from a transcendent standpoint is contingency (1971, 15).

unintelligible.) Even if we somehow thought the God's-eye-view the correct one, it seems clear that we could not sustain it. (Aristotle recognized that we are neither simply gods nor animals, though our natures may participate in characteristics of both—*Nicomachean Ethics*, Book X.) And again, even if we could sustain it, that would not show that what matters to us does not really matter to us or should not matter to us. We love and (yes) we hate, and the reasons of our hearts cannot be simply dismissed just because we can imagine a perspective from which our reasons might no longer move.

The God's-eye-view, like the perspective of determinism is not really ours. It is not what our attitudes toward others and ourselves depend upon. Perhaps we can look from such a perspective in rare philosophical moments (like looking from the point of view of the stars and seeing the earth as an insignificant little planet), but there is no reason that we should seek to shift from the perspective through which we must inevitably live our lives or give higher priority to an ultimately impossible standpoint.

While enlarged understanding may always offer some benefits, I myself would hesitate to attempt to move permanently into a wholly expansive view, not only because I don't think one could permanently succeed, but because more particular perspectives seem to me often appropriate. That something might not matter from a God's-eye-view does not mean it does not matter. And vice versa. Supposing God exists and has a purpose for us and that we could know it (which is supposing quite a lot), it does not follow that his purposes must be ours. Supposing a lamb's function from the point of the view of the shepherd is to be fatted for slaughter, would it follow that the lamb's function (from its point of view) is to become the best lamb chop possible? (See Neu 2000, chap. 1, "Mill's Pig.")

Forgiving need not take one to a God's-eye-view. The notion that to understand all is to forgive all, taken in the prescriptive sense, may sometimes be urging one take the (apparently misbehaving) agent's view. If no person willingly does evil, as Socrates thought, then understanding what the person took themselves to be doing from their point of view is to see the person as aiming at the good: intentional action always aims at the good. This is the typical claim of the person who insists "I didn't mean to" when the unfortunate nature of the outcome of their acts becomes manifest. But even an agent conceded to be aiming at the good may be wrong about what constitutes the good and their view of the good may include an insulting message for the aggrieved. (This leaves aside the deeper issues of Socrates' understanding of human motivation and intention.)

In order to preserve the inner goodness of the wrongdoer, perhaps to make it easier to go on loving the sinner while condemning the sin, people sometimes distinguish an inner (real and true) self and an outer (false and determined self). (See Lamb 1996, 82.) But the separation is as false as the Cartesian split between mind and body that it mimics— both approaches treating the real or essential self as though it were a disembodied mind. It is the schizoid vision of the self popularized by R. D. Laing in *The Divided Self* (1960) and other books of that period. The perhaps comforting vision of a well-meaning (and, in the full schizoid version, all-talented and omnipotent) self should be resisted. There are several protections against the metaphysical and moral temptation to regard one's inner or mental life as somehow "true" and one's bodily life (with its overt, observable actions) as external and somehow "false." The first is to consider carefully what "false" might mean here. In most senses (except where it is equated from the start with things bodily and visible) it can apply equally to things mental and physical. That is, emotions and thoughts may be as "false" as social roles in the sense of being, for example, undesired, unchosen, and disliked. Properly understood, the true/false distinction cuts across the mind/body distinction, rather than running parallel to it. Mind (mental states) can be false as well as true. Bodily states can be true as well as false. This connects with a second major protection against the schizoid delusion: the recognition that not all social roles are false. We build our identity partly through others' perception and recognition of us. Some of the social roles that make us who we are we in fact desire and choose. Being a parent, friend, student, lover need not be "false" just because each is a social role involving an embodied interacting life. And a third remedy to a schizoid split of mind and body is to consider what constitutes a "mental state." Philosophers such as Gilbert Ryle (1949) have emphasized the behavioral aspects of intelligence, "knowing how," vanity, etc. If I may cite Wittgenstein's formulation once more, "The human body is the best picture of the human soul" (1953, 178). The self inevitably becomes empty if it is regarded as disembodied because the attribution and existence of many psychological states depends on their bodily expression. The moral comfort of a retreat to a well-meaning inner self can be bought only at the cost of gross distortion of just what it is that makes us who and what we are. Sinners cannot shed their sins by a simple metaphysical shift in identity.

FORGIVING AND FORGETTING

It might seem that, as a moral virtue, forgiveness must be given for moral reasons and so forgetting could not be a form of forgiving. Typically we forget for no reason at all, effortlessly: forgetting is not a straightforwardly intentional activity. But then, perhaps forgiveness need not itself always be intentional (whether it then ceases to be a virtue is a further question). Of course, sometimes we are unable to forgive despite our best intentions. Still, as T. S. Eliot understood (and we noted in chap. 1), there is many a slip between an intention and its execution for all sorts of acts. The fact that an intention may not culminate in action may leave the intention intact (at least sometimes). But the intention in forgiveness involves a largely internal change, a shift in attitude. The fact that one presumably can always say "I forgive you" does not mean that forgiving itself (which involves a change of attitude, which as we have noted is a complex process) is in one's direct control. Can one choose to forgive (to change one's attitude, not just one's behavior)? Always? Certainly one can choose not to forgive. But is choosing to forgive closer to choosing to love (usually something not thought within the power of the will) than to choosing not to forgive (which like deciding to bear a grudge, or to not speak to someone, is regarded as within the power of the will)?

Control over emotions (despite the perhaps wishful thought of Sartre and others who treat all emotion as action), like control over beliefs, is limited. Belief, which aims at truth, is constrained by the evidence we acknowledge. (I think Spinoza, who refused to distinguish a separate faculty of willing in relation to belief, was closer to the truth about the relation of belief and will than Descartes, who insisted error was due to the extension of our will beyond our understanding.) Our responsibility for our beliefs does not end, however, with the limits on our will. There is always the question of whether to act on the beliefs we happen to have and the even more crucial question of what efforts and attitude to take toward gathering evidence in the formation and maintenance of beliefs. All of these complications in relation to belief, given the centrality of belief and thought in emotions, carry over to the realm of emotions, judgments, and attitudes. If forgiveness is foreswearing resentment, the question arises of whether (and if so, how) we can choose to forgive. Can we choose not to be angry? At best it seems a process, sometimes involving steps over which we have only limited control. Not that forgiveness is simply a matter of anger management—the interplay of morally appropriate (or inappropriate) attitudes is at stake.

Forgetting can, I think, sometimes be a form of forgiving—a way of letting go. (Of course, forgiving need not entail forgetting. It might indeed sometimes be foolish to forget.)[5] While forgetting may not be directly willed, it may sometimes reveal that an offense, like certain debts, no longer matters. Indeed, a creditor may sometimes release an indebted individual from their debt by telling them to "forget it." Where

5. Forgiveness does not require that one behave in the future as though the events needing forgiveness had not occurred. It would be foolish systematically to ignore evidence relevant to current and future expectations (that so-and-so is capable of betrayal, of deceit, of malicious action, and the like). Even if one does not assume the future will be like the past in every respect, only a fool would think the past contains no relevant guidance. (And Hume, who insisted on the contingency of the connection, came to the same practical conclusion [1748].)

How forgiving connects with treating and interacting with the wrongdoer, given the past act and one's understanding of what it reveals about the character of the agent, can be a quite complex matter. As Murphy points out, "If I forgive, this will primarily be a matter of my foreswearing my resentment toward the person who has wronged me—a change of attitude quite compatible with still demanding certain harsh public consequences for the wrongdoer. My forgiving you for embezzling my funds is not, for example, inconsistent with a demand that you return my funds to me or even with a demand that you suffer just legal punishment for what you have done. Neither does my forgiveness entail that I must trust you with my money again in the future. Forgiveness restores moral equality but not necessarily equality in every respect—e.g., equality of trust" (506–7). But demanding full punishment might undermine the claim to a shift in attitude (think of the parable of the unforgiving servant at Matthew 18:21–35 discussed by Murphy 1982, 512–13). Can punishment be the price of forgiveness? If forgiveness is bought at such a price, is what is earned "forgiveness"? Does forgiveness require reparation (Melanie Klein's notion) that goes beyond repentance, or does reparation function as the true sign of repentance?

a forgiver lets go of their resentment by forgetting the offense, the resentment has not been so much foresworn or renounced as simply allowed to die a natural death. (It is worth remembering that resentment has degrees and need not always be actively overcome. We expect it to fade with time, especially where the offense is minor and takes place in the context of an ongoing relationship characterized overall by caring.) Can understanding have anything to do with such forgiveness? While it is doubtful that understanding could lead directly to forgetting (given that forgetting is not itself directly willed), it might free an individual to let go—in the passive form of forgetting as well as in the active form of renouncing. The test here would come in what happens when the forgotten offense is recalled. (It might also be of interest to know what it takes to recall the offense. Is it so deeply buried that only a new offense or a direct statement about the old one can bring it back?) If a recalled offense brings back with it the old resentments, it has not been forgiven. If it doesn't, it may sometimes be that it is not just the passage of time that has made the offense cease to matter, but that a new understanding plays a role. It is significant that the new understanding may be of the offense, of the other, of oneself, or even of the world at large. (Following Spinoza's advice to consider things *sub specie aeternitatis* can be effective in overcoming anger—in the larger scheme of things, small offenses may not matter. My hesitation is in making the move to no offenses mattering.) This suggests an interesting twist in the role of understanding in forgiveness in general. When one says "to understand all is to forgive all," the object of understanding is typically assumed to be the same as the object of forgiveness. But in fact, a changed understanding of oneself or even of what matters in the world may be what enables one to forgive.

Self-understanding may be as important as understanding of others in relation to forgiveness. This is obvious in terms of recognizing one's own fallibility and proneness to faults. That is sometimes a condition of sympathetic understanding (and so forgiveness) of others. But it may equally be the case that understanding one's own tendency to attach undue importance to certain things, one's over-readiness to take offense, may free one to forgive an offense that remains unjustified or even unintelligible in one's eyes. Understanding, we may note once more, is not a necessary condition of forgiveness. (If it were, we might wonder whether children who cannot fully understand can fully forgive.

There is no age of forgiveness, unlike an age of consent. Understanding is a condition of consent, but it need not be a condition of forgiveness. Children are encouraged very early to apologize and to forgive. They may be very finely attuned to the interplay of attitudes.) Understanding may also include a recognition of one's provocativeness in producing certain offenses. In all, the object of understanding may be broader than just the object of forgiveness itself.

It might seem that if forgetting can be a form of forgiving, a shifting of attitude, perhaps changing one's attitude not for reasons having to do with the wrongdoer but for one's own sake, say for anger management or other therapeutic reasons, might also be a form of forgiveness too—this despite my earlier remarks. But then there remain the earlier doubts about whether forgiveness with such a basis, aiming simply to allow the forgiver to move on, involves a genuine shift in attitude. The offender's attitude and the offense may not have shifted at all. It is only one's attitude toward one's own state of mind that seems to have come into play.

THE ONE AND THE MANY

Does it matter who is being forgiven, who has wronged one? And does it matter whether it is just one who has been wronged, whether there were fellow victims or perhaps even a group of victims, or whether one was perhaps singled out as a victim precisely because one was a member of a group? All of these things may matter in a variety of ways, some of them affecting one's understanding of the nature of the wrong, of what needs to be forgiven or otherwise dealt with, and some even affecting who (if anyone) might be in a position to forgive. These questions about "who"—who has been wronged and who needs to be forgiven, who is the victim and who is the perpetrator (not to mention beneficiaries and perhaps not-so-innocent bystanders)—may matter as much as the many "whys" that so often complicate understanding and forgiveness.

We should start with the recognition that one is always at least among the victims when questions of forgiveness arise. Of course a mother may forgive someone for something done to her child, or a husband forgive someone for something done to his wife (or vice versa), but then the forgiver is clearly aggrieved on their own behalf as well as because of the wrong done more directly to their loved one. The notion that someone with more tenuous ties to a victim or victims might be in a position to give vicarious forgiveness is at the very least presumptuous. One may forgive on one's own account, but to offer to forgive on behalf of another is to invite the question: who does one think one is?

Only a wronged party can forgive. It is presumptuous for others to absolve those who have not wronged them. Insofar as resentment is a moral emotion, that is, insofar as it depends on beliefs about injustice, legitimate resentment requires a legitimate grievance. To foreswear a resentment one has no right to bear in the first place is to renounce what is not one's own. One can, of course, be indignant on behalf of another, angry at injustice, but to call a change of heart in such circumstances "forgiveness" is liable to mislead. It takes place outside the central interplay of attitudes.

There may be ties to perpetrators as well as to fellow victims. Is it worse to be raped by a stranger or by a date, a would-be friend? A member of one's family? The ties to the perpetrator (whatever they might be) open the possibility of additional injuries. (See Neu 2000, chap. 10, "What Is Wrong with Incest?") In particular, those injuries include betrayal of trust. What trust there might have been depends on what ties in fact there were, but we generally have less reason to trust strangers than friends. (Freud points out that the concepts of stranger and of enemy are not that distant.) Still, people regularly report feeling "violated" when their house is burglarized. Aside from the identification of their house with their person, the description suggests that we may expect something even from strangers. The character of our expectations from others and the relation of their identity to our feelings is tellingly revealed in a story told by Gandhi in his early political pamphlet, *Hind Swaraj:* "Imagine, Gandhi suggests, that you are awakened by a thief entering your bedroom and that in turning on the light you discover that the thief is in fact your own father. Would you not be embarrassed for his shame?" (Meister 2005, 104n19). As Robert Meister makes clear in his retelling of Gandhi's story, anger and resentment are not the only morally appropriate responses to a moral affront. These variant feelings, however, may also call for something like forgiveness if they are to be overcome. Which is not to say that they always should be overcome. In the political realm, as Gandhi well understood, reconciliation can take many and complex forms.[6] Much may depend on the wrong and on one's understanding of one's relation to the wrongdoer—we have seen this already in the notion of forgiving someone "for old time's sake." Forgiveness is not the only morally or psychologically appropriate response to one's own anger and resentment. Herbert Morris (1968) contrasts a regime of forgiveness to alternatives of punishment and treatment of wrongdoers. He suggests automatic forgiveness, like automatic treatment (as though all wrongdoers were somehow "sick," determined by forces outside their control, and so in need of therapy), might be a terrible mistake. Respect for the choices of the wrongdoer (which may morally require certain sorts of responses and preclude others) might be as much at stake as self-respect. And, crucially, we would lose one of the central forces for social control and harmony. Too much pity, as Bishop Butler pointed out long ago, can be a mistake. "Just indignation, he says, "is necessary for the very subsistence of the world, that injury, injustice, and cruelty should be punished; and since compassion, which is so natural to mankind, would render that execution of justice exceedingly difficult and uneasy; indignation against vice and wickedness is, and may be allowed to be, a balance to that weakness of pity, and also to anything else which would prevent the necessary methods of severity" (77).

Since we may also sometimes need to forgive ourselves, the issue of who forgives whom can become multiply complicated. Surely there

---

6. As Meister's exploration delicately brings out, there can be difficulties at every turn. If one follows the path of the unreconciled victim seeking revolutionary justice, refusing to distinguish between the perpetrators and the beneficiaries of evil, there is hope of more than a merely moral victory but there is a risk of endless struggle, of the constant creation of new enemies. If one follows the path of the reconciled victim, willing to distinguish between the perpetrators and the beneficiaries of evil, a moral victory may be claimed but there is a risk that the aftereffects of evil will persist in the form of social injustice, with the old beneficiaries reaping a reward when in fact they are no better than would-be perpetrators. Whatever its costs, a distinctive advantage of forgiveness (and other forms of reconciliation) is that it avoids the third kind of injury mentioned earlier (different from the grievous injuries done to victims and the degrading messages that injuries done with certain attitudes reflect), "the distinctively moral kind of damage that would make victims capable of doing injustice in their turn, and thus incapable of legitimate rule" (85).

are significant differences between forgiving others and forgiving one-self. The latter may be (as therapists often urge) all the more necessary because one must always be with oneself. Insofar as forgiveness is a matter of attitude, an aggrieved and unforgiving attitude toward oneself may be all the more disruptive to one's life than a similar attitude toward an often absent (or avoidable) other. On the other hand, there may be something unseemly in being too ready to forgive oneself—at least for wrongs done to others. The temptations of self-interested leniency and the issue of standing to forgive are especially problematical when one contemplates forgiving oneself for wrongs done to others. (The problem of renouncing a resentment that is not legitimately one's own may leave self-forgiveness more intelligible as a matter of overcoming guilt or shame rather than, our usual formula, foreswearing resentment.) This connects with the two faces of responsibility: taking responsibility can involve forward-looking commitments to deal appropriately with the consequences of wrongs and it can involve backward-looking acceptance of blame for shortcomings. Only the latter might be at all undermined by some deterministic explanation of how whatever went wrong was (ultimately) out of one's control. It may always be in place to take responsibility for one's failings, to clean up one's messes (however uncertain one may be about the backward-looking attribution of the mess exclusively to oneself), and here being too ready to forgive oneself may buy comfort and self-satisfaction at the price of ceasing to be worthy of respect.

The direct connection between understanding and forgiveness claimed by "to understand all is to forgive all," is as questionable in relation to self-forgiveness as forgiveness of others. As Isaiah Berlin puts the commonsense point, "Certainly it will surprise us to be told that the better we understand our own actions—our own motives and the circumstances surrounding them—the freer from self-blame we shall inevitably feel. The contrary is surely often true" (Berlin 1954, 96).

FORGIVENESS AND KNOWLEDGE

Going back to the quotation from Madame de Staël with which we started, her character Corinne's thought is actually, in context, neither simply descriptive nor simply prescriptive, but rather a kind of boast

(Book XVIII, chap. 5). Corinne there is claiming that among the virtues of "superiority of mind and heart" (her own and in general) is that it, in the form of superior understanding, makes one exceptionally indulgent and accepting, and in the form of superior depth of feeling, makes one exceptionally kind and good. Would that it were so. Leaving goodness aside (though here one should be aware that it is not unheard of for people to have great depth of feeling where they themselves are concerned, but less sensitivity when it comes to others), it is simply not the case that superior understanding leads automatically to acceptance of the foibles and crimes of others and oneself. Forgiveness, as we have seen, has other conditions. And, depending on what one thinks follows from forgiveness, that may be a good thing. Certainly a too eager readiness to forgive may expose one to more insults (of their many different kinds) than a firm expectation of treatment from others in accord with fundamental self-respect and earned self-esteem. Of course, those standards also call for us to control our own impulses to insult—whether by intention or inattention.

REFERENCES

50 Cent. 2002. "I Smell Pussy." Track 14 on *50 Cent Is the Future* (Shadyville Entertainment). Compact disc.

Abbott, Jack Henry. 1982. *In the Belly of the Beast: Letters from Prison* (New York: Vintage).

Abrahams, Roger D. 1962. "Playing the Dozens," *Journal of American Folklore* 75, pp. 209–20.

——. 1970. *Deep Down in the Jungle: Negro Narrative Folklore from the Streets of Philadelphia* (2nd ed.; New York: Aldine).

Acocella, Joan. Review of Andrea de Jorio 2000 [1832], *Gesture in Naples and Gesture in Classical Antiquity* (trans. and ed. by Adam Kendon; Bloomington: Indiana University Press) in the *New York Review of Books* of Dec. 21, 2000, pp. 48–55.

Adams, Robert M. 1977. "Invective and Insult." In his *Bad Mouth: Fugitive Papers on the Dark Side* (Berkeley: University of California Press), pp. 21–42.

Althusser, Louis. 1971. "Ideology and Ideological State Apparatuses," in *Lenin and Philosophy*, tr. Ben Brewster (New York: Monthly Review Press), pp. 170–86.

Anonymous. 1993. Note: "The Demise of the Chaplinsky Fighting Words Doctrine: An Argument for Its Interment," *Harvard Law Review* 106, pp. 1129–46.

Anscombe, G. E. M. 1963. *Intention* (2nd ed.; Ithaca, N.Y.: Cornell University Press)

Aristotle. 1984. *Nicomachean Ethics*, trans. W. D. Ross and J. O. Urmson. In *The Complete Works of Aristotle*, Vol. 2, ed. Jonathan Barnes (Princeton: Princeton University Press).

——. 1984. *Rhetoric*, trans. W. Rhys Roberts. In *The Complete Works of Aristotle*, Vol. 2, ed. Jonathan Barnes (Princeton: Princeton University Press).

Austin, J. L. 1962. *How to Do Things with Words* (Cambridge: Harvard University Press).

——. 1970a (1956). "A Plea for Excuses," in *Philosophical Papers* (2nd ed.; Oxford: Oxford University Press), pp. 175–204.

Austin, J. L. 1970b (1956). "Performative Utterances," in *Philosophical Papers* (2nd ed.; Oxford: Oxford University Press), pp. 233–52.

Ayoub, Millicent R. & Stephen A. Barnett. 1965. "Ritualized Verbal Insult in White High School Culture," *Journal of American Folklore* 78, pp. 337–44.

Baker, Robert. 1975. "'Pricks' and 'Chicks': A Plea for 'Persons,'" in *Philosophy and Sex*, ed., Robert Baker and Frederick Elliston (Buffalo: Prometheus), pp. 45–64.

Bartlett, John (1968). *Bartlett's Familiar Quotations* (14th ed.; Boston: Little, Brown).

Bateson, Gregory. 1972 (1955). "A Theory of Play and Fantasy," in *Steps to an Ecology of Mind* (New York: Ballantine), pp. 177–93.

Benjamin, Jessica. 1988. *The Bonds of Love* (New York: Pantheon).

Berg, A. Scott. 2003. *Kate Remembered* (New York: G. P. Putnam's Sons).

Berlin, Isaiah. 1969 (1954). "Historical Inevitability," in *Four Essays on Liberty* (Oxford: Oxford University Press), pp. 41–117.

Booth, Wayne C. 1974. *A Rhetoric of Irony* (Chicago: The University of Chicago Press).

Bourdieu, Pierre. 1966. "The Sentiment of Honour in Kabyle Society," in J. G. Peristiany, ed., *Honour and Shame: The Values of Mediterranean Society* (Chicago: The University of Chicago Press), pp. 191–241.

Brandreth, Gyles. 2000. *John Gielgud: An Actor's Life* (Phoenix Mill, Gloucestershire: Sutton).

Brenneis, Donald. 1980. "Fighting Words," in J. Cherfas and R. Lewin, eds., *Not Work Alone* (Beverly Hills, Cal.: Sage), pp. 166–80.

Briggs, Jean L. 1970. *Never in Anger: Portrait of an Eskimo Family* (Cambridge: Harvard University Press).

——. 1982. "Living Dangerously: the contradictory foundations of value in Canadian Inuit Society," in Eleanor Leacock and Richard Lee, eds., *Politics and History in Band Societies* (Cambridge: Cambridge University Press), pp. 109–31.

Brophy, John and Eric Partridge, eds. 1930. *Songs and Slang of the British Soldier: 1914–1918* (London: Eric Partridge at the Scholartis Press).

Brown, Norman O. 1966. *Love's Body* (New York: Vintage).

Buckley, F. H. 2003. *The Morality of Laughter* (Ann Arbor: The University of Michigan Press).

Butler, Bishop Joseph. 1970 (1726). *Butler's Fifteen Sermons*, ed. T. A. Roberts (London: SPCK).

Butler, Judith. 1997. *Excitable Speech: A Politics of the Performative* (London: Routledge).

Carroll, Lewis. 1965 (1865, 1871). *The Annotated Alice*, ed. Martin Gardner (Harmondsworth: Penguin Books).

Carter, Graydon. 2005. "Roman Holiday," *Vanity Fair*, Oct 2005, pp. 80–92.

Chantrell, Glynnis, ed. 2002. *The Oxford Dictionary of Word Histories* (Oxford: Oxford University Press).

Chatauvillard, Comte de. 1836. *Essai sur le Duel* (Paris: Imprimerie d'Édouard Proux, et comp.).

Chesterfield, Philip Dormer Stanhope, Earl of. 1795. *Advice to His Son, On Men and Manners* (Philadelphia: Jacob Johnson).

Chodorow, Nancy. 1978. *The Reproduction of Mothering: Psychoanalysis and the Sociology of Gender* (Berkeley: University of California Press).

Collins, Lauren. 2005. "Don't Laugh," *The New Yorker*, July 4, 2005, pp. 31–32.

Critchley, Simon. 2002. *On Humour* (London: Routledge).

Darwall, Stephen L. 1977. "Two Kinds of Respect, *Ethics* 88, pp. 36–49.

Davies, Christie. 2002. *The Mirth of Nations* (New Brunswick, N.J.: Transaction).

Delgado, Richard. 1993 (1982). "Words That Wound: A Tort Action for Racial Insults," in *Words That Wound*, ed. Matsuda et al. (Boulder, Colo.: Westview), pp. 89–110.

Dennett, Daniel C. (1984). *Elbow Room: The Varieties of Free Will Worth Wanting* (Cambridge, Mass.: MIT Press)

de Sousa, Ronald. 1987. *The Rationality of Emotion* (Cambridge, Mass.: MIT Press).

de Staël, Madame. 1998 (1807). *Corinne, or Italy*, trans. S. Raphael (Oxford: Oxford University Press).

Dollard, John. 1939. "The Dozens: Dialectic of Insult," *The American Imago* 1, pp. 3–25.

Dover, Kenneth J. 1978. *Greek Homosexuality* (Cambridge: Harvard University Press).

Dr. Dre. 1992. "Fuck Wit Dre Day." Track 2 on *The Chronic* (Death Row/Interscope). Compact disc.

Dundes, Alan, Jerry W. Leach, and Bora Özkök. 1972. "The Strategy of Turkish Boys' Verbal Dueling Rhymes," in John J. Gumperz and Dell Hymes, eds., *Directions in Sociolinguistics: The Ethnography of Communication* (New York: Holt, Rinehart and Winston), pp. 130–60.

Dworkin, Ronald. 1996 (1993–94). "MacKinnon's Words," in *Freedom's Law* (Cambridge: Harvard University Press).

Ekman, Paul and Dacher Keltner. 2000. "Facial Expression of Emotion," in Michael Lewis and Jeannette M. Haviland-Jones, eds., *Handbook of Emotions* (2nd ed.; New York: The Guilford Press), pp. 236–49.

Eliot, T. S. 1934. *After Strange Gods: A Primer of Modern Heresy* (London: Faber and Faber).

———. 1969. *The Complete Poems and Plays of T. S. Eliot* (London: Faber and Faber).

Elliott, Robert C. 1960. *The Power of Satire: Magic, Ritual, Art* (Princeton: Princeton University Press).

Ellman, Richard. 1988. *Oscar Wilde* (New York: Alfred A. Knopf).

Ellsworth, Phoebe C. and J. Merrill Carlsmith. 1968. "Effects of Eye Contact and Verbal Content on Affective Response to a Dyadic Interaction," *Journal of Personality and Social Psychology* 10, pp. 15–20.

Ellsworth, Phoebe C., J. Merrill Carlsmith, and Alexander Henson. 1972. "The Stare as a Stimulus to Flight in Human Subjects: A Series of Field Experiments," *Journal of Personality and Social Psychology* 21, pp. 302–11.

Ellsworth, Phoebe C. and Ellen J. Langer. 1976. "Staring and Approach: An Interpretation of the Stare as a Nonspecific Activator," *Journal of Personality and Social Psychology* 33, pp. 117–22.

Eminem. 2002. *8 Mile* (Universal). Compact disc; lyrics at http://www.stlyrics.com/lyrics/8mile/papadoc.htm.

Eribon, Didier. 2004 (1999). *Insult and the Making of the Gay Self*, trans. Michael Lucey (Durham, N.C.: Duke University Press).

Erikson, Erik. 1963. *Childhood and Society* (2nd ed.; New York: W. W. Norton & Company).

———. 1964. "Psychological Reality and Historical Actuality," in *Insight and Responsibility* (New York: Norton), pp. 159–215.

Feinberg, Joel (1970a). "The Expressive Function of Punishment," in *Doing and Deserving* (Princeton: Princeton University Press), pp. 95–118.

———. (1970b). "What Is So Special about Mental Illness?" in *Doing and Deserving* (Princeton: Princeton University Press), pp. 272–92.

———. 1985. *Offense to Others* (vol. 2 of *The Moral Limits of the Criminal Law*, Oxford: Oxford University Press).

Fish, Stanley. 1994. *There's No Such Thing as Free Speech, and It's a Good Thing, Too* (Oxford: Oxford University Press).

Fletcher, George P. 1988. *A Crime of Self-Defense: Bernhard Goetz and the Law on Trial* (New York: The Free Press).

Foot, Philippa. 1978a (1958). "Moral Arguments," in *Virtues and Vices* (Berkeley: University of California Press), pp. 96–109.

———. 1978b (1958-59). "Moral Beliefs," in *Virtues and Vices*, pp. 110–31.

Foucault, Michel. 1986. *The Use of Pleasure* (vol. 2 of *The History of Sexuality*, New York: Vintage).

Frankfurt, Harry. 1988 (1969). "Alternate Possibilities and Moral Responsibility." In *The Importance of What We Care About* (Cambridge: Cambridge University Press), pp. 1–10.

———. 1988 (1982). "The Importance of What We Care About." In *The Importance of What We Care About*, pp. 80–94.

Freud, Sigmund and Josef Breuer. 1895d. *Studies on Hysteria, Standard Edition of the Complete Psychological Works of Sigmund Freud*, ed. James Strachey (London: Hogarth, 1953–74), 2.

Freud, Sigmund. 1905c. *Jokes and their Relation to the Unconscious, Standard Edition* 8.

———. 1905d. *Three Essays on the Theory of Sexuality, Standard Edition* 7.

———. 1905e. *Fragment of an Analysis of a Case of Hysteria, Standard Edition* 7.

———. 1908b. "Character and Anal Erotism." *Standard Edition* 9.

———. 1908c. "On the Sexual Theories of Children." *Standard Edition* 9.

———. 1908e. "Creative Writers and Day-Dreaming." *Standard Edition* 9.

———. 1909d. "Notes Upon a Case of Obsessional Neurosis." *Standard Edition* 10.

———. 1910e. "The Antithetical Meaning of Primal Words." *Standard Edition* 11.

———. 1912–13. *Totem and Taboo, Standard Edition* 13.

———. 1915c. "Instincts and Their Vicissitudes." *Standard Edition* 14.

———. 1916–17. *Introductory Lectures on Psycho-Analysis. Standard Edition* 15–16.

———. 1917e. "Mourning and Melancholia." *Standard Edition* 14.

———. 1918a. "The Taboo of Virginity." *Standard Edition* 11.

———. 1919e. "A Child Is Being Beaten." *Standard Edition* 17.

———. 1921c. *Group Psychology and the Analysis of the Ego. Standard Edition* 18.

———. 1924c. "The Economic Problem of Masochism." *Standard Edition* 19.

———. 1925j. "Some Psychical Consequences of the Anatomical Distinction between the Sexes." *Standard Edition* 19.

———. 1930a. *Civilization and Its Discontents. Standard Edition* 21.

Frevert, Ute. 1995 (1991). *Men of Honour: A Social and Cultural History of the Duel,* trans. Anthony Williams (Cambridge, England: Polity).

Friend, Tad. 2001. "You Can't Say That," *The New Yorker,* Nov. 19, 2001, pp. 44–49.

———. 2002. "What's So Funny?," *The New Yorker,* Nov. 11, 2002, pp. 78–93.

Frye, Northrop. 1957. *Anatomy of Criticism: Four Essays* (Princeton: Princeton University Press).

Gates, Henry Louis Jr. 1988. *The Signifying Monkey: A Theory of Afro-American Literary Criticism* (Oxford: Oxford University Press).

———. 1994. "War of Words: Critical Race Theory and the First Amendment," in *Speaking of Race, Speaking of Sex: Hate Speech, Civil Rights, and Civil Liberties* (New York: NYU Press), pp. 17–58.

Gilligan, Carol. 1982. *In a Different Voice* (Cambridge: Harvard University Press).

Gilmore, David D. 1987. "Introduction: The Shame of Dishonor," in David D. Gilmore, ed., *Honor and Shame and the Unity of the Mediterranean* (Washington, D.C.: American Anthropological Association), pp. 2–21.

Goffman, Erving. 1967. *Interaction Ritual: Essays on Face-to-Face Behavior* (Garden City, N.Y.: Anchor Books).

Goodwin, M. H. 1990. *He-Said-She-Said: Talk as Social Organization among Black Children* (Bloomington: Indiana University Press).

Gossen, Gary H. 1976. "Verbal Dueling in Chamula," in Barbara Kirshenblatt-Gimblett, ed., *Speech Play: Research and Resources for Studying Linguistic Creativity* (Philadelphia: University of Pennsylvania Press), pp. 121–46.

Gottlieb, Robert. 2004. "The Hitmaker: Or, The Man Who Came to Broadway," *The New Yorker,* Nov. 29, 2004, pp. 142–50.

Gould, Jon B. 2005. *Speak No Evil: The Triumph of Hate Speech Regulation* (Chicago: The University of Chicago Press).

Greenawalt, Kent. 1995. *Fighting Words: Individuals, Communities, and Liberties of Speech* (Princeton: Princeton University Press).

Greenblatt, Stephen. 2004. *Will in the World: How Shakespeare Became Shakespeare* (New York: W. W. Norton & Company).

Greer, Germaine. 1971. "Abuse," in *The Female Eunuch* (New York: McGraw-Hill), pp. 259–69.

Grice, Paul. 1989 (1948, 1957). "Meaning," in *Studies in the Way of Words* (Cambridge: Harvard University Press).

Hampshire, Stuart. 2000. *Justice Is Conflict* (Princeton: Princeton University Press).

Hart, H. L. A. (1968). *Punishment and Responsibility: Essays in the Philosophy of Law* (Oxford: Oxford University Press).

Hegel, G. W. F. 1977 (1807). *Phenomenology of Spirit.* Trans. A. V. Miller (Oxford: Oxford University Press).

Heller, Zoë. 2004. "Don't Call Me Sir: Don Rickles and the Art of the Insult," *The New Yorker,* Aug. 2, 2004, pp. 32–38.

Helms, Alan. 1995. *Young Man from the Provinces: A Gay Life Before Stonewall* (London: Faber and Faber).

Hill, Thomas E. Jr. 1973. "Servility and Self-Respect," *The Monist* 57, pp. 87–104.

Hobbes, Thomas. 1968 (1651). *Leviathan* (Harmondsworth: Penguin Books).

Holmes, Oliver Wendell, Jr. 1881. *The Common Law* (Boston: Little, Brown).

Hu, Hsien Chin. 1944. "The Chinese Concepts of 'Face,'" *American Anthropologist* n.s. 46: 45–64.

Hughes, Geoffrey. 1998. *Swearing: A Social History of Foul Language, Oaths and Profanity in English* (Penguin Books).

Huizinga, Johan. 1950. "Play and Contest as Civilizing Functions," in *Homo Ludens: A Study of the Play-Element in Culture* (Boston: Beacon).

Hume, David. 1977 (1748). *An Enquiry Concerning Human Understanding* (Indianapolis: Hackett).

Ignatieff, Michael. 1993. *Blood and Belonging: Journeys into the New Nationalism* (New York: Farrar, Straus and Giroux).

Irons, Peter. 1983. *Justice at War: The Story of the Japanese-American Internment Cases* (Oxford: Oxford University Press; repr., Berkeley: University of California Press, 1993).

Jones, William K. 2003. *Insult to Injury: Libel, Slander, and Invasions of Privacy* (Boulder: University Press of Colorado).

Jorio, Andrea de. 2000 [1832]. *Gesture in Naples and Gesture in Classical Antiquity* (*La mimica degli antichi investigata nel gestire napoletano*) trans. and ed. by Adam Kendon (Bloomington: Indiana University Press).

Kant, Immanuel. 1993 (1785). *Grounding for the Metaphysics of Morals,* trans. James W. Ellington (3rd ed., Indianapolis: Hackett Publishing Company).

Kennedy, Randall. 2002. *Nigger: The Strange Career of a Troublesome Word* (New York: Pantheon Books).

Kiernan, V. G. 1988. *The Duel in European History: Honour and the Reign of Aristocracy* (Oxford: Oxford University Press).

Kolnai, Aurel. 1978 (1973–74). "Forgiveness," in *Ethics, Value, and Reality* (Indianapolis: Hackett Publishing Company), pp. 211–24.

Labov, William. 1972. "Rules for Ritual Insults," in *Language in the Inner City: Studies in the Black English Vernacular* (Philadelphia: University of Pennsylvania Press), pp. 297–353.

Lahr, John. 2003. "Chasing the Witch," *The New Yorker,* Nov. 17, 2003.

Laing, R. D. 1960. *The Divided Self* (London: Tavistock).

Lamb, Sharon. 1996. *The Trouble with Blame: Victims, Perpetrators, and Responsibility* (Cambridge: Harvard University Press).

Lawrence, Charles R. III. 1993 (1990). "If He Hollers Let Him Go: Regulating Racist Speech on Campus," in *Words That Wound*, ed. Matsuda et al. (Boulder, Colo.: Westview), pp. 53–88.

Lawrence, D. H. 1961 (1929). "Pornography and Obscenity," in *A Propos of Lady Chatterley's Lover and Other Essays* (Harmondsworth: Penguin Books), pp. 60–84.

Lazare, Aaron. 2004. *On Apology* (Oxford: Oxford University Press).

Leach, Edmund. 1964. "Anthropological Aspects of Language: Animal Categories and Verbal Abuse," in Eric H. Lenneberg, ed., *New Directions in the Study of Language* (Cambridge, Mass.: MIT Press), pp. 23–63.

Levy, Leonard W. 1993. *Blasphemy: Verbal Offense Against the Sacred, from Moses to Salman Rushdie* (New York: Knopf, 1993).

Lewis, Anthony. 1991. *Make No Law: The Sullivan Case and the First Amendment* (New York: Random House).

Linger, Daniel Touro. 1992. *Dangerous Encounters: Meanings of Violence in a Brazilian City* (2nd ed.; Oxford: Oxford University Press).

Lorenz, Konrad. 1966. *On Aggression*, trans. M. Latzke (London: Methuen).

Low, Jennifer. 2003. *Manhood and the Duel: Masculinity in Early Modern Drama and Culture* (New York: Palgrave Macmillan).

MacKinnon, Catherine A. 1979. *Sexual Harassment of Working Women: A Case of Sex Discrimination* (New Haven: Yale University Press).

———. 1989. *Toward a Feminist Theory of the State* (Cambridge: Harvard University Press).

———. 1993. *Only Words* (Cambridge: Harvard University Press).

Mandeville, Bernard de. 1732. *An Enquiry into the Origin of Honour and the Usefulness of Christianity in War* (London: Printed for J. Brotherton).

Martin, Judith. 1990. "Heavy Etiquette Theory," in *Miss Manners' Guide for the Turn-of-the-Millennium* (New York: Simon & Schuster), pp. 3–19.

Matsuda, Mari J. 1993 (1989). "Public Response to Racist Speech: Considering the Victim's Story," in *Words That Wound*, ed. Matsuda et al. (Boulder, Colo.: Westview), pp. 17–51.

Matsuda, Mari J. et al. 1993. *Words That Wound: Critical Race Theory, Assaultive Speech, and the First Amendment* (Boulder, Colo.: Westview)

McAleer, Kevin. 1994. *Dueling: The Cult of Honor in Fin-de-Siècle Germany* (Princeton: Princeton University Press).

McGrath, Ben. 2005. "Tub War" *The New Yorker*, April 11, 2005, pp. 23–24.

McPhee, Nancy, ed. 1980. *The Book of Insults Ancient & Modern* (Harmondsworth: Penguin Books).

Meister, Robert. 2005. "Ways of Winning: The Costs of Moral Victory in Transitional Regimes," in Alan D. Schrift, ed. *Modernity and the Problem of Evil* (Bloomington: Indiana University Press), pp. 81–111.

Merchey, Jason. 2004. *Values of the Wise: Humanity's Highest Aspirations* (Haverford, Pa.: Infinity Publishing Co.).

Mill, John Stuart. 1975. *Three Essays: On Liberty, Representative Government, The Subjection of Women* (Oxford: Oxford University Press).

Miller, William Ian. 1993. *Humiliation and Other Essays on Honor, Social Discomfort, and Violence* (Ithaca, N.Y.: Cornell University Press).

———. 2003. *Faking It* (Cambridge: Cambridge University Press).

Mitchell, Joni. 1998. "Lead Balloon." Track 4 on *Taming the Tiger* (Warner Bros.). Compact disc.

Morgan, Marcyliena. 2002. *Language, Discourse and Power in African American Culture* (Cambridge: Cambridge University Press).

Morris, Herbert (1968). "Persons and Punishment." *The Monist* 52, pp. 475–501.

Murphy, Jeffrie G. 1982. "Forgiveness and Resentment," *Midwest Studies in Philosophy* 7, pp. 503–16.

———. 2003. *Getting Even: Forgiveness and Its Limits* (Oxford: Oxford University Press).

Muzio, Girolamo. 1550. *Il Duello* (Venice).

Nagel, Thomas. 1979 (1971). "The Absurd." In *Mortal Questions* (Cambridge: Cambridge University Press).

Neu, Jerome. 1977. *Emotion, Thought, and Therapy* (London: Routledge & Kegan Paul; Berkeley: University of California Press).

———. 2000. *A Tear Is an Intellectual Thing: The Meanings of Emotion* (Oxford: Oxford University Press).

———. 2002a. "Reply to My Critics," *Philosophical Studies* 108, pp. 159–71.

———. 2002b. "To Understand All Is to Forgive All—Or Is It?" in Sharon Lamb and Jeffrie Murphy, eds., *Before Forgiving: Cautionary Views of Forgiveness in Psychotherapy* (New York: Oxford University Press), pp. 17–38.

———. 2002c. "An Ethics of Fantasy?," *Journal of Theoretical and Philosophical Psychology* 22, pp. 133–57.

Nietzsche, Friedrich. 1967 (1901). *The Will to Power*, ed. and trans. Walter Kaufmann and R. J. Hollingdale (New York: Random House).

Nisbett, Richard E. and Dov Cohen. 1996. *Culture of Honor: The Psychology of Violence in the South* (Boulder, Colo.: Westview).

Nye, Robert A. 1993. *Masculinity and Male Codes of Honor in Modern France* (Oxford: Oxford University Press).

Onians, Richard Broxton. 1951. *The Origins of European Thought: about the Body, the Mind, the Soul, the World, Time, and Fate* (Cambridge: Cambridge University Press).

Onions, C. T., ed. 1966. *The Oxford Dictionary of English Etymology* (Oxford: Oxford University Press).

Paglia, Camille. 1992 (1991). "Junk Bonds and Corporate Raiders: Academe in the Hour of the Wolf," in *Sex, Art, and American Culture* (New York: Vintage).

Partridge, Eric. 1966. *Origins: A Short Etymological Dictionary of Modern English* (New York: Macmillan).

Paumgarten, Nick. 2005. "Fighting Words: Whatever," *The New Yorker*, July 11 and 18, 2005, p. 38.

Peltonen, Markku. 2003. *The Duel in Early Modern England: Civility, Politeness and Honour* (Cambridge: Cambridge University Press).

Pitt-Rivers, Julian. 1966. "Honour and Social Status," in J. G. Peristiany, ed., *Honour and Shame: The Values of Mediterranean Society* (Chicago: The University of Chicago Press), pp. 19–77.

Plato. 1989 (c. 380 BC). *Symposium*, trans. Alexander Nehemas and Paul Woodruff (Indianapolis: Hackett Publishing Company).

Post, Robert C. 1988. "Cultural Heterogeneity and Law: Pornography, Blasphemy, and the First Amendment," *California Law Review* 76, pp. 297–335.

Rabelais, François. 1955 (1532–52). *Gargantua and Pantagruel*, trans. Thomas Urquhart and Peter Motteux. Vol. 24 in *Great Books of the Western World* (Chicago: Encyclopædia Britannica).

Radcliffe-Brown, A. R. 1952. *Structure and Function in Primitive Society: Essays and Addresses* (Glencoe, Ill.: The Free Press).

Rawls, John (1971). *A Theory of Justice* (Cambridge: Harvard University Press).

Richards, Norvin. (1988). "Forgiveness." *Ethics* 99, pp. 77–97.

Riesman, David. 1950. *The Lonely Crowd: A Study of the Changing American Character* (New Haven: Yale University Press).

Riggin, Judith M., ed. (1992). *John Wayne: A Bio-Bibliography* (New York: Greenwood Press).

Rostand, Edmond. 1971 (1897). *Cyrano de Bergerac*, trans. Anthony Burgess (New York: Alfred A. Knopf).

Roth, Philip. 2000. *The Human Stain* (Boston: Houghton Mifflin).

Roughgarden, Joan. 2004. *Evolution's Rainbow: Diversity, Gender, and Sexuality in Nature and People* (Berkeley: University of California Press).

Ryle, Gilbert. (1949). *The Concept of Mind* (London: Hutchinson).

Sachs, David. 1981. "How to Distinguish Self-Respect from Self-Esteem," *Philosophy and Public Affairs* 10, pp. 346–60.

Sagan, Carl. 1977. *The Dragons of Eden: Speculations on the Evolution of Human Intelligence* (New York: Random House).

Sartre, Jean-Paul. 1956 (1943). *Being and Nothingness: An Essay on Phenomenological Ontology*, trans. Hazel E. Barnes (New York: Philosophical Library).

"Shakespeare Insult Kit." http://www.pangloss.com/seidel/shake_rule.html.

Shakespeare, William. 1969. *The Complete Pelican Shakespeare*, ed. Alfred Harbage (Penguin Books).

Snoop Doggy Dogg. 1993. "Tha Shiznit." Track 5 on *Doggystyle* (Death Row/Interscope). Compact disc.

Spelman, Elizabeth V. 1989. "Anger and Insubordination," in Ann Garry and Marilyn Pearsall, eds., *Women, Knowledge and Reality: Explorations in Feminist Philosophy* (Boston: Unwin Hyman), pp. 263–73.

Sperling, Samuel J. 1953. "On the Psychodynamics of Teasing," *Journal of the American Psychoanalytic Association* 1, pp. 458–83.

Spinoza, Baruch de. 1985 (1677). *Ethics.* In *The Collected Works of Spinoza*, Vol. 1., trans. E. Curley (Princeton: Princeton University Press).

Stocker, Michael. 2002. "Some Problems About Affectivity," *Philosophical Studies* 108, pp. 151–58.

Strawson, P. F. 1974 (1962). "Freedom and Resentment." In his *Freedom and Resentment and Other Essays* (London: Methuen).

Sullivan, Kathleen M. 1992. "The First Amendment Wars," *New Republic*, Sept. 28, 1992, pp. 35–40.

Sumner, L. W. 2004. *The Hateful and the Obscene: Studies in the Limits of Free Expression* (Toronto: University of Toronto Press).

Swift, Jonathan. 1967. *Swift: Poetical Works*, ed. Herbert Davis (Oxford: Oxford University Press).

Talbot, Margaret. 2006. "The Agitator: Oriana Fallaci Directs Her Fury Toward Islam," *The New Yorker*, June 5, 2006, pp. 58–67.

"*The Alternative Afrikaans Dictionary.*" http://www.notam02.no/~hcholm/altlang/pdf/Afrikaans.pdf.

Tribe, Laurence H. 1988. *American Constitutional Law* (2nd ed.; Mineola, N.Y.: Foundation).

Trillin, Calvin. 2004. *Obliviously On He Sails: The Bush Administration in Rhyme* (New York: Random House).

Updike, John. 2005. "Incommensurability: A New Biography of Kierkegaard," *The New Yorker*, March 28, 2005, pp. 71–76.

Vanggaard, Thorkil. 1972. *Pallós: A Symbol and Its History in the Male World* (New York: International Universities Press).

Wetzsteon, Ross. 2002. *Republic of Dreams: Greenwich Village: The American Bohemia, 1910–1960* (New York: Simon & Schuster).

Williams, Bernard. 1973 (1965). "Ethical Consistency." In *Problems of the Self* (Cambridge: Cambridge University Press).

——, ed. 1979. *Obscenity and Film Censorship* (Cambridge: Cambridge University Press).

——. 1993. *Shame and Necessity* (Berkeley: University of California Press).

——. 2002. *Truth and Truthfulness: An Essay in Genealogy* (Princeton: Princeton University Press).

Wittgenstein, Ludwig. (1953). *Philosophical Investigations*, trans. G. E. M. Anscombe (Oxford, Basil Blackwell).

Wollheim, Richard. 1979. "Wish-Fulfilment," in R. Harrison, ed., *Rational Action* (Cambridge: Cambridge University Press).

Zoglin, Richard. "The Power of One," *Time Magazine*, Dec. 20, 2004, pp. 155–56.

Zuckerman, Solly. 1932. *The Social Life of Monkeys and Apes* (New York: Harcourt, Brace).

INDEX